1.99
1/7

THE GREAT CHEESES
OF BRITAIN AND IRELAND

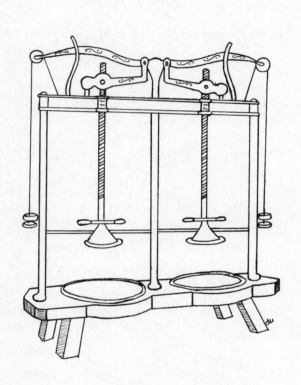

The Great Cheeses
of
Britain and Ireland

A GOURMET'S GUIDE

Robert Smith

AURUM PRESS

ACKNOWLEDGEMENTS

Special thanks to Trevor Knights for patiently checking the manuscript
and to Steve Macallister for his helpful comments on the text.

Line drawings by Karen Macallister

First published 1995 by Aurum Press Limited
25 Bedford Avenue, London WC1B 3AT

2 4 6 5 3 1
1996 1998 1997 1995

Text copyright © Robert Smith 1995

A catalogue record for this book is available from the British Library.

ISBN 1 85410 338 5

Frontispiece: Cast-iron double cheese press at Westway Dairy, Avon

Book design by Roger Lightfoot
Typeset by Action Typesetting Limited, Gloucester
Printed in Great Britain by Hartnolls Ltd, Bodmin

Contents

KEY TO THE CHEESES SHOWN ON THE FRONT COVER

1 Unpasteurised traditional Cheddar from S.H. and G.H. Keen & Sons
2 Traditional Cheshire from Appleby's of Hawkstone
3 Double Worcester from Anstey's of Worcester
4 Devon Oke from Curworthy Cheese
5 Berkswell Manchego from Ramhall Dairy
6 Somerset Brie from Lubborn Cheese
7 Staffordshire Organic from M. and B. Deaville of Acton, Staffordshire
8 Wensleydale from Hawes Creamery
9 Capricorn goats cheese from Lubborn Cheese
10 Shropshire Blue from Long Clawson Dairy
11 Swaledale Applemint from Swaledale Cheese Company
12 Cornish Yarg from Lynher Valley Dairy
13 Rosary from Clare Moody of Landford, Wiltshire
14 Goats cheese ash pyramid from Cerney House, Gloucestershire
15 Cropwell Bishop Stilton from Somerset Creameries
16 Double Gloucester from Diana Smart of Birdwood, Gloucester

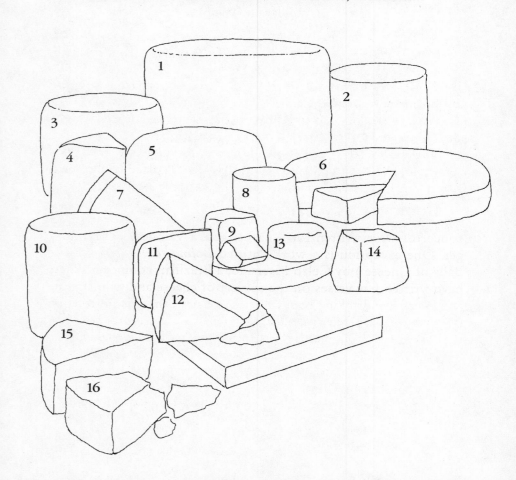

Introduction

CHEESE IS PART of our history, its discovery and development aiding our progress towards civilisation. In many ways cheese combines the old and the new; its manufacture can be a highly sophisticated process involving expensive modern technology or it can gracefully proceed in a manner little changed over twenty centuries.

Cheese is part of our being; it has shaped the teeth in our heads and the stone walls around our fields. Only recently has meat become commonplace in our diets, and for many centuries the ploughman's lunch really did consist of bread and cheese, whilst meats *rost and boyled* were a rare treat. Men have lived on little else but bread and cheese and, doubtless, found such a diet tiresome. Nevertheless, the inherent goodness of cheese has stood the test of time. Cheese, like wine, was created not merely to meet our needs but also to gratify our excesses, and many cheeses improve with long keeping in cool cellars so that the pleasures of anticipation can be added to the delights of indulgence.

Cheese has been neglected, despite its vital place in our diet. The making of cheese is an art but the other arts have treated it with disdain. Seldom does it form the subject of a still life, and musically it has been largely ignored, even if the Mozart horn concertos were written for Igna Leitgeb, a Viennese cheesemonger. One exception is a work entitled *Bolinos de Queijo* ('Little Balls of Cheese') by Celso Machado, a Brazilian composer. Poets have written few verses on the subject of cheese and, whilst wine and beer have drinking songs to raise a thirst, there is no rousing chorus to accompany the eating of cheese. In literary works, cheese generally only merits a mention in passing.

H.V. Morton, in his classic *In Search of England* (1927), sang the praises of simple fare: 'How, I wonder, have I refrained so long from praising bread, cheese, and beer, the most significant, romantic, delicious, satisfying food that can pass the parched gullet of a wayfarer!' Alas for Mr Morton and for us all, bread, cheese and beer were soon to be less deserving of praise as mechanised methods displaced ancient arts and skills. Post-war Britain discovered cotton-wool bread and plastic cheese, and devoured them with relish. Fifty years on, the improvement in British bread has been little less than astonishing, while hardened campaigners have won their battle to bring real ale back to our pubs. Yet there have been fewer voices raised to champion the cause of cheese. Why should this be? Never before have there been so many cheeses to choose from, and the greater part of those on offer are now made better than they have ever been. Could it be, in an age when we are told what to think, that cheese consumption has been mostly unaffected by advertising?

Let us begin by asking, What is cheese? It might be defined in the same way as wine: 'The fermented juice of freshly gathered grapes, made in the region in which the grapes are grown, according to local custom and practice.' The substitution of 'fresh whole milk' for 'freshly gathered grapes' coupled to a requirement that such milk should be processed near to the point where the cows are grazed 'according to local custom and practice' would take us close to a working definition of cheese. Cheese, like wine, is a preserve and the two have much in common.

In the Western world, *milk* is usually taken to mean cows milk. As you travel east, sheep and goats milk are more common but it does not end there. Milk from asses, banteng, bison, camels, guar, gayal, reindeer, yak and zubu have all been found fit for the purpose, and buffalo milk is used to make a cheese similar to Mozzarella in India today.

Milk does not turn spontaneously into cheese; a controlled process of separation has to take place, allowing the solid elements to break free from the liquid that holds them in suspension. The milk solids, called the *curd*, must be parted from the liquid, known as *whey*. The more nutritious solid part is then usually scalded, salted and pressed into firm rounds which are ripened or matured before being eaten.

What a lucky people we are, in that we have cheese in plenty and even cheese to spare. The same cheese that enabled our distant ancestors to preserve milk in times of surplus so as to provide a store of food. The same cheese that fed the prophet in the desert, the Roman soldier on the march, the rich man in his castle and the poor man under his thatch. When times were hard, game was scarce or fruit out of season, we were reared on bread and cheese.

Cheese is a practical food. Nutritious, portable and delicious, it does without the mystique of caviar and oysters, the sentiment surrounding real ale or the snobberies of wine. Best of all, cheese is still a luxury that everyone can enjoy. Buy the quantity that fits your purse and your appetite. There is no need to economise on flavour for even a poor man can afford a little of the richest cheese on offer.

Bread and cheese – eat and enjoy!

1

The History of Cheese

CHEESE IN ANCIENT TIMES

ANY HISTORY OF cheese must necessarily suffer from the impermanence of its subject. There are few concrete examples for archaeologists to exhume and display, even though milk from domesticated animals has been a valuable food source for thousands of years. As nomadic farmers drove their flocks before them, they sought a way to preserve surplus milk for use in times of hardship. By accident or design, milk was left in shallow vessels, where it evaporated in the sun, and the dried residue was collected. It was discovered that this process was more successful if the cream was skimmed off the surface of the milk first, and the skimmed milk reduced to a powder that could be reconstituted with water.

The surplus cream or whole milk would have reacted to acidic residues in unglazed pottery or leather containers to form a solid curd, which some hungry individual found good to eat. This was a curd cheese and it was then but a short step to the discovery that the texture could be improved if the mixture of curds and whey was strained. The primitive cheesemaker probably used a basket as a strainer; wicker baskets for the making of cheese were known to the Greeks as *formos*. In Latin, this word became *forma*, meaning *mould* or *shape*, from which came the Italian word for cheese, *formaggio*. The early French *formage* later became *fromage*.

Sadly, no inventor has his or her name writ large in the annals of cheese. However, archaeologists are still discovering early examples of cheese moulds and drainers. Near Lake Constance a pottery colander, for draining whey from the curds, has been found, dating back to the Stone Age. It is known that cheese was made in the cradle of civilisation, the fertile crescent between the rivers Tigris and Euphrates, for bread and cheese have been identified as two of the staple foods consumed in settlements which existed here between 7000 and 6000 BC. In ancient Egypt, the Pharaohs so appreciated the value of cheese that they carried it into the tomb, ensuring adequate provisions for their journey to the after-life.

In the Sumerian city of Ur, around 2500 BC, people worshipped the moon god, and the temple priests collected offerings from the faithful which included pots of butter and rounds of cheese. Cheese has been found in the tomb of Hories-Aha near to Ur in the Chaldees, the city of Abraham.

Near Jerusalem there is a valley bordering the temple hill known as *Tyropoeon*, the Valley of the Cheesemakers. It is recorded in the First Book of Samuel that David was out delivering cheeses on the day he met Goliath: 'And Jesse said unto David his son, Take now for thy brethren this corn, and these ten loaves, and run to the camp with thy brethren; And carry these ten cheeses unto the captain.' Later, when crowned King, David was served 'cheese of sheep and kine' when he visited Shobi, son of Nahash, at Mahanaim. Such cheese was preserved by pickling in brine before being dried rock-hard in the sun. It was probably grated before use. The Jewish *kashruth* ritual laws permit the carrying of a cheese-grater on the Sabbath, though carrying other tools is forbidden.

Cheesemaking skills may have been introduced to the Mediterranean region by the Aryans of Central Asia. They were accomplished herdsmen who, as a migratory people, did not pause to develop cereal growing but remained dependent upon their animals. In their constant search for better grassland they migrated west into Europe, bringing their dairying skills with them.

The ancient Greeks believed that cheese was a gift from the gods, brought down to earth by Aristaeus, son of Apollo. Cheese was regarded as no less valuable than ambrosia from Mount Olympus, and offered back to the deities at their temples. The first Olympic athletes trained on a diet heavy in cheese, while the island of Delos even engraved cheeses on its coinage. Sheep and goats provided milk for the cheesemakers of ancient Greece, as the milk of cows was reserved for making *boutyron* (i.e. 'cow-cheese'), which we now call butter. In the *Odyssey* of Homer, Odysseus found cheese drying on racks, together with barrels of whey, when he entered the lair of the Cyclops.

Cheese has long been amongst the rations issued to soldiers on the march, for it is easily carried and requires no cooking fire. When Alexander the Great defeated Darius at Damascus in 331 BC, the lives of 13 cheesemakers from the Persian monarch's entourage were spared, doubtless because of their value to the military. The ancient Greeks also used to give their children little cheeses, as today we hand out sweets, except that cheese is better for the teeth. In classical literature good children are affectionately referred to as 'little cheeses'.

The Romans also used their word for cheese, *caseus*, as a term of endearment (broadly equivalent to 'darling'). More importantly, they developed advanced agricultural systems and skilled dairying methods, and by the time of the Emperor Diocletian (245–313 AD), the industry had become so successful that a limit was set on prices, possibly the first recorded instance of government intervention in the dairy trade. Brand names are no more recent an invention, for amongst the price controls issued by Diocletian is a maximum price for *Lunar*, a cheese with its own 'Horns of the Moon' trade mark. It is to be hoped that Capricorn, a cheese from Somerset, does not infringe some Roman copyright after 20 centuries!

The Romans had a taste for cheese enhanced by herbs and spices, and could choose from varieties flavoured with thyme, green pine nuts, garlic, pepper, marjoram, mint, coriander and onion. As well as dusting the outer surface of their cheese with chives and salt, they bought cheeses that had been basted with new wine, or smoked over boughs of apple wood. In larger Roman houses there was a separate cheese kitchen, the *caseale*. The word 'dairy' comes from the Latin *dey* (meaning female servant) and *ery*, a suffix of Roman origin, so that *dey-ery* indicated the place where the women's duties were carried out. The duties of the 'dey-ery' continued to be regarded as women's work right up until the twentieth century.

It was common practice for Roman soldiers to be discharged with a grant of land around garrison towns when their military service was completed. In his work *De Re Rustica*, written around 50 AD, a Roman named Columella, himself an ex-army officer, provided detailed instructions for those new to farming, including a set of basic rules for cheese manufacture that still hold good after 2,000 years. The writings of another Roman, Palladius, are also of particular interest, for the author mentions cheese from a garrison town called Chester, situated in one of the Empire's less important colonies. Chester cheese travelled to Rome, making it the first British cheese to be known and recorded outside its own area. When the legions were recalled from Britain in the fourth century, cheesemaking survived, eventually becoming part of our agricultural heritage.

BRITISH CHEESE EMERGES

Just as rudimentary cheesemaking had spread to Europe, Asia and India from the fertile crescent of Sumeria, the greater skills developed in the Roman Empire were bequeathed to Goths, Teutons and Celts. The convenient and compact meal of cheese that was carried in every Roman soldier's knapsack became part of the staple diet throughout Europe, each area developing its own methods of manufacture.

New skills in cheesemaking were introduced not only by the Romans but also by the Vikings, who transported live cattle in their longships. The large brown cows of Normandy and the Jerseys and Guernseys of the Channel Islands owe their existence to a knowledge of selective breeding passed on by the Vikings, who may even have carried the secrets of cheesemaking to the Moors in Spain.

In a Britain that came to lose even its network of Roman roads, improved methods of preserving surplus milk (available after spring calving) for consumption later in the year could only be spread by word of mouth. This role was performed by itinerant monks, especially the Celtic monks of Ireland who were not affected by the violence that struck Europe after the fall of Rome. They travelled the country spreading the Christian gospel as well as their practical skills. Monks had a personal interest in improving the taste of cheese, for those in holy orders were forbidden meat on fast days, and with over a hundred of these in the calendar (not to mention compulsory fish every Friday), bread and cheese dinners would have been decidedly monotonous. Inside monastic institutions, running a dairy was not without staff problems. Comely dairymaids were known to distract the brothers from religious observances, and one prior ordered that only 'old and ill-favoured females' were to be employed.

The earliest British writings on cheese are of Irish origin, although the Saxons were knowledgeable sheep farmers with common flocks maintained by the villages. The shepherd had an important job, guarding the flock with his fierce dogs, milking the ewes twice a day and making cheese. Unlike the shepherd, the cowherd didn't make any butter or cheeses, for this was the duty of the cheesemaker, who was female. Cows milk cheeses were principally made for the aristocracy, but when King Offa, the ruler of Mercia, who died in 796, demanded 40 cheeses from Westbury-on-Trym (now in Avon), he allowed the cheesemaker to keep the buttermilk and whey. To preserve these for future use, she would have made skimmed-milk cheeses and whey butter.

Bread has long been the staff of life but, for centuries, the consumption of meat depended on permission to hunt, money to buy or fuel for cooking. Recent research into the history of English forests has revealed that timber shortages, long attributed to the felling of trees for shipbuilding during the Tudor period, actually occurred much earlier. Forests were ravaged to provide timber for houses, bridges, fences and fuel. Landowners guarded their trees as jealously as the game on their estates and, as a result, the peasant never tasted much meat. Instead, it was cheese that provided an almost universal source of protein. Plentiful, portable, affordable, storable and ready to eat without cooking, cheese was so valuable that it served as currency.

The pipe rolls of the Bishops of Winchester in 1210–11 record cheeses not only being collected as rent (Tichborne contributed 20 to the total) but paid as a perquisite to shepherds for their duties. The Winchester records are incredibly detailed and we know, for example, that in the years 1274 to 1281 Sevenhampton-with-Stratton, Wiltshire, made 1,691 cheeses from a herd of 228 cows. Later, between 1281 and 1287, the herd had shrunk to 159 and only 1,373 cheeses were made. With records as detailed as these being kept, there can be no doubting the importance of cheese. Ewes were the primary milking animals, and the sheer magnitude of the flocks managed by the estates is astonishing. In Yorkshire it has been calculated that in the thirteenth century the abbeys of Jervaulx, Fountains and Rievaulx each yielded 10,000 fleeces a year, with Malton contributing another 9,000.

The fleeces and the ewes milk cheeses were valuable exports. Cheese from the Cotswolds (Minchinhampton and Avening being mentioned as sources) was exported from Southampton, and produce from Povington in Dorset was exported from

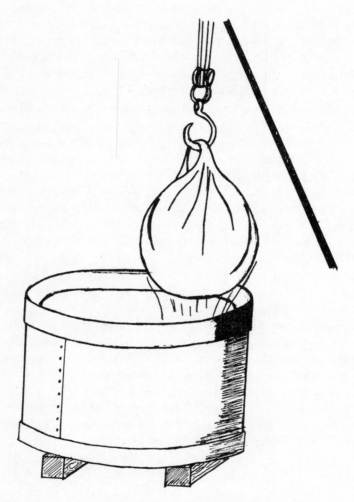

Curds hanging in a cloth suspended from a hook: an early method of draining off the whey.

Wareham. Flemish ships collected 100 *weys** of cheese from London in 1361, and in 1386, Richard II had his serjeant-at-arms buy 60 weys of Essex and Suffolk cheese at Ipswich market for shipping to Calais.

The Dissolution of the Monasteries helped to spread the

*A *wey* was a unit of weight varying from 168 to 182 lb (76 to 82 kg).

knowledge of cheesemaking. Before 1536 much of English agriculture was controlled by the religious foundations, which owned
vast tracts of land. When the monks were displaced, many were
forced to seek work on local farms. They carried their cheesemaking and dairying skills with them, and many a former monk might
have taught a farmer's wife how to make good cheese in exchange
for accommodation. The methods were passed down from
mother to daughter. Regional differences in methods and raw
materials have led to the great variety of cheeses found in Britain
and Ireland today.

The regular publishing of agricultural journals began during the
Tudor period. In 1573 Thomas Tusser, in *Fieve Hundredth Pointes
of Good Husbandrie*, recommended that a housewife should make
her own cheese, or answer for the consequences:

> Ill housewife unskillful to make her own cheese
> though trusting in others, hath this for her fees:
> Her milkpans and creampots so clabberred and sost
> that butter is wanting and cheese is half lost.

Clabberred is an archaic word meaning 'curdled' and *sost* means
'messed up'. Tusser was particularly concerned with the education
of Cicely, his dairymaid, and presented her instruction in poetical
form. The verse below concerns cheese that was 'hoven and
puffed', possibly needing to be pierced with a bodkin to free the
'strong wind of disagreeable smell'. The richness of medieval
smells can even pervade written history.

> If cheeses in dairy have Argus his eyes
> Tell Cisley the fault in her housewifery lies.
> Tom Piper hath hoven and puffed up cheeks,
> If cheese be so hoven, make Cisse to seek creekes.
> Leave Lot with his pillar dear Cisley alone
> For much salt in the whitemeat is ill for the stone.

In Tusser's time, dairy products (which sometimes included eggs)
were referred to as 'white meats'. William Caxton, writing in
1483, makes reference to 'fysshe, mylke, egges or whyte mete'.
White meats were brought into London from the surrounding
countryside but, by the late fifteenth century, all was not well
beyond the city's limits. With the demise of the feudal system,

landowners submitted to the tempting concept of the cash crop. No longer was land tilled to provide today's food and tomorrow's store; the object of the exercise became the creation of wealth. Wool was the growth industry and peasants were evicted to provide space for sheep. The flocks demanded vast tracts of land but few workers, and if the poor starved, what of it? Sheep required so much less labour than mixed farming that unemployment rose steeply. Deprived of their land, villagers grew less of their own food. The more the rich waxed fat on the profits of wool, the more the poor came to depend on their cheese. With so many sheep, cheese commonly meant ewes milk cheese.

The notion of our ancestors being great meat eaters dies hard, perhaps because of the popular image of a merry monarch gnawing on a haunch of venison and carelessly tossing the bone over his shoulder. Contemporary pictures depicting prosperous farmers and merchants established the reputation of England as a meat-eating nation, but the truth is that the majority survived on a meagre diet. Bread, cheese and beer were the staples. Even when meat became available, its consumption was frequently limited by religious observances. After Henry VIII broke up the large monasteries and sold off their estates in the 1530s, cows milk was increasingly used to make cheese. Only in the remoter parts of Scotland did the making of ewes milk cheese continue, finally dying out in the eighteenth century. There is no doubt that elsewhere the milking of ewes became much less common and remains so today.

By the seventeenth century even cows milk cheese was increasingly regarded by the rich, in England, as inferior food for the common people. Paintings of Tudor and Stuart banquets, attended by the ruling classes, rarely show cheese on the table. No such stigma existed in Ireland, Scotland or Wales, but the English idea that cheese was more appropriate for the lower orders persisted for a very long time. By this piece of snobbery, the rich did themselves out of a valuable part of their diet. An increase in the incidence of rickets was one price they paid.

2

The Making of Cheese

Milk does not turn spontaneously into cheese, but raw (unpasteurised) milk left standing in a warm atmosphere will sour naturally after a few hours and eventually form a curd. Milk has been mostly supplied by cows since the sixteenth century although, in the medieval period, ewes milk was of considerable importance. Large flocks of sheep and goats grazed the Mendip Hills at the time of the Norman Conquest and sheep were equally numerous in the eastern counties. In the Domesday survey there were 130,000 sheep, 11,000 goats and 9,000 cattle or oxen in Norfolk, Sussex and Essex alone.

Ewes milk provided the raw material for cheesemaking in Yorkshire until the sixteenth century, and its use was still commonplace in Northumberland two hundred years later. In Wales, ewes milk was mixed with cows milk to make Glamorgan cheese, and in the remoter parts of Scotland, the milk of cows, ewes and goats was mixed for sale until recent times.

All milks are complex emulsions of fat globules in water, but there are marked differences between the three milks commonly used by cheesemakers:

Milk	Protein %	Fat %	Lactose %	K/cals per 100g	Calcium mg per 100g	Water %
Cows	3.5	3.5	4.5	73	152	88
Goats	3.0	4.0	4.0	77	110	89
Ewes	6.0	6.0	5.0	102	210	82

The difference in protein levels is what affects cheesemakers. To make 1 lb (0.5 kg) of cheese requires 10 lb (5 kg) of cows milk, whereas it takes less ewes milk to achieve the same result. Whatever the source, there cannot be good cheese without good milk and, all down the western side of the British Isles, we are blessed with the rainfall, the soil, the grassland and the dairying skills to provide the ideal raw material. Milk has to be clean, wholesome, and free from taints. The age of the animal, the breed, the way in which it is fed and the stage of lactation all affect the milk and, in turn, the quality of the cheese. Milk from animals suffering from mastitis, a disease of the udder, is not suitable for cheesemaking, and if the animal has been treated with antibiotics, or other medicines, the milk cannot be used. Such milk would affect the *starter* (of which more later) and, in any case, antibiotics should not be allowed to enter the food chain at random.

Alvis Brothers of Redhill, near Bristol, have been making superb Cheddar for thirty years so I cannot do better than repeat John Alvis's comments concerning cows milk, which would equally apply to milk from other sources:

> It is true to say that high quality milk is absolutely fundamental to the flavour, body and texture of the cheese produced. The milk must be extremely hygienic and antibiotic free, produced from healthy cows fed on natural foods (mostly grass) which are known not to give rise to 'taints' in the milk which, in turn, would produce off-flavours in the cheese. Some cattle feeds could give rise to milk which produces soft or weak bodied cheese, which does not keep very well.

Milk is now tested to a degree that makes it one of the most wholesome of foods but this was not always the case. Milk was, for many generations, commonly dirty, diluted and downright

The first essential for cheesemaking is a supply of high-quality milk.

dangerous. It was not until the 1850s that a new breed of landowner emerged, prepared to invest heavily in showpiece farmsteads and model dairies. These were an astonishing improvement on anything that had existed before. Examples include Bemerton Farm on the Wilton estate near Salisbury, Tattenhall Farm in Cheshire, Lord Wantage's Ardington Dairy in Oxfordshire and, most famous of all, Prince Albert's dairy at Sandringham. The Sandringham windows, said to be Albert's own invention, contained an ingenious system of louvres designed to admit air but exclude direct sunlight and keep the dairy cool.

Sadly, on smaller farms the bad old ways persisted. Dairies were constructed as part of the farmhouse, convenient for the farmer's wife, who did most of the work. However, as the cowsheds were commonly some way distant, one can only hazard a guess at what foreign bodies the milk attracted as it was carried across the yard. A series of measures, beginning with the Dairies, Cowsheds and Milkshops Order of 1885, empowered local authorities to enforce new bylaws designed to ensure cleaner milk.

Even when cattle are properly housed and fed, there is a variation in the composition of whole milk. The fat percentage usually falls from March to June, when the cows are turned out on to spring grass, building up through the summer and falling again in the winter months. Casein, the major protein, is at its peak through the spring and summer but falls as the days shorten. Even when animal feed is carefully balanced and fortified with nutrients there is still a seasonal variation in quality, and the best cheese is said to be made after autumn calving.

Making allowances for seasonal variation, typical constituents of 100 grams of cows milk might be:

Water	88.0 g
Lactose (milk sugar)	4.5 g
Fat	3.5 g
Proteins (casein, albumin, globulin)	3.5 g
Vitamins and minerals include:	
Calcium	152 mg
Vitamin B2	150 mg
Vitamin C	2 mg
Vitamin D	0.05 mg
Iron	0.03 mg
Vitamin A	150 international units

The milk of ewes and goats also varies with the seasons and their lactation period is shorter. A cow gives milk for eight to ten months after calving, while a ewe might give milk for less than six months before drying off.

PASTEURISATION

Before cheesemaking begins, milk has to be agitated to ensure that the fat (which is lighter than water) does not rise, as a layer of cream, to the top. Most milk is then pasteurised by being heated to 160°F (71°C) for 15 seconds and then cooled to 85°F (29°C) to kill off unwanted bacteria. This process has advantages from the health point of view, as milk must be free from *Mycobacterium tuberculosis*, but it does destroy some of the natural *lipase* that gives character to the cheese. The enzyme *phosphatase* is also inactivated by pasteurisation, and to test for phosphatase is a reliable way of ensuring that milk is adequately treated.

Unfortunately, however, pasteurisation may cause a portion of the calcium to become insoluble and some of the whey proteins to be lost. The level of calcium is vital to the formation of a *coagulum* or junket and it may be desirable, at some times of the year, for the cheesemaker to add calcium in the form of calcium chloride. Some cheeses are made from partly or fully skimmed milk but most are made from full cream milk, to which the cheesemaker may add milk powders to 'standardise' the solids content. The process that turns milk into some type of cheese consists essentially of five stages:

1. Acidification of raw milk or treatment with a starter.
2. Coagulation or 'setting' by the action of rennet.
3. Cutting and heating the curd to remove most of the whey.
4. Ladling the curd into a suitable container (soft cheese) or milling, salting and pressing in a mould (hard cheese).
5. Ripening or maturing the partly dried curd.

Given time, fresh milk will set by the action of lactic bacteria alone. Such *acid curd* cheeses are still made today, but the manufacture of most types of cheese requires the action of rennet. Rennet only performs well if the milk is allowed to acidify, i.e. if part of the milk sugar (lactose) is allowed to turn to lactic acid.

This happens naturally when raw untreated milk is left standing but must be encouraged in pasteurised milk by the action of a starter.

STARTER, THE HEART OF A CHEESE

Some cheesemakers who have direct control over their milk supply, and smaller specialist producers, still use unpasteurised milk but the majority of cheese is made using pasteurised milk. As this treatment kills off valuable as well as harmful bacteria the 'good bugs' need to be replaced. To do this, cheesemakers add a collection of specific starter bacteria which enables the process to be controlled. The choice of starter affects both flavour and character, and the starter has been referred to as 'the heart of a cheese'. Lemon juice, whey and other simple acids have been used as starters but many of the problems encountered by cheesemakers can be avoided if a carefully regulated combination of bacteria is employed. These are supplied, ready for use, by specialist laboratories.

RENNET – THE CLOTTING INGREDIENT

The discovery of rennet as a clotting agent might well have resulted from a fortuitous accident. Curd from the stomach of a newly slaughtered calf might have been placed in a bowl and its action on surplus milk observed. It would have been found that just a small part of the stomach itself, or merely water in which the stomach had lain, could provide an effective clotting action. The stomachs or *vells* were subsequently dried and salted for future use. The stomachs of goats, lambs and hares yield rennet but it is the fourth stomach of a calf that has been accepted as the most reliable source. Just before it was killed, a calf was fed so that there would be digestive juices in its stomach, and a lump of curd was left in the stomach bag to keep it active. After a few hours the bag was washed clean and salted. Instructions for producing rennet are given in Marshall's *Rural Economy of Gloucestershire* (1789):

> To two gallons of water, made salt enough to bear an egg, add one pennyworth of mace, one pennyworth of cloves, a handful of

sweet briar and hawthorn buds, a quantity of alum (about the bulk
of a small walnut), the same quantity of sal prunellae [nitrate of
potash], a small pinch of cochineal (the bulk of half a hazel nut)
and, if to be had, two or three bay leaves. Pound the alum, salt, salt
prunel, & etc. and, having mixed the several ingredients with the
salt and water, add five vells; or if small six or seven. In ten days the
rennet will be fit for use.

The function of the herbs was probably no more than to counteract any bad flavours in the rennet, and the results, at best, would
have been highly unpredictable. Commercial 'standardised'
rennet (i.e. of measured strength) became available after the
Copenhagen factory of Christopher Hansen was established in
1874.

Modern rennet is not usually extracted from an animal as there
are now a number of synthetically derived substitutes. (See
Vegetarian Cheese, p. 24.) Back in the days when any scientific
knowledge was regarded as magic, rennet was known as *cheese lip*.
The word came from the old English *lybb*, meaning poison,
derived in turn from *lupp*, of old High German origin, or the old
Norse *lyf*, both meaning 'medicinal herb'. In old Gothic, this
same word root leads to *lubjaleisei*, meaning witchcraft!

CHEESEMAKING ON THE FARM

When cheese is made today, on the farm or in the smaller creamery,
it is the combination of traditional skills and modern controls that
results in the best possible product. It takes one gallon of cows
milk to make one pound of cheese (or 5 litres to make 0.5 kg) and
it takes a real expert to do it properly. Of course, the cheesemaker
does not work with one gallon of milk; 2,000 gallons would be a
typical quantity. After collection, milk needs to be gently agitated
until it is used, to prevent the cream, which is lighter, rising to the
top. Once cream has separated it cannot merely be stirred back in;
before the advent of mechanised stirring, cream from the evening
milk was skimmed off, warmed and returned to the vat with the
morning milk.

The milk is normally pasteurised and then poured into a stainless-steel cheese vat, which has double walls so that steam can
pass through for heating purposes. The starter is added, with the
amount and type employed being very much part of the cheese-

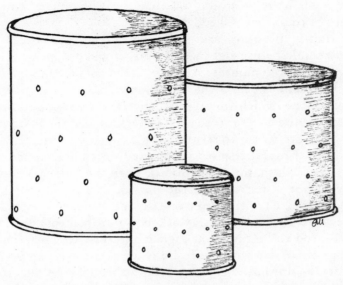

Cheese moulds, also called vats or chessets, come in various shapes and sizes. They were formerly made by the village cooper from oak or elm bound with iron hoops. Stainless steel is now more commonly employed.

maker's skill. This process converts part of the milk sugar into lactic acid. Afterwards, rennet is stirred in, causing the mixture to clot. After around 45 minutes, this junket of clotted milk is cut into small pieces by mesh screens, known as knives, and the curds and whey are successively cut and heated. As stirring continues, the acidity rises and the curd particles shrink. This is a highly skilled part of the process, as the curd is scalded and stirred until the correct firmness is achieved.

The choosing of the right moment to run off the whey, so that the curd can be tipped or *pitched* into the cheddaring pans, varies each day, depending on a multitude of factors, even the weather. In the wide, flat pans the curd goes through the repeated stacking and turning process (heavy manual work) that we call *cheddaring*, until the thick blocks or parcels of curd have achieved the right acidity and moisture content. When the curd arrives at a texture that resembles cooked chicken breast, it is passed through a mill that cuts the mass into small pieces, like potato chips. At the same time salt is added to provide flavour and act as a natural preservative. The salted curd is then pressed into round moulds or hoops, each holding around 60 lb (27 kg) of cheese, to form truckles of traditional Cheddar.

The newly pressed curd is known as 'green' cheese. It is scarcely edible before eight weeks and only becomes a good mild cheese after three months. A complicated balance of the acidity, fat content and salt level within this new cheese gives rise to the natural process which we call maturing, and the temperature and humidity of the cheese store need to be monitored constantly if a really good product is to result.

Traditional round cheeses are pressed, in a mould lined with a coarse cheesecloth, for a day or two. Then they are taken out and bathed in hot water, to melt the outside and form a rind. Each truckle is greased with butter or lard and bandaged with a fresh cheesecloth. Even then, the work is far from over as 'rind-on' cheeses need to be turned at regular intervals to ensure an even distribution of fat within the body of the cheese. Any excess moisture or unwanted gas can escape through the cheesecloth, before the rind hardens, as the rich and strong flavour develops. This is real cheese, and there is nothing to compare with the flavour. However, the costs of handling and maturing have forced the industry to concentrate on rindless blocks, and truckles have become the preserve of the specialist.

The manufacture of rindless cheese proceeds as described above until the curd is pressed, whilst still warm, into rectangular moulds of stainless steel or plastic to form 40 lb (20 kg) blocks. These are easier to cut into prepacked portions of cheese. The cheese develops inside its plastic wrapper and can never emulate the character of traditional cheese but a good maker can still produce an excellent product. Rindless blocks often win prizes at cheese shows much to the chagrin of the traditionalists.

CHEESEMAKING IN A LARGE CREAMERY

Creamery production commenced in England with the opening of a factory, in Derby, by the Derbyshire Cheese Factory Association on 8 April 1870. Just four years later there were five more factories in Derbyshire alone, and today most of the cheese we eat is factory made. There are inevitable differences between the cheese produced by a small farm and that of a large creamery. The former should have the ability to make a more individual cheese whilst creameries are geared more to the needs of the mass market. Creameries can, and do, make excellent cheese, although their priority must be the most effective use of liquid milk. As this is collected over a very wide area, they are unlikely to make a product with local characteristics. The creameries have well-equipped laboratories on site, where the contents of each tanker are checked before being pumped into bulk silos and stirred continuously. An analysis of the milk's constituent parts is carried out, and the milk may be standardised by the addition of milk powders. Milk is converted to cheese by the sealed-vat method, introduced from Denmark in the 1970s, which provides a greater yield of product per litre of milk. The vat has integral cutting and stirring devices to handle the curd, and the injection of starter and coagulating cultures is carefully controlled. The curd is progressively cut, stirred and heated in a process which takes around two and a half hours, until the whey is drawn off by suction. At this point, the nature of the process differs dramatically from the farm method, with the curd being blown, by compressed air, to the top of a Cheddar Master Tower. In the 40 ft (12 m) high tower the temperature is maintained at 90–100°F (32–8°C) and any residual whey is drawn off through a perforated lining. Slowly the curd settles and fuses into a fibrous mass under its own weight. At the foot of the tower, the curd is cut and milled into finger-sized pieces and mechanically dosed with salt before being pressed into moulds under enormous hydraulic pressure. In a controlled process like this, cheesemaking can proceed automatically with a very high output and continuous flow. The end product is uniform, of good quality but lacking in individuality.

The final pressing of the curd into the one-tonne moulds is carried out at a much higher pressure than for farm-made cheese, and the absence of natural fissures within the product, together with a greater level of whey extraction, usually leads to a less satisfactory flavour. The final product may be condemned by the connoisseur but cheesemaking has progressively been concentrated in large creameries. Uniform block cheeses convert readily into prepacked wedges, which are easy for supermarkets to display. This has proved a more profitable market for cheesemakers than meeting the needs of the connoisseur.

THE ARTISAN MAKER

Artisan producers leave the creameries to press on with making cheese by the cartload. Theirs is a different task, that of making cheese to meet the needs of customers who demand an individual flavour and character that is true to the cheese's type and its origins. Artisans may keep goats, ewes or cows, even a pedigree herd, and many choose to work with raw milk, which is no easy task. Their presence in the industry is vital for they work to only one standard, perfection. As one Lancashire maker comments:

> I know and treat my animals [goats] like pets and only milk them myself. If they as much as look off colour, I don't make cheese from their milk. If their udders are hot or if there is a spot of blood in the milk it is rejected. When the cheese is made, anything that doesn't ripen exactly as I want goes to the pigs. The only cheese that I offer for sale is perfect, just perfect.

Many artisan makers have a limited production, only enough to sell direct or to a couple of shops, but it is to be hoped that they will eventually find it financially viable to bring their cheese to a wider public. Artisan products include mould-ripened cheeses (which are not pressed but left to drain naturally on mats), fresh cheeses and cheeses which develop a rind, adding another dimension to their flavour. Perhaps more than any other food, artisan cheese should reflect the farm where it is made: the south-facing slope, the chalk in the soil or the herbs in the pasture. A combination of such small factors adds up to the birth of a truly great cheese. Please God, let artisan makers ever be allowed to keep making cheese in their own natural way.

3

Different Types of Cheese

Cheeses vary according to the type of starter and amount of rennet used, and the manner in which the curd is cooked, pitched, pressed and moulded. The way the surface is treated will also create a different end product, and finished cheeses may be bathed in brine, larded and bandaged, dusted with rice or flour, waxed or wrapped in plastic film. The variations are infinite and each produces different characteristics; some of these appeal to local tastes, while others find wider acceptance. Countless named cheeses are produced throughout the world (1,000 or so in the British Isles alone) but, all too often, a new name merely indicates a cosmetic change in the shape or outer wrapping. It is possible to group nearly all of the world's cheeses under a dozen main categories, which will be examined in this chapter.

FRESH CHEESES

Normally produced from pasteurised milk, these cheeses have a short life. They are unpressed and high in moisture. The curd is cut, moulded and naturally drained. The finished cheese might be so soft as to be sold in a tub, and yoghurt and fromage frais could be included in this group. Fresh unripened cheeses include the cream and double-cream varieties, which are blended with cream during the manufacturing process to produce a fat content of 60 per cent or more. Nevertheless, most fresh cheeses are light in texture and lower in fat than hard cheeses such as Cheddar. Examples include Crowdie, curd cheese and cottage cheese.

RIPENED UNPRESSED CHEESES

These cheeses are produced from raw or pasteurised milk treated with starter and rennet. The curd is seldom cut but whey is allowed to drain naturally. Unpressed cheeses have a limited shelf life. They remain high in moisture and are not matured but allowed to ripen for a short period, often forming a soft rind. An example would be Sussex Slipcote.

SCALDED PRESSED CHEESES

Most of the cheese produced in the British Isles falls into this category, made from pasteurised or raw milk treated with starter and rennet. Annatto colouring (see p. 119) may also be added. The curd is cut and briefly scalded (not cooked), pitched for piling and turning (cheddaring), then milled and salted before moulding. The finished cheese may be allowed to form a traditional rind or wrapped in plastic to be sold as rindless cheese. Cheeses in this group can be eaten after three months, but they mature well, usually over a long period. Cheddar, Double Gloucester, Red Leicester, Derby and Dunlop are well-known examples.

COOKED PRESSED CHEESES

Cooked cheeses are produced from milk treated with starter and rennet. A number of different starters are used, including *Lactobacillus bulgaris* and *Lactobacillus lactis*. Such starters may cause a secondary fermentation, converting part of the lactic acid to propionic acid, acetic acid and carbon dioxide gas. It is this process which forms the 'eyes' or cavities commonly found in Swiss-type varieties. The curd is scalded at a high temperature (126–34°F / 53–7°C), held for a period to cook in the whey, and then brined or dry salted. Such cheeses keep for many years. The manufacture of cooked pressed cheese is more widespread in continental Europe but there are British examples, including Parmesan and Lyegrano.

MOULD-RIPENED CHEESES

Mould-ripened cheeses are produced from pasteurised or raw milk treated with starter and rennet. The curd is not usually pressed, merely drained and ladled into moulds. A surface 'flora' may be encouraged by spraying the cheese with a mould culture. For example, Camembert and Brie, both of which fall into this category, are sprayed with *Penicillium candidum*, sometimes followed by *Bacterium crythrogens*. The white surface is to be eaten and enjoyed. Examples of British mould-ripened cheeses include Sharpham and Somerset Brie.

WASHED RIND CHEESES

These cheeses are produced from raw or pasteurised milk treated with starter and rennet. After the curd is moulded and pressed, the surface is repeatedly washed using brine, beer, cider, wine or other liquids to produce the most pungent of cheeses. The outer rind may be smeared with *Breyibacterium linens* to encourage the development of an orange-red surface coat. This type of 'rind' is not normally eaten. Examples include Cloisters and Stinking Bishop.

PASTA FILATA CHEESES

Normally produced from pasteurised milk treated with starter and rennet, these cheeses have a curd that may be ripened and is 'stretched' in hot water before moulding. The finished cheese may be brined, dry salted or sold fresh. An example is Mozzarella.

WHEY CHEESES

Produced from whey, or a mixture of whey and buttermilk, which is heated until the protein coagulates and rises to the surface. This curd is drained and subjected to other treatments before being packed. Ricotta is a whey cheese.

GOATS MILK CHEESES

In the UK the production of goats milk more than doubled between 1970 and 1989, and demand continues to increase. Goats milk has a distinctive odour and taste, the result of three fatty acids, *caprioc*, *caprylic* and *capric*. It has smaller fat globules and the fat is much easier to digest than butterfat. The differences in fat composition are reflected in the cheese, especially as many makers use unpasteurised milk. Goats milk cheeses are normally softer and have a more crumbly texture than cows milk varieties. They do not harden as cows milk cheeses do when the whey is pressed out of them and, if allowed to mature, they become sharp and almost 'peppery'. They can have a distinctive earthy flavour that develops ferociously as the cheese matures. The goats cheese industry is still small but the taste for cheeses such as Chavannes and Pant-ys-gawn is growing.

EWES MILK CHEESES

Ewes milk is sweeter than that of cows and richer in vitamins. Its fine fat globules are naturally homogenised, resulting in a cheese which is usually very close textured and has a marked creaminess. Many producers choose to work with unpasteurised milk. In Britain, the milking of sheep is not common and no cheese is produced on the scale of French Roquefort, the most famous ewes milk cheese. That this should be the case is curious, as ewes provided the milk for our medieval cheeses, including Wensleydale and Caerphilly. Ewes milk cheeses are generally mild, although there are exceptions, and all have a rich, creamy texture. Few are noticeably salty. Examples include Ashleigh, Duddleswell, Nepicar, and St Finans.

BLUE CHEESES

This is not a true sub-group as many cheeses, hard-pressed or semi-soft, can be induced to blue by the introduction of *Penicillium roqueforti*, Stilton and Dorset Blue Vinney being the most famous examples. A machine was invented in 1953 to pierce Stilton with steel needles so as to create uniform blue veins.

Hard-pressed cheeses, such as traditional Cheddar, may show a thread vein of blue, and several of the lighter-pressed cheeses, such as Cheshire and Wensleydale, have been known to blue spontaneously after picking up mould spores occurring naturally where they were stored.

PROCESSED CHEESES

Processed cheese is a blended product, containing cheese, water and other ingredients such as butter or milk powder. A mixture of ground cheese, water, emulsifier and other chemicals is heated to a minimum of 150°F (66°C) and the mixture is stirred or agitated before being extruded into barrier wrapping or aluminium foil. The emulsifier prevents separation and the end product is pasteurised, so it does not ripen. Processed cheese is virtually inert and has an extended shelf life. It is higher in water and lower in nutritional value than real cheese. Many expensively packaged cheese products originating in continental Europe are cleverly processed cheese with added ingredients or coatings.

OTHER VARIETIES

Beyond the dozen basic categories, the sub-divisions are complex and misleading. A normal hard-pressed cheese might take on a new identity as a result of being blended with wine, herbs, spices, fruits or pickles. Sage Derby is the best known 'additive' cheese, whilst the makers of Ilchester produce a famous range of blended products.

Feta, Halloumi and a group of similar cheeses originating from the eastern Mediterranean and Asia form a distinct group of 'pickled' cheeses. They vary widely in taste, texture and mode of manufacture but all are preserved in brine. Although the cheeses are now made around the world they emanated from an area with a hot climate. The practice of brining was adopted to extend the life of the product in the days before refrigeration.

Coloured rind gives cheeses like Cloisters or Hereford Red their distinctive appearance. England's Choice, Five Counties and Huntsman are made up of more than one cheese sandwiched together. The outer surface of many cheeses might be smoked,

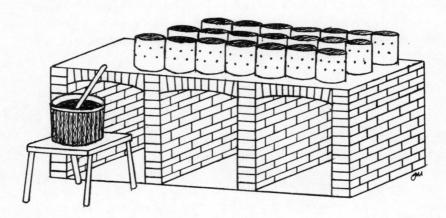

Cheese moulds waiting to be filled.

studded with nuts, dusted with ash or rolled in oatmeal. 'Tendale' and 'Shape' are trade names for reduced-fat cheeses, where taste is of secondary consideration.

VEGETARIAN CHEESE

Vegetarian cheese is not another type of cheese. Any cheese can be described as vegetarian, provided it is made with non-animal rennet. Taste and texture are not affected.

The active enzyme in rennet, *chymosin*, was traditionally extracted from the fourth stomach of a newly slaughtered calf, although almost any ruminant animal will suffice. Non-animal substitutes have been in common usage for over ten years; these are based on synthetically derived chymosin or microbial setting agents. Both are totally safe and perform successfully, enabling cheesemakers to practise their craft without resort to killing an animal. Those who object to animal rennet, because they hold vegetarian sympathies or are strict observers of Jewish dietary laws, have frequently been asked to pay a premium for their preference. As 'vegetarian' rennet costs no more than that derived from animals, this should not be the case. The majority of cheese made in the UK is now set with non-animal rennet or a microbial setting agent and can be correctly described as 'suitable for vegetarians'. It makes no difference whether the product carries the 'V' symbol of the Vegetarian Society or not. This change should also benefit the small number of people who have an allergy to animal rennet, and the many more who complain that eating cheese gives them a headache. A general move towards the use of non-animal rennet is taking place in the cheese industry.

4

Cheddar: God's Gift
to Somerset

Cheddar, the most noted place in all England for making
large, fine, rich and pleasant cheeses.
NATHAN BAILEY (1721)

Nowhere is good cheese more respected than in Somerset. Wise
heads nod appreciatively if it is said of somebody, 'He knows a
good piece of cheese when he sees it', for that is no small acco-
lade. And when in Somerset, to speak of cheese is to speak of
Cheddar. The excellence of Cheddar cheese was noted as early as
1586 when William Camden, a leading antiquary, wrote, 'West of
Wells just under the Mendippe Hills, lies Cheddar, famous for the
excellent and prodigious great cheeses made there, some of which
require more than a man's strength to set them on the table.'

John Houghton, writing in a letter on 5 July 1695, attributed
the success of Cheddar to the 'warm and fertile soil', with farms
exposed only to south-west winds and sheltered by the Mendips.
He was also the first writer to mention the co-operative system of
cheesemaking, under which farms pooled their surplus milk.
However, it was left to Daniel Defoe to write the most famous
description of Cheddar cheese. He must have found it to his
liking, for in his *Tour Through the Whole Island of Great Britain*
(1724–7) he reported at length:

> In the low country, on the other side of the Mendip Hills, lies
> Cheddar, a village pleasantly situated under the very ridge of the
> mountains; before the village is a large green or common, a piece of
> ground in which a whole herd of cows belonging to the town do

feed; the ground is exceeding rich, and as the whole village are cowkeepers, they take care to keep up the goodness of the soil by agreeing to lay on large quantities of dung for manuring and enriching the land. The milk of all the cows is brought together every day in a common room, where persons trusted for the management, measure every man's quantity and set it down in a book; when quantities are adjusted, the milk is put together, and every meal's milk makes one cheese, and no more. By this method, the goodness of the cheese is preserved and, without all dispute, it is the best cheese that England affords, if not that the whole world affords.

After Defoe's report the fame of Cheddar spread and demand increased beyond the capacity of the original village makers. The price rose alarmingly and for a time Cheddar appeared only at rich men's tables. It was only with the coming of the eighteenth century and a more organised and efficient approach to farming, pioneered by such agricultural reformers as Arthur Young and William Cobbett, that ample supplies of Cheddar became available. This was largely due to the efforts of one man, Joseph Harding.

JOSEPH HARDING

Joseph Harding (1805–76) was one of a new breed of intelligent and articulate farmers. Working with his family at Marksbury, near Bath, he developed and recorded cheesemaking methods that were to be imitated all over the world. His recipes and equipment, largely unchanged, were still in use until just before the Second World War. Harding was a working farmer, not the owner of a great estate, but his influence was such that J.G. Davis (a leading scientific authority on cheese) wrote in 1976, 'On the evidence available it is probable that Harding made a greater contribution to Cheddar cheesemaking than any other person.' Harding's dictum was, 'Cheese is not made in the field, nor in the byre, nor even in the cow, it is made in the dairy.' He and his wife emphasised the importance of training young cheesemakers, as well they might with seven sons and six daughters.

Harding's improvements even formed the subject of a government inquiry. In 1899 F. J. Lloyd was commissioned to carry out an investigation into Cheddar cheesemaking, and described

Harding's system in his report. The milk was passed through a hair strainer before it entered the cheese tub (even this simple precaution was not a common practice elsewhere). Harding worked with unpasteurised milk, which was kept cool to arrest acid development. Sour whey was added to act as a starter. (Specific starter bacteria had yet to be discovered.) The milk was heated to 84°F (29°C) by means of a steam boiler and the temperature checked with a thermometer. A measured quantity of standardised rennet, newly introduced from Denmark by Christopher Hansen, was added, and an hour allowed for coagulation before the curd was 'carefully and minutely broken' by Mrs Harding and her niece. F. J. Lloyd noted that 'servants were never entrusted with this part of the work'. The cutting, scalding and pitching of the curd was carried out in an equally precise manner, and each step was carefuly timed. The cheese tub was made with a convex bottom so that the curd could be cut from the sides and placed on the elevated centre. It was carefully heaped up and allowed to drain under its own weight before being cut, turned, and left yet again for any remaining whey to drain away.

The cooled curd was packed into moulds and lightly pressed. After an hour the cheese was removed from the moulds and broken up into finger-sized pieces by a curd mill. Salt was evenly distributed, at a rate of 1 lb to 56 lb of curd (500 g to 28 kg), and the green cheese was repacked in the moulds, using clean cheesecloths, to be matured for several months.

Harding achieved a remarkable degree of consistency in the production of his Cheddar, even heating the dairy in the winter months so that cheesemaking might proceed at the correct temperature. His improvements exposed the deficiencies of old-fashioned makers who worked solely by taste and experience. He published pamphlets and delivered lectures to pupils from all over Britain and from abroad. His daughter shared in his success, taking prizes at many shows, including a gold medal at the 1865 French Exhibition, for cheese made by her father's methods. Lastly, and farmers are not least affected by financial considerations, Harding costed his cheesemaking operation and showed that it gave improved returns. Harding's demand for hygienic dairy construction led him to insist that the cheesemaking be set apart from the animals on the farm. Dairies at that time usually consisted of little more than a whitewashed room, preferably on the shaded side of the farmhouse, with a copper tub standing on a

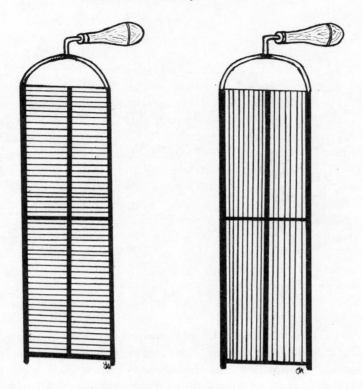

Cheese knives in the Museum of Rural Life at Glastonbury. Cuts from the vertical and horizontal blades would reduce the curd to even-sized cubes.

wooden base. More enlightened farmers kept their dairy room cool by lowering the floor below ground level or covering the roof with thick thatch. In suitable locations streams were diverted around, or even under, the dairy. There is a re-creation of what Harding's cheese room might have looked like in the Somerset Museum of Rural Life at Glastonbury.

DEVELOPMENTS IN CHEESEMAKING EQUIPMENT

As the Empire expanded, no country was more inventive than Great Britain, but even here cheesemaking equipment was still made by rural craftsmen such as the blacksmith, the cooper and the wheelwright. The cheese moulds, sometimes called *vats* or

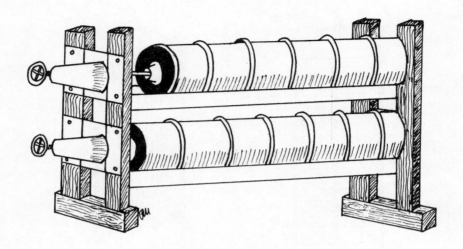

Cheddars in a gang press at Chewton Dairy, Somerset.

chessets, had not changed for centuries. They were strong wooden buckets, made from elm to withstand regular washing, and bound round with hoops of wood or iron. At a later stage, a metal screw-thread was mounted across the 'bucket' to force down a *follower*, a round disc of wood or slate that pressed the cheese into the mould. Early cheese presses simply consisted of a large weight placed on the follower. A single large block of stone, or box of gravel, was hard to raise and lower, and systems of ropes and pulleys were devised. (There is a fine example in the town museum at Aberystwyth.) The design of cider presses may have led to threaded metal rods being used to wind up heavy stone blocks but, gradually, the lever-action cheese press came into common use, with cheeses subjected to a controlled pressure of up to 1.5 tons (1,500 kg). It was not until the 1840s that the cast-iron cheese press was invented, combining a screw and lever. Later came the development of the *gang press*, a system whereby cheese is pressed in slightly tapered moulds, each fitting inside the other on a horizontal rail. By this means, the turning of a single screw can uniformly press a series of cheeses in their moulds. Every aspect of cheesemaking entailed hard physical work, not least the effort required to turn the 60 lb (27 kg) truckles. A system of pivoted shelves, called *tumbling cheese racks* or *turning dales*, was invented in the 1850s by William Blurton of Fieldhall, near Uttoxeter. This enabled 50 cheeses to be turned in one movement. Turning dales are still used on a farm at Newton St Cyres, near Exeter.

WEST PENNARD'S GIANT CHEESE

For the wedding of Queen Victoria, in 1840, the villagers of East and West Pennard made a giant 11 cwt (560 kg) Cheddar cheese. It was 9 ft 4 in round and 20 in deep (2.8 m × 0.5 m) taking the day's milk of 737 cows. A huge octagonal vat and a special press were built by local craftsmen. The wooden follower was intricately carved with the royal coat of arms on a piece of Spanish mahogany 5 in (13 cm) thick. On Friday 28 June 1839 nearly 50 dairymaids assisted in making the cheese at the farm of Mr George Naish. The day was marked by the ringing of the church bells and the firing of a gun at 5 o'clock in the morning! A poem was written to celebrate the occasion:

The Pennard Men they built a cheese, the like was never seen.
T'was made and pressed and fit to please our Gracious Lady Queen.
And, Wedded to her Royal Love may blessings on her fall,
And Pennard cheese at dinner prove the best thing – after all!

Despite the proud words, the omens were not good from the start. The cheese refused to budge from its mould, the follower had to be prised off and the curd ground again. A second attempt was more successful and the newly bound Cheddar was exhibited for a week, raising a tidy sum for local charities. On Queen Victoria's wedding day the cheese was 'guest of honour' at a village party, when 30 hogsheads of cider were drunk in loyal toasts.

Come February of the following year, a deputation of villagers presented themselves and the cheese at Buckingham Palace. Their gift was duly examined by Her Majesty who, after sampling a morsel, indicated that something with more flavour would be preferable. The farmers were asked to take the cheese back and mature it further, for which service Her Majesty would donate £100 to the poor of the village. The farmers agreed to this sensible proposal but, instead of removing the cheese to some cool cellar, they decided to display it to the public. A wire cover surmounted by a crown was made to protect the cheese from flies and rodents, and the cheese was exhibited at the Egyptian Hall in Piccadilly. Exhibitions all over the country were planned but, ultimately, the cheese travelled only to a few of the larger Somerset towns. Sad to say, those charged with guarding it neglected their duties. The giant cheese was poked and prodded, subjected to all manner of indignities, and deteriorated badly. On its second presentation it was wisely refused by the Palace and returned to its makers, who then compounded their folly by arguing long and hard over its ownership until it was no longer fit for consumption. Its final resting place is unknown but I suspect that the pigs had it.

WILLIAM SMALL

No account of the history of Cheddar cheese would be complete without mentioning William Small's famous cheesemongery. Mr Small came from a cheesemaking family; his mother had secured a post as cheesemaker in Cheddar village 'at £80 a year an' her living' fer makin a 100-cow dairy cheese'. She was made to sign an undertaking that she would not smoke, eat onions or suck peppermints. Her son's modest cheese store, established in 1876, became *the* place to buy cheese, for William was an acknowledged expert and, though not a big man, was said to have sampled over 3 million cheeses. A photograph taken outside his shop on 6 June 1901 still survives, showing a horse and cart loaded with 3,547 lb (1,600 kg) of 'genuine Cheddar cheese' for the first British National Antarctic Expedition led by Captain Robert Falcon Scott. A proud moment in the history of Cheddar.

Alas, after William Small left the business in 1925, the village of Cheddar was connected only in name with its famous cheese. Any visitor hoping to acquire some real cheese was to be disappointed, as T.A. Layton describes in his book *Choose Your Cheese* (1957):

> As for Cheddar, the messy, straggling, dreary little village must be one of the worst examples of an unworthy place giving its name to something which is *hors concours* in its class. How the cheese came to be named after the village, not a soul in the place knows or cares.

The village had lost its birthright. Visitors still came to see the towering Gorge and to enter the Caves but thought not of cheese. Despite tales to the contrary, Cheddar Caves were never used to store cheese for, until the last century, they remained inaccessible to all but climbing enthusiasts.

Happily the village renewed its connection with cheese when, in 1988, John and Shirley Hammond opened The Cheddar Gorge Cheese Company at the foot of the Gorge. Here they show visitors the process of Cheddar-making, past and present, and provide an opportunity to buy Cheddar from Cheddar. It is certainly an innovative idea, and one of the better tourist attractions on offer. Down the road at Draycott, not so far distant, Peppy D'Ovidio of Times Past Cheese Dairy (a highly respected local maker) is making traditional Cheddar by hand, and Cheddar cheese is once again being sold at William Small's premises, now trading as The Original Cheddar Cheese and Cider Company, in the famous Gorge. Real Cheddar cheese is to be found in Cheddar again. Long may it continue.

THE CHEDDAR TOAST

The following poem was said to have been exhibited in the windows of the 'better grocers' of Shepton Mallet, Somerset. Despite many visits to the town I have yet to see it so displayed, but I applaud the sentiments.

> Come fill ye up the cider cup
> And drink to Cheddar Cheese,
> Good luck be with the hoof and horn,
> Good luck with flock and fleece.
> May the milk pail fill, the hayloft swell,
> The root crops still increase,
> May our land be crowned with plenty,
> Good temper, wealth and peace.

5

The Cheshire Harvest

In an age when soporific blandness rules, some people have only experienced two county cheeses: a crumbly white one variously described as Lancashire, Wensleydale, Caerphilly or Cheshire, and the alternative orange, soapy one variously called Double Gloucester or Red Leicester, depending on the whim of the retailer. What a deceit! Take the time to seek out the traditionally made real article and you'll never settle for plastic imitations again. Enough of my hobby-horses, but it is a travesty to grant many of these characterless blocks of white fat the proud name of Cheshire cheese. Cheshire is a *round* cheese, drum-shaped like Stilton, never block-shaped.

Originally known as Chester, Cheshire was the earliest English cheese to be exported, and was respected by the Romans. The flat landscape of north Cheshire is one reason for its excellence; west-facing, well-watered and well-drained, this is unmistakably cow country. There is limestone beneath the surface, as in Lancashire and Yorkshire, although in those two hilly and exposed counties, early cheeses were made from ewes milk. Nobody has suggested that Cheshire was ever anything but a 'cow' cheese. Perhaps the skills required to get the best out of cattle developed early because the native breed of the area, the Welsh Black, was small in stature and thus easier to catch and control. The breed is a very old one, descended from the cattle which ancient Britons took into the mountains of Wales when they retreated from the Saxons. Cheese was made in Cheshire before the craft began in Somerset, where tidal marshes abounded until the Somerset Levels were drained. Boggy ground is not well suited to keeping cattle. Also, Somerset lay in the kingdom of Wessex, further removed from the main trade routes.

Documentary evidence is scant, there being no mention of Cheshire cheese in the Domesday Book, but it survived the Dark

Ages and appears to have retained its reputation, being described in 1425 as 'greene cheese that will greese your cheeks'. ('Greene' meaning fresh, not a reference to the colour.) The Elizabethan cartographer John Speed had Cheshire in mind when he wrote:

> The champion grounds made glad the hearts of their tillers; the meadows imborderred with sweet-smelling posies; and the pastures make kines [cows'] udders to strout [bulge] to the paile, from whom and wherein the best cheese in all Europe is made.

During the Civil War 300 tons of Cheshire cheese were purchased in a single year to feed Cromwell's army. An entry in the diary of Celia Fiennes (who omitted precise dates but made entries from 1695–7) suggests that cheese was being made in Cheshire on the same co-operative basis as in the Cheddar area:

> Nantwich is a pretty large town and well built; this is a pretty Rich land but what I wondered at was that tho' this shire is remarkable for a greate deale of greate Cheeses and Dairys I did not see more than 20 or 30 Cows in a troope feeding, but on Enquiry find ye Custome of ye Country to joyn their milking together of a whole village and so make their greate Cheeses.

It was indeed 'greate' cheese, the historian Frederick Maitland calculating, from port receipts, that 5,665 tons were shipped to London in the year ending 25 March 1770. By the time of William Marshall's farming survey of 1775 production was around 9,000 tons per year, enough to support cheese fairs at Chester, Ellesmere, Market Drayton, Nantwich, Shrewsbury and Whitchurch. This was a prodigious quantity, when one considers that at that time an average cow could barely yield enough milk to make 300 lb (136 kg) of cheese in a year. Such figures would suggest the Cheshire herds amounted to something over 67,000 head of cattle, despite Celia Fiennes's observation. The rich pastures, the deposits of salt lying just below the surface and the long tradition of cheesemaking in the area all contributed to the excellence of the Cheshire product.

The original Cheshire cheese was a pale-golden colour and its reputation was so good that naughty Welsh farmers were tempted to pass off their inferior product as the real thing to coach travellers on the London to Holyhead route. The Welsh cheese had a quite different flavour; in many cases a proportion of goats milk was mixed with the cows milk. When it was sold in London, the howls of dissatisfied customers brought the real Cheshire into disrepute. Pressure was applied to make the Welsh farmers colour their product red so as to distinguish the inferior cheese from true Cheshire, but, just to show how contrary customers can sometimes be, the red colouring proved so popular that the Cheshire makers found themselves obliged to add it to their cheese. Perhaps the passengers on the Holyhead coach, having once bought red 'Cheshire', would not thereafter accept pale cheese as the genuine article.

By the eighteenth century the quantity of Cheshire cheese being sent to London was so great that road transport alone was inadequate. Cheese was collected at Frodsham for the cheese factors of Liverpool, who combined with the cheesemongers of London and ran a fleet of no less than 16 ships between London and Liverpool. Larger estates, such as those maintained by Lord Crewe and the Duke of Westminster, built superb dairies, incorporating all the latest improvements.

A distinctive feature of a Cheshire dairy was the *cheese oven*. This was a brick cavity, warmed by an adjacent chimney, within which the milled and salted curd was left overnight. The warmth assisted the expulsion of whey and raised the acidity. Better cheese rooms were even heated by hot water pipes. With improvements in roads and canals making it possible to transport food over greater distances, it was not long before Cheshire appeared in the shops of all the principal English towns. The cheese sometimes crossed the Channel, where the French persist in calling it *Chester* cheese.

POETIC CHESHIRE

Poets have been strangely silent on the subject of cheese, but Cheshire is one of the very few that can boast verses written in its honour. I have not been able to trace the author of a poem which relates to the old rivalry between England and Spain. A Spaniard boasts of his land being so fertile that two crops could be ripened in a single year, but as the fruit of the Cheshire grassland is cheese, produced twice a day, the Cheshireman is less than impressed.

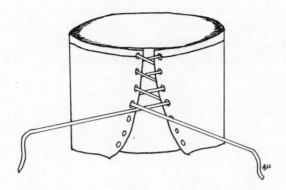

A lace-up cheesecloth from Overton Hall, Cheshire. These were usually made of strong calico.

A Cheshireman sailed into Spain, to trade for merchandise;
When he arrived from the main, a Spaniard him espies.
Who said, You English rogue, look here! What fruits and spices fine
Our land produces twice a year, thou hast not such in thine.

The Cheshireman ran to his hold, and fetched a Cheshire cheese,
And said, Look here, you dog, behold we have such fruits as these.
Your fruits are ripe but twice a year, as you yourself do say,
But such as I present you here, our land brings twice a day.

TODAY'S CHESHIRE CHEESE

Today, a range of Cheshire cheeses is available, besides the traditional white variety. You can find Cheshire coloured red with annatto, as well as white and blue-veined cheese.

Blue Cheshire with its famous 'green fade' is no longer made in the county but has been re-created by Long Clawson Dairy in Leicestershire. Genuine Cheshire Cheese is made on around half a dozen farms, one of which, Appleby's of Hawkstone, still uses unpasteurised milk. Take the trouble to seek out real Cheshire cheese; anything prepacked is unlikely to have the character of the traditional article.

Sizes vary but the cheese is normally made in truckles around 15 in (38 cm) high. The cheesecloth may be pasted to the cheese with a flour and water paste, not larded, as in the case of Cheddar.

The cheese is ready for eating around six weeks after production, and the preferred texture is loose and crumbly, with a mild and slightly salty flavour. Cheshire is delicious eaten with fresh fruit or fruitcake, but its keeping qualities are poor and it can quickly turn acid and bitter in flavour. Enjoy your Cheshire cheese whilst it is still young and enjoy it often.

6

Gloucester:
The Cheese We Nearly Lost

Gloucestershire was once noted for the excellence of its cheese but two world wars virtually extinguished the craft until a recent revival. Cattle still graze the lush pastures of the Severn Vale but they are not Old Gloucesters, and the milk is required for purposes other than cheesemaking.

Long before the Old Gloucester breed was established, Cotswold sheep provided milk for cheese. At the time of the Norman Conquest the Manor of Minchinhampton, granted to the nuns of Caen by King William, had 1,700 sheep grazing the common land. Between May and September 1307, 445 cheeses were made, each weighing 7 to 8 lb (3.2–3.6 kg). As early as 1498 there was so much cheese being traded in Gloucester that a permanent cheese market was established at Kings Board in Eastgate Street, still the site of Gloucester's indoor market.

By the time of the Tudors, cows milk had taken the place of ewes milk and cheese was being made across the north of the county, through the Vale of Berkeley and as far south as Bristol. At some risk of inflaming old animosities, I repeat the story that one William Cheddar was making cheese in the Sodbury area during the 1700s (a century before Joseph Harding was born) and that William was the true originator of Cheddar cheese! Whatever the truth of the matter, Gloucestershire had some very discriminating cheese eaters. Thomas Blisse of Painswick recorded in 1667 that he had 43 different kinds of cheese in his cellar.

Milk was provided by Old Gloucester cows, which had become a distinct breed by 1700. These cows yielded 500 gallons (2,300 litres) per year (considered high in those days) and the milk was ideal for cheesemaking, as the small fat globules made for a fine, even-textured cheese. The fat droplets from Old Gloucester milk rose to the top of the milk so slowly that the cream had to be skimmed off twice. There is a theory that this double skimming accounts for the name 'Double' Gloucester.

Cheesemaking became the major industry of Gloucestershire, taking the place of the Cotswold wool trade as weaving went into decline. Gloucester cheese was sold all over the country and exported from Bristol to Ireland, America and the West Indies. Output continued to grow until the middle of the eighteenth century. Sadly, in the years 1745–6, a great cattle plague struck the county and the Old Gloucester breed was virtually wiped out, eventually being replaced by the longhorn. By the time herds had been rebuilt, cattle plagues in other parts of the country, particularly around London, combined with improvements in transport, made it more profitable for Gloucestershire farmers to sell fresh milk.

A survey carried out in 1789 estimated that over 1,000 tons of Gloucester cheese was produced each year, its reputation rivalling that of Cheddar. Scarcely a vestige of that great industry remains but the eighteenth-century passion for detail has left us a legacy of farming reports. William Marshall, in his *Rural Economy of Gloucestershire* (1796), meticulously set down the minutiae of cheesemaking:

> The presses which I saw in this vale, were mostly loaded with gravel, in cubical boxes, raised by rollers, and made to fall horizontally upon the cheese. The young cheese are carried immediately from the press to an upper room, fitted with shelves for the purpose. Here they are turned, generally once a day, until they have acquired a sufficient degree of texture to undergo 'washing': a work which is gone through every three, four, or five weeks. In the operation of washing, the firmness or solidity of the cheeses is seen in their specific gravity; by observing which of them sink, and which of them swim. If they sink they are of a sufficiently close texture: if they swim, they are 'hove'; that is, either porous, or hollow in the middle.

Who was that latter-day Archimedes, realising that it was possible to calculate the specific gravity of cheese by immersion in water? Marshall also records the appearance of a natural blush on the surface of some Berkeley cheeses:

> Cheeses rich in quality, and well produced; more especially, I

believe, the produce of some particular soils; acquire, by age, a variegated color; particularly, at and near the surface; which becomes clouded with red. I have seen instance of this effect, in some Gloucestershire cheeses, of a curiously fine quality and great age.

Fifty years after Marshall's survey, Gloucester cheese was still held in high regard. In June 1854, *Farmer's Magazine* praised the care with which Gloucester cattled were tended and set out the qualities to be expected of the cheese.

The marks of the true Gloucester cheeses are their richness and sweetness; the yellow, golden hue of their edges; a smooth, close and wax-like texture; a very mild and rich flavour; not crumbling when cut into thin slices, not parting when toasted, with the oily matter they contain, but softening without burning.

Lesser makers were unfortunately inclined to pass off their wares as better-known varieties but expert cheesemakers were officially recognised and their products stamped. It was the powerful cheese merchants or factors who ultimately rewarded those who turned out the best product. The Gloucestershire historian Samuel Rudder, writing in 1779, confirmed the influence exerted by the factors:

The produce of the vale of Berkeley, like that of the vale of Gloucester, is all purchased by what are called 'cheese factors'; though, in reality, cheese merchants. Almost the whole produce of the vale passes through the hands of two men, Mr. Bigland of Frocester and Mr. Hicks of Berkeley. Each purchaser has his own particular dairies: which he takes, year after year; at such prices, as their several specific qualities are entitled to; and the market price, at the time of delivery, will afford.

THE LAST GLOUCESTER CHEESES

Gloucestershire finally ceased to be a cheesemaking county when a flood of low-priced imports, and the easier profit derived from fresh milk, killed off the trade at the end of the nineteenth century. Ken Pickford in his book *Country Days* (Peter Watts

Publishing, 1984) describes how cheese was made at Standish Court in the 1920s and eaten in large quantities, not least by his own Uncle Oswald, who is credited with having said, 'A cheese is good if you can eat a pund on't it wi'out bread.' In 1925 there were a handful of makers left around Berkeley (and even a cheese section in the annual fair at Lechlade) but none of them survived the Second World War. Gloucestershire lost its cheese, just as Wiltshire had done. It is little realised today how Wiltshire cheese was once the pride of the county, rivalling Gloucester and Cheddar, but that is another story.

DOUBLE OR SINGLE

There are several explanations on offer as to how the descriptions 'Double' and 'Single' came to be applied to Gloucester cheese. The one I believe to be correct is that evening milk was enriched by the addition of cream skimmed from the morning milk, so that the real *Double* Gloucester was made with *double* the amount of cream. The cheese was pressed in discs 20 in (50 cm) round and 5 in (13 cm) thick. For less affluent customers, a *Single* Gloucester was made from the residual skimmed milk and pressed thinner, so that the customers could see at a glance which they were getting. As the larger, richer Double Gloucester had better keeping qualities, the smaller Single Gloucester dropped out of favour. The manufacture of an excellent Single Gloucester cheese has fortunately been revived by Charles Martell at Dymock, while a highly acclaimed Double Gloucester is made by Diana Smart at Birdwood. Seek out their products; you'll be glad you did.

7

The Battle of Wensleydale

The story of Wensleydale is the story of a battle. The people of Wensleydale, on more than one occasion, have successfully fought to maintain the distinctive individuality of their local cheese. It is fortunate that Wensleydale production has persisted when other county cheeses have succumbed, as this product, at its best, is well worth fighting for.

Wensleydale is a close-textured, pure-white cheese, ready for eating after three weeks. It is a little dry on the palate, but a remarkably 'light' cheese. As I was raised on mature Cheddar, my first taste of Wensleydale came like a light, dry Moselle after an excess of heavy port or sherry.

We know that cheese was being made in the Dales 2,000 years ago because a curd strainer from that period was unearthed at Bainbridge Roman fort, east of Hawes. Cheese was later made by monks, who were granted vast tracts of land by William the Conqueror. The Cistercians, already noted sheep farmers and horse breeders, established a monastery at Fors but soon moved to a better site at Jervaulx and later founded abbeys at Fountains and Kirkstall. They were forbidden meat, except as a remedy during illness, and their cheese must have meant a lot to them. (As well as to the Conqueror's troops, who were reportedly dissatisfied with their rations.) The monks erected farm buildings and contained their flocks of ewes within miles of limestone walls, laid quite differently to the Cotswold variety. Such walls are still a major feature of the landscape. The milk was carried to centres, known as 'granges', where managers were employed to produce food and clothing adequate for the monks' needs, as well as wool to sell. The excellence of the cheese made for the monks' use at these granges was noted as early as 1150.

Monastic influence ended in 1537 when the last abbot was executed and the monasteries destroyed but, in truth, today's Wensleydale has only a passing acquaintance with the cheese of the Tudor period, which was made with ewes milk and might have resembled a Camembert-type cheese called *augelot*.

At some time between the Dissolution of the Monasteries and the seventeenth century, the ewes were replaced by shorthorn cows and the cheese became more like the Wensleydale, Swaledale, Cotherstone and Coverdale cheeses we know today. The name Wensleydale was not commonly used for cheese made in the valley of the river Ure until 1840, when the cheese fairs held in Leyburn's wide, sloping market-place became famous throughout the county. The three-day Yarm Fair, held in October, also provided an outlet, as merchants from all over the north of England vied to secure stock for the Christmas trade. The making of cheese, like knitting, was such a part of everyday life that it passed into the language. A nosey-parker would be dismissed with, 'There's a cheese on the cross', whilst 'Not for a cheese' expressed reluctance to perform an unwelcome exercise. 'There's a cheese for the last' was a salutary warning for anyone late about their business.

It used to be held that perfect Wensleydale could only be made in early spring, when the cows were released for their 'first bite' of the spring grass whilst winter snow still lingered in the hollows. They would graze on the young alder shoots growing by the streams and this was said to impart a special flavour to the curd.

Wensleydale cheese should be mild and creamy, made from a finely cut curd that is only lightly pressed, so as to retain the high moisture content that makes it slightly crumbly and flaky. It should never be oily or brown round the edges. Traditional Wensleydale is the same shape as Stilton, if a little smaller, and is best eaten fresh, to savour fully the honeyed aftertaste. It is at its best when eaten with apple pie or a crisp, fresh apple. There is also a blue-veined version of Wensleydale, a robust cheese that takes six months to mature and has a flavour comparable to Stilton.

One custom that persisted long in Yorkshire, reflecting local appetites, was the buying of a whole cheese as opposed to fiddling little slices. The author James Herriot had one such served during his honeymoon, 'a foot-high Wensleydale cheese, the old kind of "wet" Wensleydale which perhaps did not satisfy the technical purists but was exquisite to eat.'

Old Wensleydale cheese had its peculiarities. The milk was renneted by adding a piece of calf vell (called a *keslop*), or a 'black snail' (possibly a leech) instead of conventional rennet. The cheesemakers were said to add three or four eggs per cheese, and the cheese was salted in brine 'strong enough to float an egg'. The dry-salting of Wensleydale was only introduced in 1890, when John Benson from the Dairy Farmers' Institute at Aylesbury visited farms in the Dales and developed a recipe for adding salt to the curd, so dispensing with the pickling process.

The manufacture of Wensleydale had declined by the end of the nineteenth century, as farmers found it easier to sell fresh milk in the nearby industrial areas. Such cheese as continued to be made was sold direct to local grocers or to corn merchants on a 'cheese-for-flour' barter system. To make an extra shilling, some farmers' wives turned out a *kirn milk* cheese, using skimmed milk, but this was a hard and tasteless product. In response to this inferior cheese, provision dealer Edward Chapman set up his own dairy at Hawes in 1897, taking in around 200 gallons (900 litres) of milk each day during the summer months. He soon moved to larger premises in an old woollen mill, where his business prospered, inspiring others, including the chocolate manufacturer Alfred Rowntree, to open factories at Askrigg, Bainbridge, Borough-bridge, Coverham, Darley, Dent, Kirkby Malzeard, Masham, Redmire and Thoralby. Many of these producers did not survive the depression of the 1930s, when prices fell below production cost. Wensleydale cheese might have disappeared altogether were it not for the efforts of Hawes's finest son, the King of Wensleydale, Kit Calvert.

THE KING OF WENSLEYDALE

Born in 1903, the son of a penniless quarryman, Kit Calvert had watched his grandmother making cheese and knew the process well. He was one of a number of farmers who sent their surplus milk to Hawes Creamery, an old mill beside Duerley Beck, where cheese had been made since 1898. Kit saw his profits plummet during the agricultural crisis of 1933, when cheese couldn't be sold for the rock-bottom price of 8d a pound.

In the summer of 1933 the Hawes Creamery faced bankruptcy. The former army captain who managed the dairy called a meeting of suppliers and told them there was no money left to pay for milk they had already supplied. The situation was equally desperate for the farmers, who had no alternative customers for their milk. The farmers decided that it was vital that the creamery survived, and formed a committee to run it. They struggled on for a month or two until, in October 1933, the Milk Marketing Board was established. The Board was set up to take all good milk from farmers, pay a nationally agreed price for it, and sell it on to the various users. The Hawes farmers were offered an astonishing deal by the Board. They hoped to pay 5½d per gallon for cheesemaking milk, and would have paid more, but the Board decided Hawes Creamery would be charged a penny halfpenny per gallon, with a discount of a halfpenny if they collected the milk themselves! Within three months the creditors had been paid off and the business handed back to the captain, but within a year a letter was sent out telling his suppliers the creamery faced bankruptcy again!

The farmers met a second time to decide the future of Hawes Creamery. Express Dairy now came into the picture, offering to buy their milk but, without the creamery, the farmers felt they would be dealing with a monopoly buyer. Kit Calvert decided to take over the business himself. 'Take no notice of that Kit Calvert,' some said. 'He knows nowt about cheese. He'll go bust t'same way as t'captain, you'll see.' But the Milk Marketing Board put its weight behind Calvert, who mortgaged his own farm to raise capital and managed to extract £25 out of each of the farmers in return for a place on the Board of Directors. (It is a bold man who can persuade farmers in the Dales to part with their brass.) Kit Calvert had to make Hawes Creamery pay its way, and his solution to its problems was a one-pound cheese.

The traditional Wensleydale had always been a big cheese, which took weeks to mature and became a millstone round the necks of small grocers' shops. The one-pound cheese was ready to sell after three days. With a bit of luck it could be made and sold before the cheque for the milk was cashed by the MMB. This solved Kit Calvert's cash-flow problems and Hawes Creamery prospered, but there were more battles to be fought.

As a result of government restrictions, Wensleydale cheese almost disappeared during the Second World War, and it was only through the determined efforts of Calvert and his team that markets were regained. Changing patterns of supply reduced the number of creameries (by 1976 only the factories at Kirkby Malzeard, Coverham and Hawes were to survive), and it was decided to secure the future of the operation by selling to the

Milk Marketing Board. Just before Kit Calvert retired, Hawes Creamery was sold to the MMB for £487,000, not a bad return for the Dales farmers who had grudgingly agreed to invest £25 back in 1935.

Kit Calvert achieved a great deal for Wensleydale. After his retirement he wrote extensively on farming in the Dales and opened a book shop in Hawes, famous for the old pillar box which served as a till, payment being posted in the slot. Kit became a great local benefactor, travelling the Dales in a cart drawn by his horse Dolly, and seldom seen without his dog and old-fashioned clay pipe. He did much for his Methodist chapel, paid for a local children's playground and was honoured by the award of an MBE in 1977. A devout Christian and a complete Dalesman, he became known as the 'King of Wensleydale' before he died, in 1985. A well-deserved title for a great man.

ANOTHER BATTLE

History repeats itself, for in the spring of 1992 Dairy Crest, the trading arm of the Milk Marketing Board, decided that Hawes Creamery was an unnecessary appendage to its operations and should close. The manufacture of Wensleydale cheese was to be transferred to Longridge in Lancashire. It was not only the farmers who were dismayed; cheese lovers faced a future without Wensleydale made in its true home and, again, Yorkshire passions were roused. Prepared to fight for their local creamery, banner-waving residents turned out in force and, as a protest, let the cyclists in the famous Milk Race pass through the town in silence. It is a serious matter, losing 59 jobs in a community of 1,000, not to mention the folk who make the Wensleydale cheese dishes, and grocers like Elijah Allen & Son who sell the cheese. Harry Hansen, as coordinator of the rescue committee, offered Dairy Crest £160,000 to take over the existing business, but the asking price was half a million. There was talk of local cheesemakers moving to premises nearby and setting up with secondhand equipment, leaving Dairy Crest to 'stew in their own juice', but such investments are not undertaken lightly. The saga was long and tedious and it was November of that year before the deal was done, at a price of £300,000, and the Hawes Creamery was saved again. Kit Calvert would have been proud of them.

The new owners completely refurbished the creamery, and a
visitor centre, with a viewing gallery, now awaits your pleasure.
Do go and see it. Hawes is a delightful centre for touring the
Dales – and, while you're there, buy some of the cheese.

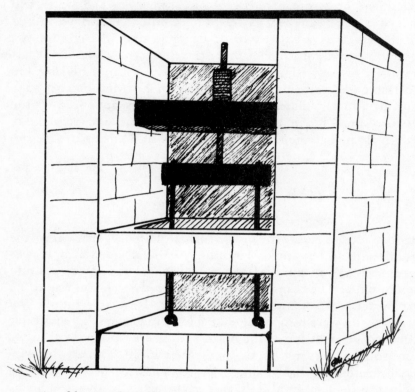

An old stone cheese press of a type commonly found in the Dales.

8

Lancashire and the Leigh Toaster

The making of this cheese is purely local, being confined
to the county bearing its name.
G. SUTHERLAND THOMPSON (1925)

The cheeses of the northern counties of England are as individual
as the people who make them. Northerners know better than to
shrink in horror from a cheese that crumbles against the knife. In
Lancashire you will find shops called The Crumbly Cheese,
whereas the Home Counties would rather have their cheese like
India rubber than suffer a few loose crumbs. Lancashire cheese,
like its Cheshire neighbour but to a greater degree, has been
bastardised out of existence outside its own county. For too long
cheese bearing no resemblance to Lancashire but carrying that
name has been foisted upon a largely uncaring public by those
who have the temerity to suggest that they are giving us what we
want.

Cheese from the Lancashire uplands has a long and illustrious
history. Even in medieval times there were huge cattle farms,
almost ranches, the property of the landed families who turned
over their hunting grounds in the forests of Bowland and
Rossendale to cattle. Preston was awarded its first royal charter in
the reign of King John, and became the principal market for
Lancashire cheese. The best cheeses were said to come from the
'black land' of the Fylde, a coastal area north of the Ribble. When
the Industrial Revolution arrived, this cheese was to become the
staple food of the mill-workers, who were crammed into miser-
able back-to-back houses with little or no cooking facilities.

Lancashire is undoubtedly the king of toasting cheeses. When melted it has a soft and silky, custard-like texture, and the aroma is pure magic. The standard joke about Welshmen was based on their love for toasted cheese, but, when times were hard and butcher's meat a rarity, the poor folk of Lancashire made a filling meal of just such cheese, the famous Leigh Toaster.

JOSEPH LIVESEY

One Lancastrian who knew poverty at first hand was Joseph Livesey of Walton le Dale. He was born an orphan and trained as a weaver, but when the weaving trade went sour he was reduced to picking over the leavings of the local market to feed his family. He would buy leftovers that the stall holders could not be bothered to carry away, including small lumps of cheese, and so successfully did he procure these bits and pieces that he was able to sell them to other poor labourers outside the gin shops. Eventually Joseph gave up weaving and devoted all his time to cheese trading. He became a familiar figure at the markets of Wigan and Chorley and was soon buying direct from the farms. He took advantage of the seasonal surplus available in farming areas and sold it in the towns. He never forgot his humble origins even when his business prospered and he rose to become a respected public figure, launching the *Preston Guardian* and using his position to champion the temperance movement. Preston market still prospers, with its gigantic canopy over a multitude of stalls, and provides a fitting memorial to its most famous son.

GORNALL'S VAT

As late as 1850, the *hafod* system was still being employed around the Forest of Bowland, with cattle being moved to higher pastures during the summer months. The methods of cheese manufacture were diverse and there was no such thing as a common type of Lancashire cheese until late in the century, when the County Council employed Joseph Gornall of Claylands Cabus to tour the county's farms offering instruction in cheesemaking. Gornall succeeded in establishing a definitive Lancashire cheese; he wrote a number of books on the subject and his teachings were closely

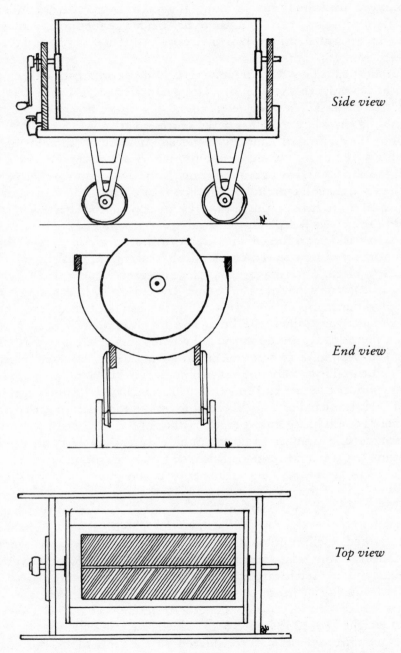

Side view

End view

Top view

Gornall's vat, as shown in the original patent application of 1892.

followed until the 1950s. (Some of his methods are still employed today although, since 1945, there has been a tendency to replace the delicate curd of high-moisture cheese with a drier variety that keeps longer.) Gornall was responsible for the invention of the *Gornall's vat*. This was a revolving cylinder, contained within an outer vessel, with a section of its lid perforated to permit drainage of the curd. The device retained heat within the curd, whilst enabling the whey to be extracted more effectively.

For the making of Lancashire cheese, the evening and morning milks were mixed, warmed and renneted to produce a moderately firm curd, dry and sweet to the taste. Annatto dye was sometimes added and the milk might be skimmed a little, but this was discouraged. 'If more than a tithe of the cream be taken, the cheese will be the poorer,' was Joseph Gornall's advice. A portion of the curd was then set aside and mixed with fresh curd after a day or two, the proportion of new to old curds in the final mixture varying from place to place. What makes Lancashire cheese unique is the mixing of curds from two or more milkings. The reason for this practice is unclear but many of the farms along the banks of the Wyre, the Grizedale, the Calder, the Loud and the Ribble are not blessed with good roads, and up in the fell country roads scarcely exist at all. Carrying milk to a central point would have presented many difficulties. How much more sensible to rennet the milk where it was produced before carrying the curd to a dairy to be pressed and salted. It is my belief that this was the reason for curds one, two or three days old being mixed together, but in the absence of written evidence, one can only speculate. Such a system was certainly used in the Carpathian Mountains, where the curds of mountain tribesmen were carried to central factories called *brynziar* to make a white cheese known as *Bryndza* or *Brinzen*.

When fresh Lancashire curds were mixed with curd that had been kept for several days, the acid level ran high, giving the cheese its markedly white colour. One source records that curds were held for 'as long as a fortnight'. The finished cheeses were cloth bound and pressed in large flat moulds, one 14 in (36 cm) in diameter producing a cheese of 44–50 lb (20–3 kg). There was also a smaller size, 8 in (20 cm) in diameter, producing a finished cheese that weighed 10–12 lb (4.5–5.5 kg). Both sizes are still used.

Lancashire cheese was considered to be a profitable variety, each gallon of milk yielding over a pound of cheese, but production declined as it became more advantageous to send fresh milk to the conurbations of Liverpool and Manchester. The situation exactly paralleled that of other areas such as South Wales and Gloucestershire, where farmers abandoned cheesemaking to obtain greater profits from fresh milk. For many years barely enough Lancashire cheese was produced to meet local demand, and it largely disappeared from the market. The cheese was entirely a farmhouse product until 1913 when Wolfen Mill Dairy was opened by the Procter family in the village of Chipping. Even within its home county, Lancashire cheese came perilously close to extinction. Before the Second World War there were 200 farms and creameries between the river Lune and the river Ribble making Lancashire cheese. As a wartime measure they were starved of their raw material and only 22 returned to cheesemaking after 1945. Now, there are less than a dozen.

The traditional Lancashire is the most crumbly of the English cheeses, although it may spread like butter when three months old. If you bought a pound of this cheese, you could expect a half-pound lump and a further half-pound of crumbs in a bag! Before 1939 it was made without a starter, so the cheese 'came on' much slower and could mature for months without becoming strong. Today's Lancashire cheese is usually made from pasteurised milk, although a better cheese might be made from raw milk. Low levels of starter are used and the curd is cut around an hour after renneting. The curds and whey receive little or no scalding and the curd is pitched whilst still very soft. The curd is drained then lightly pressed and rebroken four or five times until it is considered to be sufficiently dry. At the salting stage, it is mixed with an equal measure of 24- or 48-hour-old curd; it all depends on the individual cheesemaker's technique. About 2½ per cent salt is added before the curd is pressed to produce bandaged or waxed rounds. The finished product is sold as a mild cheese within three or four weeks, although it can be matured on.

Good cooks regard Lancashire as the best cheese for cooking, as it crumbles readily, and sprinkle it over Lancashire hotpots to provide extra nourishment and richness.

MAKING LANCASHIRE CHEESE

I watched Lancashire cheese being made at Wolfen Mill Dairy near Chipping. This is wild and windy country, magnificent for walking if you're not afraid of a little rain. (There are always the warming Lancashire cheesy-topped potatoes to look forward to after a bracing stroll.) The dairy gets through 4,000 gallons (18,000 litres) of milk a day, much of it going into their Lancashire cheese. Evening and morning milk is mixed in the Gornall's vat with its perforated lid, which is tilted to drain off excess whey. As only a very gentle pressure is applied to the curd, it may take an hour before it is drained adequately. The curd is cut with a perforated revolving screen, until reduced to particles the size of wheat seeds. The whole of the curd may be set aside for the next day, or 50 per cent fresh curd mixed with 50 per cent from the previous day. Temperature control is vital at this stage, with the curd needing to be maintained at a steady 68–70°F (20–1°C). The final cheese used to be pressed in 40 lb (18 kg) rounds, but now an easier-to-handle 28 lb (13 kg) disc is preferred. These are often dipped in hot water for about 30 seconds, to give the cheese a smooth outer coat.

THE NEW LANCASHIRE CHEESE

A revolution came about in the 1960s with the development of 'new' Lancashire, not made by the two-curd method. Designed for the exigencies of mass production, the new cheese was roundly condemned by the locals. The new or *fatty* Lancashire is still made with very little starter, and to avoid the difficulty of keeping large quantities of curd for more than a day, it is produced by a 'single-curd' method. This is a good-keeping and smooth-cutting cheese that can be shipped around easily, but such advantages are likely to be dismissed by the locals who think that people down south don't know how to appreciate crumbly cheese. The larger creameries are the major manufacturers of the new single-curd Lancashire. Still snowy white but only slightly crumbly, it is sharper than the original but this is the only Lancashire that most of the population will ever encounter.

9

Toasted Cheese from Wales

In the heart of Powys, near the point where the river Llynfi breaks through the Black Mountains to link up with the Wye, the peaceful town of Talgarth stands astride an old bridge over the Ennig stream, guarded by an ancient tower. Talgarth is not only a convenient centre for holidaymakers and hill walkers. Excellent cheese can be bought here from Gwynne and Son, grocers extraordinary, who have traded in the market square for more than a century. However, the good citizens of Talgarth, and the many summer visitors, are largely unaware of the fact that this was once a cheesemaking area of renown. Indeed, Talgar cheese was of such importance that it found particular mention in the ordinances of the Cheesemakers Company, dating from 1377. This document deals at length with the enforcement of restrictions designed to stop the buying and selling of cheese by middlemen, before it was offered for open sale: 'Whereas strangers do come and bring to the City [of London] cheese of Wales, called "talgar", and house the same in Fletstrete and Holbourne, and other places within the City as without, and there sell it in secret, against the ancient custom....'*

I have been unable to trace much information regarding Talgar cheese, but as the hills around Talgarth provide ideal sheep grazing, it seems likely that it was made from ewes milk. Wales is a conservative country where old ways are long respected and tradition dies hard, and Talgar was probably an antecedent of Caerphilly, the close-textured, white cheese favoured by Welshmen, particularly miners:

> Blackened men hew coal on hands and knees,
> Then dine in the dark on snow-white cheese.

*Quoted by Ambrose Keevil in *The Story of Fitch Lovell* (Phillimore, 1972)

The attractions of Caerphilly are four-fold. First, in a mining community, it has a saltiness which helps to counteract salt lost through perspiration during the men's labours. Second, it is mild and, as an ex-miner explained to me, miners believed that a 'strong' cheese would cause indigestion if eaten by someone doing hard manual work within the confines of the pit. Whatever the truth of this assertion, it is a fact that in South Wales, Derbyshire, Yorkshire, the North-east and other mining areas (some of which have not had working pits for a generation) the preference is most certainly for a mild cheese.

The third advantage benefits the farmer, in that Caerphilly is ready to be eaten only two weeks after being made (no long maturing period is required). Finally, Caerphilly is ideal for toasting. 'If you can toast cheese in Wales and boil rice in Turkey, then you can call yourself a cook' is an old adage dating from the early seventeenth century. Before this, Welsh tastes were mocked by Dr Thomas Cogan, physician to Elizabeth I, who said that 'Roasted cheese is more meet to bait a trap, to catch a mouse or rat, than to be received into the body.' An oft-repeated joke concerning the Welshman's love for toasted cheese appears in *Merry Tales, Wittie Questions and Quicke Answers* by Andrew Boorde, published in 1567:

> Fynde wryten amonge olde jestes how God made St Peter porter of heven. And that God of his goodness suffred many men to come to the kyngdome with small deservyng. At which tyme, there was in heven a grete company of Welchmen which with theyre rekrakynge [quarrelling] and babelynge trobelyd all the others. Wherefore God says to St Peter that he was wery of them and he would fayne have them out of heven. To whome St Peter sayde, 'Good Lorde, I warrent you that it shall be done.' Wherefor St Peter went outside of heven gayts and cryd with a loude voyce, 'Cause Babe!', that is as moche as to say 'Rosty'd Chese!' Which thynge the Welchmen heryng ran out of heven at a grete pace. When St Peter sawe them all out he sodenly went into Heven and lokkyd the dore! and so aparyd all the Welchmen out!

As much as the Welsh loved their toasted cheese, by 1900 farms were finding it more profitable to sell their milk in the mining valleys. This made it necessary to import cheese from Somerset, and large quantities were shipped across the estuary on steamers from Bridgwater dock.

A double-walled trolley vat once used for making Caerphilly cheese.

THE DUCKETT FAMILY

Mary Duckett is a member of a cheesemaking family who farm land at Wedmore in Somerset; they have been making Caerphilly for 60 years. Her father was a dealer at Highbridge, where there used to be a weekly cheese market, for which her mother made the cheese. Each week the Agricultural Institute at Cannington, near Bridgwater, would send an instructress to the farm to teach the youngsters cheesemaking. Each one had to make up a small tub of cheese, and Mary found this great fun. As soon as she left school, she started work in the dairy. At first, cheesemaking was done in a round copper vat holding just 80 gallons (140 litres) of milk. For the scalding, Mary had to dip off whey into a 7 gallon (12 litre), two-handled 'warmer', stand it in hot water, then pour it back into the curd, continuing this process until the correct temperature was reached.

When Mary married a farmer in 1942, only 'Government' Cheddar cheese was being made as wartime regulations did not permit products like Caerphilly, Lancashire and Wensleydale.

All the cheese was collected by the Milk Marketing Board and the family was allowed to keep back just one cheese a month for their own use. Mary used to help the lady employed to make the cheese and, as electricity was not installed until after the war, this meant tending the fire in the steam boiler. In the summer her duties included pumping water by hand from a well to cool the milk tank. (Well water was ten degrees colder than tap water.) When the war was over the Duckett family started making Caerphilly again. It was a case of regaining lost markets but, luckily, some of their pre-war customers were still around. The Duckett family are still making their Caerphilly, and it continues to win numerous awards. Buy it when you see it, for it really is exceptionally good.

CHEESEMAKING RETURNS TO WALES

The demand for fresh milk in the mining valleys was so great that cheesemaking was of little importance in Wales for many years from the late nineteenth century onwards. The loss of the Principality's national cheese was the cause of a complaint by Evan Jones in his *Book of Cheese* (1976):

> Caerphilly, the white unaged cheese that bears the name of the Welsh town dominated by its sprawling, moated castle, has for years been made in a score of alien places. In fact, when my wife and I picnicked there between the castle and Nay-y-Gledyr Brook there wasn't a crumb of local Caerphilly to be bought.

The town still cannot boast any cheese made in its environs but the manufacture of Caerphilly has returned to Abergavenny, not too far distant.

GLAMORGAN SAUSAGES

Glamorgan, a famous white cheese made from the milk of Gwent white oxen (long before the county of Gwent was invented), has been lost to Wales for many years, but the tradition of making sausages from cheese instead of meat has survived. These sausages were recalled by George Borrow, an expert commentator on cheese and beer but something of an eccentric,* in his book *Wild Wales* (1826): 'The breakfast was delicious, consisting of excellent tea, buttered toast and Glamorgan sausages, which I think are not a whit inferior to those of Epping.'

Happily, Glamorgan sausages, or *Selsig Sir Forganwwg* in the Welsh tongue, are once again back on the market. Since Glamorgan cheese is as extinct as the Gwent cattle, the sausages are now made from a mixture of Farmhouse Cheddar and Caerphilly cheeses, blended with leeks and spices, by Abergavenny Fine Foods. Along with a host of other small dairies based all over the Principality, Abergavenny Fine Foods are successfully creating new cheeses and reviving old varieties, proof of the dedication and innovation of today's Welsh cheesemakers.

Gwynfor and Thelma Adams of Caws Cenarth, Pontseli, Dyfed, should be credited with ploughing the first furrow of this revival, and other fine artisan makers have followed. It is an illustrious list: Leon and Joan Downey of Castle Morris, who have gained an enviable reputation for the excellence of their Llangloffan cheese; John Savage-Onstwedder with his incomparable Teifi; Dougal Campbell's Ty'n Grug (astonishingly good cheese); the Merlin goat cheeses and many others. Abergavenny Fine Foods have introduced a whole range of Welsh cheeses, all of them well worth trying. There's a welcome in the hillside, when you try the cheese of Wales!

*Burrow was convinced that the Welsh nation was the lost tribe of Israel. His researches, which extended over many years, sought to prove that a connection existed between the Welsh and Hebrew tongues.

10

Stilton: The Royal Blue

Cheeses to be taken to the portals of heaven and offered to the gods.
T. A. LAYTON

If anything were needed to exemplify the natural union of bread and cheese then it is the miracle of blue-veined cheeses. The specific mould that creates those veins, *Penicillium roqueforti*, was first raised on rye bread. I have heard the old tale of a shepherd boy from the banks of the Adour, in south-west France, who accidentally left his meal of rye bread and ewes milk cheese in a cave. When he returned several days later the white cheese was lined with blue. He tasted it, and Roquefort was discovered.

We cannot say with any degree of certainty who first discovered Stilton, but the cheese was noted by Daniel Defoe in his *Tour Through the Whole Island of Great Britain* (1724–6). Defoe found Stilton 'a town famous for cheese', praised as 'the English Parmesan'. Over the years, the identity of the inventor of the famous blue cheese has been the subject of much debate, including a lively correspondence in *The Times.* One school of thought held that this noble cheese was first made at Belvoir by one Mrs Stilton, head dairymaid to the fifth Duchess of Rutland, but this claim is weakened by the absence of documentary evidence.

Most accounts credit Miss Elizabeth Scarbrow, the housekeeper at Quenby Hall in Leicestershire, who took the recipe for what was then called Quenby cheese with her when she married a Mr Orton and set up home at Little Dalby, not far from Melton Mowbray. The year was 1720. The newly married Mrs Elizabeth Orton was not averse to letting the rumour spread that her cheese could only be made with the help of her husband's cows, fed on a small meadow called Orton Close. Her method stayed a family secret until one of her two daughters married an innkeeper and moved into the Bell Inn at Stilton in Cambridgeshire. The other daughter married a farmer, a Mr Paulet from Wymondham near Melton Mowbray. The new Mrs Paulet would almost certainly have made Quenby cheese to her mother's recipe, and it is equally certain that she would have supplied her brother-in-law, Cowper Thornhill, the landlord of the Bell Inn. This old coaching inn served travellers on the Great North Road from Aldersgate Street to Glasgow and the fame of 'Stilton' cheese spread even though it was not made in the village from which it took its name.

Whenever the story of Stilton is told, the name of Mrs Paulet must receive due mention but any claim of her having been the inventor of the cheese is weakened by a couplet in Alexander Pope's *Imitations of Horace* which appeared in 1733, when she was not yet of marriageable age:

> Cheese, such as men in Suffolk make,
> But wish'd it Stilton for his sake.

Whoever was the true innovator, Stilton has been made in the Vale of Belvoir for generations and also in the Dove Valley of Derbyshire, first by farming families and later by small dairy companies. What a success it has been! William Pitt in his *Survey of Leicestershire* (1809) gave a detailed recipe for the making of Stilton, which begins 'Take the milk of seven cows and the cream of the same number; heat a gallon of water scalding hot, and pour it upon three or four handfuls of marigold flowers that have been bruised a little.' The advantages afforded by the marigold flowers must have been significant for blue Stilton sold at 2s 6d per pound in London when Cheddar cheese fetched only 6–8d and Cheshire cheese only 2½d.

Stilton was also mentioned in Jane Austen's novel *Emma* of 1816: 'She was come ... for the Stilton cheese, the north Wiltshire [cheese], the butter, the celery, the beet-root and all the dessert.' In 1823, the essayist Charles Lamb wrote to thank his friend Thomas Alsop for a gift of Stilton cheese: 'Your cheese is the best I have ever tasted. Mary has sense enough to value the present; for she is very fond of Stilton. Yours is the delicatest, rainbow-hued melting piece I have ever tasted.'

Stilton still takes pride of place where British exports are concerned. It has been shipped abroad for 200 years, and remains the only British-made cheese to enjoy real success beyond our shores since the Romans praised the cheese made in Chester.

CHEESE MITES

Should Stilton have mites or should it not? There are those who say that it should. Stilton has traditionally been infested with small black living specks, the *Tyroglyphus siro* or cheese mite. Such cheese is still sought out by some connoisseurs today, who insist that it is those mites and, presumably, their excrement that gives the king of cheeses its particular flavour.

In September 1991 the magistrates at Alnwick in Northumberland threw out a case brought by the county's trading standards department, who claimed that the cheese was 'unfit for human consumption' because of the infestation. In a spirited defence, Mr Adrian Williams, appearing for the supermarket chain Safeway, told the magistrates: 'Here is a product which has been English to the bone from the 1700s onwards. It has had mites in it ever since that day and whatever the European Community says it is going to have mites in it in the future.'

Mr Williams might have recalled what Daniel Defoe wrote: 'Stilton is brought to the table with mites or maggots round so thick that they bring a spoon with them for you to eat the mites with as you do the cheese.' The eating of maggots is revolting in principle, but the cheese mite is tasteless and small enough to be inoffensive. Its presence should be regarded as a fortuitous accident and any concerns dismissed with this piece of doggerel:

> The cheese mites asked how the cheese got there,
> And warmly debated the matter;
> The orthodox said it came from the air,
> And the heretics said from the platter.

It is a fact that microscopic organisms are an integral part of Stilton's maturing process. Their presence is first betrayed by a light 'powder' at the bottom of the cheese. The Stilton is still perfect, and is often lightly dressed with cornstarch, anyway. A different situation arises if the cheese carries a coating of brown 'dust', for it is then heavily infested with cheese mite, which does indeed spoil it. To guard against this, the cheese store may be 'flushed' with a gas which kills off the infestation, but the process involves technical difficulties. Only skilled handling and storage can obviate the problem, and a well-made Stilton deserves to be handled with care right up until the time it is eaten. It has been remarked, 'Except that they make no noise, Stiltons are more trouble than babies.'

LONG CLAWSON: STILTON MANUFACTURER

The creamery at Long Clawson, Leicestershire, was established in 1911 and, with its sister dairy in the nearby village of Hose, produces 3,000 tonnes of Stilton each year, some 30 per cent of the UK total.

At Long Clawson milk is carefully checked and pasteurised before being poured into one of the eight 1,000 gallon (4,500 litre) vats. Special starters and the micro-organism *Streptococcus lactis*, which 'makes' Stilton, are then introduced. Rennet is added about 40 minutes later, to create the curds and whey. After pitching, the drained curd is allowed to stand for a day before being cut and milled into walnut-sized pieces. Salt is added and the curd is tipped into plastic tubes 2 ft (60 cm) long and 1 ft (30 cm) in diameter. This curd is not pressed in any way; liquid is allowed to drain naturally out of perforations in the tube. The tubes are turned once a day for five days to prevent the ends drying out. Before the week is up, the developing cheeses are removed from their moulds and wrapped in plastic film to prevent premature development of the blue veins. After three weeks, or thereabouts, the cheeses are removed from the film and left to stand in a *ripening room*, where the temperature and humidity are closely monitored. If left to its own devices the cheese would now ripen into creamy-white Stilton, a versatile product that makes an excellent sauce, but most Stilton is encouraged to 'blue'. At six weeks, the cheeses are skewered from the side by long needles (now a mechanised process), which admit air and initiate the formation of those famous blue veins. The cheese should be at its peak of perfection around 11 weeks after manufacture, still firm and creamy-white but with an even distribution of blue veins radiating out from the centre. It is cheese to be savoured, cheese to be enjoyed, cheese like no other.

THE ROYAL BLUE

Less than 10 dairies in all the world, most of them in the Vale of Belvoir, are allowed to describe their cheese as Stilton: Colston Bassett, Long Clawson, Millway, J.M. Nuttall (Dairy Crest), St Ivel (Unigate), Somerset Creameries, Tuxford and Tebbutt (The Cheese Company) and Webster's Dairy. Nowhere else can real Stilton be made; it is therefore a unique product. J.G. Davis, a mentor of the industry, asserted that the best Stilton is made around Melton Mowbray because the iron in the soil enhances the production of blue mycelium by the *Penicillium* bacteria, but there is no scientific evidence to support this claim. Patrick Rance, in his *Great British Cheese Book* (Macmillan, 1983), makes special mention of the smallest dairy, Websters of Saxelby, where Margaret Callow produces Stilton by the most traditional method. I share his opinion that Websters is one of the best Stiltons, but I'm sure you'll enjoy trying them all.

11

Cheese from Scotland

Kyle for man, Carrick for coo
Cunningham for butter and cheese
And Galloway for woo.*

Outside its own borders, Scotland seldom receives the respect it deserves where cheesemaking is concerned. As early as the sixteenth century dairying formed an important part of the Scottish economy and dairy products were used to pay rent. In outlying areas the milking of ewes and goats remained commonplace long after cows milk had become predominant south of the border. The making of soft or 'porridge' cheese, composed of lightly pressed or unpressed curds for quick consumption, has always been of greater importance in Scotland than in England and Wales. However, the difficulties of communication meant that there was no definitive 'Scottish' way of making cheese. Although there were radical differences between Highland and Lowland farming, farms in both areas tended to be small and cheeses made singly. This was how a lady in Kirkintilloch made cheese in 1820:

> The contents of my churn I put in an iron pot over a slow fire. As the buttermilk curdles, the curd sinks, and the next morning, when cool, I pour off the whey, and work the curd, giving it a little salt to taste. The curd is then put in a strong linen cloth, tied tightly, and hung for the remainder of the day to drip, and then retied, and hung up to dry for four weeks, when the cheese is fit for use. If a little bit of butter be worked into the curd, and the cheese kept for three or four months, it will be very good; at least it will taste like ewe-milk cheese, and it can be made with only one cow.

*The meaning of 'woo' in this old poem is far too indelicate for the author to specify.

In parts of the country the system of *transhumance* was practised, i.e. moving cattle from the valleys to higher pasture during
the summer months. In Wales, the temporary hilltop farmstead
was known as the *hafod*. The system is still practised in
Switzerland to this day. The farmworkers would drive the stock
that had survived the hardships of winter up to their new
grazing. During the summer, the men lived in a communal hut.
As the flow of milk increased after the spring calving, workers
who had finished the sowing came up and joined the mountain
dwellers in the daily round of milking, churning butter and
making cheese. In some areas they even utilised the water power
of the fast-flowing mountain streams. The helpers from the
valley brought up tubs of oatcakes – as bread would not have
kept fresh – and the tubs went back down the hill filled with
rounds of butter and cheese.

The cheeses would have received a dusting of oatmeal from
residues in the tubs, and several Scottish cheeses are sold with an
oatmeal coating to this day. The mountain workers lived on
oatcakes, butter, cheese and curd dishes all summer, looking to
the wild herbs such as garlic, thyme and sweet gale to provide
variation, just as we still add herbs to blander cheeses. After
tending the stock all day, they would have made up the peat fires
in the evening under cauldrons of whey. The cheese tubs would
first have been filled with water, and red-hot stones thrown in
until the water boiled. In this way the tubs were scalded, whilst
smoke from the peat fires drifted across the cheeses, adding a
smoky flavour. To lighten the darkest hours, some kind of spirit
was distilled from the whey. I can find no record of the flavour
but its effects I can easily imagine.

Cheese also played a part in the celebrations for Hogmanay.
The last day of the year originally gave licence to Scottish youngsters to call at cottage doors chanting rude rhymes and
demanding cheese and oatcakes:

> Get up, gude wife, and binno sweir*
> And deal your cheese while you are here
> For time will come when you'll be dead
> And neither need your cheese, nor bread.

*Be not lazy.

Scottish recipes for cheese have an individual character. J.G. Davis refers to a 1743 recipe for cream cheese 'which involved hanging unrenneted cream in an ox bladder for three weeks, and then, after removal, dry salting for a further eight days'. Ewes milk continued to be important in Scotland long after it had been replaced by that of cows south of the border. In a 1790 statistical report it was noted that Ettrick in Selkirkshire had 30,000 sheep.

BARBARA GILMOUR

Barbara Gilmour was one of the most influential characters in the history of Scottish cheese. Born in Dunlop in Ayrshire, she was one of the many Scottish Presbyterians known as Covenanters who fled to Northern Ireland in the 1670s to escape religious persecution under Charles II. In 1692, Barbara returned to the village of her birth, married John Dunlop of Overhill Farm and rapidly established a reputation for the excellence of her cheesemaking. Whether she developed some new technique, copied Irish methods or simply changed to making cheese with whole milk rather than skimmed is uncertain but, by whatever means, Barbara Gilmour created a Dunlop cheese which the cheese merchants of Kirktown carried to Glasgow. Here it sold at 4½d per pound, a good price in those days. Her descendants continued the business after her death (the family tomb bears only one date, 1732), and one of her stone presses can still be seen at the farm.

The milk provided by Ayrshire cattle is particularly suitable for cheesemaking as its fat content is suspended in very fine droplets, like that of the Old Gloucester breed. Dunlop cheese became famous all over Scotland during the nineteenth century but its quality varied and, with considerable foresight, the Ayrshire Agricultural Association sent a deputation to Somerset to see how things might be improved. Joseph Harding was invited to Scotland to demonstrate his methods at first hand and, as a result of his teaching, the Cheddar system of manufacture was adopted. Cheshire cheese was also made from time to time, probably as a result of immigrants from Cheshire seeking new opportunities in the north, but it was Dunlop that became the Scottish counterpart of Cheddar cheese.

CROWDIE

In the middle of the eighteenth century Crowdie was a soft unripened cheese consisting of two-thirds curds and one-third double cream, but it developed from far humbler origins. The name goes back to the Vikings and may have derived from the Lowland word *crud*, meaning curds. In 1773 Samuel Johnson noted how vital a foodstuff curds were to a family of goatherds at Loch Ness. He was informed that they lived 'all the Spring without meal, upon milk and curds and whey alone'. John Jamieson, in his *Dictionary of the Scottish Language* (1808), defines Crowdie as 'curds with the whey pressed out and mixed with butter, nearly in an equal proportion'.

Pre-war Crowdie was a sour-milk cheese, made by penurious crofters and eaten with oatcakes. Susannah and Reg Stone of Knockbreck, in the Scottish Highlands, revived the making of Crowdie after the Second World War. It is now generally defined as a skimmed-milk cheese, although the curds may have single or double cream added later. Ewes milk cheeses were common in the eighteenth and nineteenth centuries but the craft almost disappeared in the 1940s and has been revived only recently. Amongst current makers, Ann Dorward, who has a farm between Dunlop and Stewarton in Ayrshire, has collected many prizes at the Royal Highland Show for her Swinzie cheese. With the revival of interest in Scottish cheeses, the small cheesemakers of Ayrshire, Dumfries and Galloway have rescued old varieties from obscurity and developed new recipes. Some have joined together to promote the 'hand-made cheeses of Scotland' and now Bonchester, Caboc, Dunsyre Blue, Galic, Gowrie, Gruth Dhu, Howgate, Stichill, Sgriob-Ruadh and others prove what glorious cheese is to be found north of the border.

12

Ireland: The Green Cheesemakers

Ireland is a country steeped in mist and mystery, not least where its cheeses are concerned. It is a cattle country *par excellence*, with its superb natural pastures benefiting from gentle rainfall and mild climate. With grasslands that really do boast forty shades of green providing abundant natural feed, Irish cheesemakers merit the description 'green' in this ecologically sensitive age.

Ireland has a dairying tradition of incalculable age, aided by a monastic influence that survived the fall of Rome and has developed over the ensuing 2,000 years. With all these advantages it is surprising that Ireland has never been famed for its cheeses like France or Switzerland, and that domestic consumption has never reached high levels. Doubtless, there were home-produced cheeses but they remained unknown abroad and the Irish people do not regard themselves as great cheese-eaters, even though old Irish chronicles record that *cais* was one of the dishes served on gold plates to the kings of Tara.

It is only in the twentieth century that Irish cheeses have come out of the mist, so to speak. The reasons for this lie outside the scope of this book, but it had much to do with the subdivision of property under the laws of Irish inheritance. Farms became smaller, unable to sustain large numbers of cattle and, where there was any surplus milk, Irishmen did not hit upon the use of co-operatives to make cheese as early as their counterparts in England. Perhaps it was simply that milk was required for immediate consumption or, where larger herds existed, their milk went into dairy products that fed an export market rather than the indigenous population. The situation mirrored that of the Channel Islands, long famed for cream and butter, which similarly lacked any native cheeses. (There has never been a specific

'Jersey' cheese, and cheesemaking in commercial quantities has only recently been introduced by the States Dairy on Guernsey.)

Dairying began in Ireland during the pre-Celtic period; cattle were milked and butter was being made as early as 2000 BC. In ancient times the price of a female slave was three cows, and marriage dowries were paid in cattle, as they still are in parts of Africa today. The romance of dairy farming was a theme much employed in Irish poetry and love songs. '*Mile uair go mbthearr lion thú ná ba na Mumham is bainne acu ...*' the old song goes, and I am indebted to Aidan McCarthy for the translation: 'A thousand times I would prefer you than all the cows of Munster and they full of milk....' Was there ever such a pretty lyric?

Ireland once venerated Brigid as goddess of the dairy. Brigid was a pagan deity, not a Christian saint, and was credited with the ability miraculously to conjure up endless supplies of food for the poor. The early Christians had no compunction in adapting local legends to their own purpose, so the pagan Brigid became St Bridget, Abbess of Kildare, who could turn milk into butter or cheese. Dairying was usually regarded as women's work and, according to a Gaelic law over 1,000 years old, a divorced woman was entitled to one-sixth of the dairy produce after her husband had left her.

There is no doubt that the milking of cattle was important to the Irish domestic economy and that butter and curds, *gruth* in the Gaelic, were a standard and substantial part of the Irish diet right up to the end of the seventeenth century. One of the earliest Irish cheeses was called *faiscre grotha*, literally meaning 'pressed curd'. The Rev. R.H. Ryland in *The History, Topography and Antiquities of the County and City of Waterford* (1824) noted that: 'Cheese made from skimmed milk and called Mullahawn was formerly an article of commerce in Waterford and was exported in large quantities.'

Consumption of cheese declined with the unhappy deterioration of Irish agriculture, culminating in the famine of the 1840s, and by the turn of the century the industry was long dominated by seasonal production of indifferent Cheddar for the English market. After 1945, however, there were great advances in Irish cheesemaking and the country soon had some of the world's largest and most progressive cheese factories. Yet T.A. Layton, in his *Choose Your Cheese* (1957), dismissed Irish cheese with the words 'This country has no traditional cheeses or if they did they have been forgotten.' Similarly, J.G. Davis in his classic *Cheese* (1965) regarded Ireland only as a source of imitations of English territorial varieties.

The first Irish Farmhouse cheese appeared in the 1970s and shortly afterwards Milleens, an unpasteurised cows milk cheese made by Norman and Veronica Steele at their farm on the Beara Peninsula in West Cork, received international acclaim. Other cheeses soon followed, Durrus, Baylough and Gubbeen being amongst the best known. Jane and Louis Grubb's Cashel Blue has established a reputation for strength and sheer excellence amongst lovers of blue cheese, whilst Abbey Blue Brie and Chetwynd Blue are also gaining an enthusiastic following.

Despite these successes over the last 25 years, Irish Farmhouse cheese has only a limited following, under 3 per cent of the domestic market. There are around 40 farms responsible for something like 70 cheeses in all, but total production is still below 1,000 tonnes. The majority of producers make less than 10 tonnes each year, a very small figure in terms of the international market. For the moment, the best way to enjoy Irish Farmhouse cheeses is to holiday in Ireland and find them at source. Frequently, it is the poetry in the names of cheeses that makes one want to seek them out. Who could possibly resist Knockanore from Ballyneety and Carrigaline from Clondalkin?

Today, it is the 'commodity' area of the cheese market that is mostly served by the Irish dairy industry. Mozzarella and Feta are both exported in huge volumes, as is the ubiquitous Irish Cheddar. There is, perhaps inevitably, a Cheddar made (by St Ivel) with Guinness. The manufacturers of Cheddar in Ireland have improved the quality of their cheese after long years of producing only the 'mousetrap' variety, with premium quality mature cheeses like Old Charleville from County Cork, Rinkippen from Galway and Ryefield from County Cavan.

There is a great deal to look forward to where Irish cheese is concerned. What is already on offer is good and, with the Irish climate, grassland, stock management and dairying skills, there will surely be many more cheeses in the future.

13

Curious Customs and Bizarre Beliefs

Cheese has been important in our diet for so long that it has become part of our folklore. Manners and customs connected with cheese abound, not least those dating from when times were hard and food in short supply. Bread and cheese have traditionally been eaten during short breaks from work – fast food is no recent invention. The morning break we call 'elevenses' was formerly called *beaver* or *cheesing*, the word 'beaver' giving us the modern 'beverage'. Eton College used to have *bever days*, when bread and cheese were issued for the boys to entertain visitors.

CHEESE DOLES

Bread and cheese have long provided succour for the poor, and such charity was known as *doles* in many country areas. At St Briavels, in the Forest of Dean, bread and cheese were thrown to the poor on Whit Monday. Tradition affirms that this boon was granted by the Earl of Hereford at his wife's instigation but only after she agreed to the terms on which Lady Godiva gained privileges for the citizens of Coventry. Dole was distributed in the church or, just as often, in the yard outside, and a stone 'cheese table' still stands in the churchyard at Powerstock in Dorset. Bread and cheese were given to the poor at Ebrington in Gloucestershire, Ripon and Wath-on-Dearne in Yorkshire, Paddington in London and Drayton Beauchamp in Buckinghamshire. At Clifton Reynes, also in Buckinghamshire, the food was issued after the parish bounds were walked on Ascension Day.

A dole with a most curious history was dispensed at Biddenden in Kent. Two girls, said to be Eliza and Mary Chulkhurst, were born as Siamese twins, joined at the hips and shoulders. They survived for 34 years and left 20 acres of land, still known as 'Bread and Cheese Land' for the relief of the poor. Each year, the dole was faithfully issued to the poor in the parish church until the end of the seventeenth century, when proceedings became unruly and the alms-giving was removed, first to the church porch and then to the workhouse. Records show that in 1872 nearly 500 people (most of the population of the village) queued for the dole. Thankfully no workhouse exists at Biddenden today but the owners of Bread and Cheese House, as it is now called, allow a dole which includes a wafer embossed with a picture of the Chulkhurst twins to be given out from one of the windows.

MILKMAIDS

Tales of comely dairymaids date back many centuries. Their reputation may come from the days when any mention of beauty was likely to be accompanied by the words 'unmarked by the pox'. The immunity of dairy-workers to smallpox was due to their exposure to cowpox, and accounted for their smooth complexion. Milkmaids also enjoyed a diet rich in dairy fats in an age when a generous figure was considered desirable.

Whether as a result of their contours or complexions, it was reported in 1894 that female entrants in the Bath and West Society's butter and cheesemaking competitions were attracting proposals of marriage. Several of these had led to matrimony and the *Wiltshire Times* of 16 June 1894 expressed a concern that a shortage of dairymaids might result.

At one period, milkmaids were indeed maids, too young to be considering marriage. Elihu Burritt in his book *Walk from London* (1868) mentions that he was taught cheesemaking by a girl only nine years old. Richard Surflet in his book of agricultural instruction *The Country Ferme* (1600) required dairymaids to be of clean appearance, writing, 'young girls should not have scabbed or scurvie hands as such filthiness hinders curdling and makes cheese full of eies'. Surflet noted that, in some dairies, only girls below the age of puberty were allowed to handle the curd, a custom connected with very old superstitions concerning menstruation.

An old country saying 'The bigger the milkmaid the better the cheese' refers to the hard manual work involved in lifting milk churns and cheese moulds. It was said that in one Cheshire village church there stood a chest with a very heavy lid. Any girl who could not lift the lid with one hand was considered too weak to be a cheesemaker and her marriage prospects were duly diminished. Yet milkmaids received little enough reward for their efforts. Porcelain figurines depicting pretty girls gaily tripping along with a yoke across their bare shoulders belie the drudgery involved in carrying full buckets of milk. In 1800 milkmaids might expect to earn £3 to £4 per year for getting up at dawn to milk the cows by hand, carrying milk to the vat, making the curd, filling the moulds, and stacking finished cheeses. The truckles had to be turned regularly for many months to ensure an even distribution of fat. 'If you'll have a good cheese and have'n old, you must turn'n seven times before's cold' the saying went, for truckles needed turning, turning and turning again.

CHEESE ROLLING

At Cooper's Hill, near Cheltenham, each Spring Bank Holiday, contestants scramble downhill after a Gloucester cheese, which is decorated with red, white and blue streamers. Some books state that the event is connected with grazing rights, whilst other sources hint at pagan origins. Cooper's Hill is a high ridge covered with trees except for a steep clearing about 50 yards wide. At 6 pm, vast crowds gather at the starting point, a maypole topped by a weathercock, and watch the Master of Ceremonies, wearing a top hat decorated with ribbons, start the rolling of a 7 lb (3 kg) cheese down the 1 in 3 slope. The competitors, brave or foolish depending on your point of view, madly rush after it, tumbling and turning as they go. The first to reach the base of the hill (alive) is pronounced the winner. Cheeses were also rolled down Dragon Hill at Uffington, in Berkshire. This race started from a patch devoid of grass, said to have been poisoned by the blood of a dragon slain by St George.

The ancient custom of parading cheeses through the streets of Randwick, a Gloucestershire village with stunning views of the Stroud valley, was revived in 1971 by the late Rev. Niall R. Morrison and forms part of the Randwick wap celebrations. On the first Sunday in May, a cheese-rolling service is held at

Randwick parish church, when three cheeses, decorated with flowers and ribbons, are carried in procession to the altar. After the service the cheeses are rolled anti-clockwise round the church before one of them is cut up and distributed amongst the congregation. The other two cheeses feature in the secular element of the celebrations on the following Saturday. The wap 'Mayor' delivers his inaugural speech while sitting in the village pond, retaining his dignity throughout. He and his attendants, accompanied by a brass band, are then carried in procession on litters bedecked with flowers and ribbons. At Well Hill there is another rolling of the cheeses, after which they are available for eating. It is possible that in bygone days the cheese formed part of a dole to the poor, but the main purpose of the revelry was to secure grazing rights on the nearby Selsley Common. The cheese rolling formed only part of an entertainment which included an old ladies' competition called 'chattering for a bladder of snuff'. Sadly, the rules of this game have not survived. In Victorian times the wap festivities led to licentious behaviour (the origin of the word 'wap' suggests activities of considerable impropriety) and the proceedings became so unruly that they were suppressed, but the ceremony is now conducted quite respectably.

CHEESE FOR EVERY OCCASION

Yorkshire folk once observed the curious custom of leaving a piece of Wensleydale cheese, with the sign of the Cross scraped on the surface, for the fairies or 'farisees' on Christmas Eve. A similar custom was found in Derbyshire, except that in this county it was Sage Derby that was left for the little folk. The old soldiers who live at the Royal Hospital at Chelsea still continue the ceremony of 'cutting the Christmas cheese', whch dates from 1692. The veterans have long enjoyed their cheese, and records show that in 1802 each Pensioner ate over 2 lb (1 kg) of cheese a week. Their consumption might have dropped since then but, at Christmas, the best British cheeses, donated by well-wishers, are displayed in the Hospital's Great Hall before being cut and sampled with due ceremony.

Shrove Tuesday was another time of year at which cheese was traditionally eaten, since dairy products were forbidden during the 40 days of Lent. In Dorset, Oxfordshire, Somerset, Wiltshire and the Isle of Wight, children went from door to door begging gifts of cheese. Something similar took place in Devon a day earlier on 'Collops Monday'.

The origins of 'Cheesecake Monday' are uncertain, but on 29 June 1895 the *Leeds Mercury* recorded that:

> A quaint custom is celebrated at Bilton, near Hull. It follows the annual camp meeting of Primitive Methodists. Young men go round the village soliciting at each door a gift of cheesecakes. At 8 o'clock the villagers, including the children, assemble, the cakes are produced, and the 'small fry' it is said, 'did ample justice to them'. Persons who have no cakes to give, contribute cash for non-intoxicating beverages.

In the West Country a belief existed that if a maiden fasted all Midsummer's Day and then, at midnight, laid a clean cloth with bread, cheese and ale, her destined lover would join her. With bread, cheese, ale and whatever other incentives might have been on offer at midnight, I have little doubt that this custom had some basis in fact!

Children who now look forward to their annual birthday cake might be surprised if it was replaced by a birthday cheese. In darker days, when the birth of a child was attended by secrecy and superstition, a cheese called the *kenno* was provided for the women who attended the confinement. The kenno was so named from *ken*, meaning to bear a child. After all had eaten, small pieces were despatched to relatives in the same way as we distribute wedding cake today.

Just as cheese was eaten to celebrate a new birth, so it also served to mourn life's passing. William Stout of Lancaster, a prominent Quaker shop-keeper, recorded in 1851 that he had 'sold much cheese to funerals, from 30 lbs to 100 lbs weight, as the deceased was of ability, which was shived into two or three slices to the pound and given with a penny manchet or loaf to all attendants'.

CHEESE FOR HEALTH

A curious mixture of Greek, Roman and Arab teachings held that our bodies were ruled by four *humours*, the balance of which determined a man's nature. According to his predominant humour, an individual might be sanguine, choleric, phlegmatic or melancholic. Different types of food were considered to possess particular humours and cheese was deemed to be heavy and cold, suitable for persons of a hot, dry, choleric temperament but to be avoided by people of a cold, moist, phlegmatic type. This poem is from *The School of Salernum*, translated by Sir John Harington in 1608:

> For healthie men new cheese be wholesome food,
> But for the weake and sickly 'tis not good,
> Cheese is an heavy meate, both grosse and cold
> And breedeth Costivenesse [constipation] both new and old.

Alexander Barclay (1475–1552), rector of All Hallows, Lombard Street, London, also asserted that mature cheese caused constipation:

> New sweet and fresh Cheese nourisheth plentifully; middle aged Cheese nourisheth strongly, but old and dry Cheese hurteth dangerously; for it stayeth seige [constipates], stoppeth the Liver, engendereth choler, melancholy, and the stone, lieth long in the stomach undigested, procureth thirst, maketh a stinking breath, and a scurvy skin.*

It was widely believed, too, that milk products caused flatulence: 'Cows and ewes milk', wrote one sixteenth-century commentator, 'is nutritive, but it is not good for them that have gurgulations in the belly.'[†]

The avoidance of certain types of cheese was also recommended by Gervase Markham in his book *The English Huswife* (1615):

> There is sortes of chese, which is to say, grene chese, soft chese and harde chese. Grene chese is not called grene by reason of colour, but for the newness of it, for the whey is not halfe pressed out of it. Soft chese, not new nor to olde, is best. Harde chese is hot and dry and wyll to digest. Chese ought not to be tough nor bruttel; it ought not to be swete nor sowre, nor tarte, nor salte, nor to fresshe. It must be of good savour and taledge, nor full of iyes, nor myters, nor magottes.

---

*From *Cooper's Thesaurus* (1565)
[†]From *A Looking Glass for London and England* (1594)

The advice to avoid cheese full of 'myters' and 'magottes' was repeated by Mrs Beeton in her *Book of Household Management* (1861):

> It is well known that some persons like cheese in a state of decay and eaten alive. There is no accounting for tastes, and it may be hard to show why mould, which is vegetation, should not be eaten as well as salad (or maggots as well as eels) but, generally speaking, decomposing bodies are not wholesome eating.

Mrs Beeton's attitude to cheese was usually hostile:

> Cheese in its commonest shape is only fit for sedentary people, as an after dinner stimulant, and in very small quantity. Bread and cheese, as a meal, is only fit for soldiers on the march, or labourers in the open air, who like it because it holds the stomach a long time.

One might choose to take issue with Mrs Beeton on this subject and suggest that some latent snobbery, associating bread and cheese with the working classes, must have coloured her judgement. The majority opinion has long been that moderate cheese eating is beneficial to health. Ben Jonson referred to 'digestive cheese' and a character in Shakespeare's *Troilus and Cressida* remarks, 'My cheese, my digestion.' Cheese was even used medicinally, one prescription stating that 'an old cheese all mouldie, braied and mixed with the decoction of a salt gammon of bacon, and applied in the form of a cataplasme doth soften all the hard swelling of the knees'. The efficacy of this remedy remains to be proven.

IS CHEESE GOOD FOR YOU?

In 1944, an unabashed T.A. Layton described in his book *Restaurant Roundabout* how he served a customer with a 'beautiful' Double Gloucester that just happened to be richly infested with maggots. There was no talk of environmental health officers or adverse publicity, merely a reasoned discussion as to whether a glass of Madeira or a Cockburn 1935 port would provide the requisite antidote. This might seem to us to reflect a cavalier attitude to food freshness but Tommy Layton really knew his cheese.

Healthy eating is now in vogue and any food, such as eggs, that gets a bad press is in for trouble. Worries about lysteria in the mid-1980s reduced sales of unpasteurised soft cheeses (nearly banned by the UK government on the flimsiest of evidence), but manufacturers responded by instituting rigorous quality controls. They were well aware that any breakdown in food safety procedures could lead to alarmist headlines. As a precautionary measure, high-risk groups (defined as the sick, the very young, the elderly and pregnant women) were cautioned against eating unpasteurised soft cheeses. While some areas of the food industry remain open to criticism, cheese has regained its reputation as a safe and natural food, and cases of cheese-related food poisoning are almost unknown. Anybody who dares suggest that health and hygiene legislation has gone *too* far risks being pilloried by the media, but the effect of some regulations has been the adoption of trade practices that border on the ridiculous. It is now common for cheese to be displayed at temperatures below 34°F (2°C); so low, in fact, that the product might be permanently damaged.

On a less serious note, cheese is one of a number of foods that sometimes cause headaches. Chocolate, bananas and red wine are often similarly accused. The reasons for this unfortunate side-effect are complex, but there may be a cure, as related in the *Country Housewife and Ladies Director* of 1727:

> Some gentlemen that had been hunting found a cottage to refresh themselves and were forced to take bread and cheese, there was nothing else to be had. One of the company was so unfortunate as to have an aversion to cheese, however, being very hungry, he resolved to venture upon it and ate heartily. But, about an hour after he was taken so very ill with purging and vomiting that in a short time his life was despaired of. After he had lain in that condition for a week he got strength enough to go homeward. Happening to stop at an Inn, he found a wagon load of Cheshire Cheeses and, finding a strong appetite to eat some of that sort, had one cut on purpose. He ate heartily of it, without suffering the least inconvenience, and has ever since been a great lover of cheese.

Cheese has long been regarded as a good source of calcium, but Prof. John Hargreaves of Alberta University, Canada, has suggested that eating cheese can help to harden tooth enamel. In tests carried out on 100 children he found that a diet of cheese, in combination with exposure to sunlight, not only prevented the formation of cavities but could actually reverse tooth decay. The sunlight encouraged the body to manufacture vitamin D, essential for calcification of the teeth. Prof. Hargreaves was even able to measure an increase in the 'hardness' of enamel on the teeth of patients who had eaten cheese. Hard cheese like Cheddar was found to give the best results. Just 2 oz (55 g) of Cheddar per day provides the adult daily requirement of calcium.

All foods are best eaten in moderation as part of a varied diet, but cheese can truly claim to be one of the most delicious, cheapest, safest and convenient sources of protein. Cheddar contains over 25 per cent protein, whilst beef steak contains only 16 per cent. Cheese does contain fat; a hard cheese is around 30 per cent fat, a medium-fat cheese 10–20 per cent, and a low-fat cheese below 10 per cent. However, some of the low-fat cottage cheeses, made from skimmed milk, are almost fat free, so there is a suitable cheese for everyone. The average ingredients in 4 oz (110 g) of cheese are:

	Cheddar	Stilton	Cottage
Energy (kilojoules)	1700	1487	500
Energy (kilocals)	406	355	120
Protein (grams)	26	20	16
Fat (grams)	34	31	4
(of which saturated fat	22	24	8)
Carbohydrate (grams)	1	1	4
Salt (grams)	1.8	2.3	1

Cheese is a good source of energy. Virtually carbohydrate free, it contains three times more energy than the same weight of bread. Bread provides fibre (especially brown bread), and cheese sandwiches are a valuable item in a balanced diet. Cottage cheese and curd cheese are usually low in calories and can be eaten liberally, even by those on a diet. Cheese supplies other minerals, as well as small amounts of vitamin B, although it is low in iron.

Reduced-fat cheeses are a curious notion, which I have placed outside the scope of this book. Reduced-fat 'Cheddar' typically has 14 per cent fat in dry matter but such products have little else going for them, and the taste and texture can be abominable. Better to buy some really good-quality cheese and eat sparingly.

14

Testing and Tasting

My mother always kept her cheese on a plate in the sideboard. It never went mouldy, probably because it never remained there long enough and houses were cooler in those days. Now almost everyone stores their cheese in a refrigerator and it is important that we remember to take it out again before serving so that the flavour and aroma are given time to develop. Cheese probably tasted better in the days of the marble slab and cool larder, a storage temperature of 45°F (8°C) being ideal. If you wish to enjoy your cheese at its best, you might do well to follow the advice given to a young bride on her wedding night: 'Keep everything clean, keep everything cool, and keep everything covered until the last possible moment!'

Cheese needs to be taken out of the refrigerator about an hour before serving to allow it to return to room temperature and develop its full flavour but, as no foodstuff is improved by hopping in and out of cold storage, try to cut as much as is required for the occasion. Do not make small off-cuts that will dry out. Trim away the rind from traditional cheese and lift the wax off coated cheeses. Food wax protects but is not meant to be eaten so trim away a little of the surface cheese, too.

Cut cheese is best wrapped in aluminium foil; not all cling films are suitable. Place the cheese in a container with a lid to prevent it from picking up other flavours. Semi-hard cheeses can be wrapped in a cloth that has been wrung out in brine or vinegar and water, for short periods.

Blue cheeses are best stored under a cheese bell, where the confined atmosphere enables them to breathe but does not allow them to dry out. It is often recommended that the surface of crumbly cheeses be smoothed with the flat of a knife to prevent moisture loss, but wrapping in foil achieves the same end. You can freeze cheese, but the texture almost always suffers, so freeze only cheese that is intended for use in cooking. If hard cheese has grown a slight surface mould it is safe to trim this away and use the rest.

The 'best before' dates of fresh, soft cheeses and cottage cheese need to be treated with respect. Goats cheese can change markedly in a short time so, unless one is partial to very strong flavours, it is best bought and eaten on the same day. Don't believe gourmets who suggest that Brie-type cheeses should ripen until they give off a strong ammonia smell. This is not the mark of a ripe cheese, it is the mark of a cheese past its best, which can be dangerous to eat.

A cheeseboard should provide a choice of mature, mild, blue and soft varieties. Copy the best restaurants and serve cheese with crusty bread, a variety of biscuits (sweet and plain), crisp apples, fresh celery and fruit. Wine should be red as often as white, and chilled tomato juice also makes a delicious accompaniment. Buy the best cheese on offer; go for quality before quantity and serve it to its best advantage by offering it before the dessert. Cheese will refresh the palate and make dessert more enjoyable. It also provides time to finish the dinner wine before starting on the sweet flavours. Cheese is not expensive when compared with other protein foods; it is quick and easy to prepare and there is no waste. If there are leftover pieces, grate them and store in a tub in the freezer to use in cooking. When making cheese sauce, add the cheese last, over a low heat, as over-cooking will toughen it. When cooking with soft cheeses, melt the cheese very slowly or it may go hard and lumpy. When cooking with Cheddar, buy the best mature. It won't cost any more as less can be used, and the flavour is so much better.

THE CHEESE GRADER

The retailer seldom finds it convenient to go out and buy cheese direct from the maker, even in country areas. Larger retailers rely on expert graders visiting dairies to buy cheese at a price they are prepared to pay, which means they do not always buy the best.

Cheese graders could save a lot of time and energy if they reverted to the method of testing recommended in 1711 by J. Distaff, who stated in his book *Don Sacheverellio*: 'The richness of a Cheese is discovered by the multiplicity of its Mites.'

Environmental health officers would hardly be impressed by this selection process but even in the eighteenth century there were more rational approaches:

> To choose cheese: when you buy cheese, observe the coat; for if the cheese be old, and its coat be rough, rugged, or dry at the top, it indicates mites, or little worms. If it be spongy, moist or full of holes, it is subject to maggots. If you perceive on the outside any perished place, be sure to examine its deepness.*

Cheese factors used to walk over cheeses to determine their firmness. The historian Thomas Rudge noted in 1807 that 'those which yield to the tread are said to be *heaved*, or *hoved*, and unfit for the London market'. Cheese graders today are less pedestrian in their deliberations!

It is easy to take for granted the consistent product that reaches our shops. Excellence will always be hard to find but at least we no longer have to tolerate the downright bad food often sold in bygone days. An experienced grader will have called on dairies regularly and built up a relationship with cheesemakers, getting to know the characteristics of their particular product. One Cheddar maker might concentrate on mild cheese for a quick turnover, another might look for the long-term rewards of holding cheese to maturity. Graders are often former cheesemakers, so their position is one of poacher turned gamekeeper. The grader will normally check at least one cheese from every vat. Cheddar is graded at around eight weeks, Cheshire at two weeks and Caerphilly even earlier. Cheeses must be true to type and free from damage, taint or mould intrusion. The grader looks for a smooth exterior or *finish*, an indication of how well the curd has been packed into the moulds.

Some cheeses 'stop' and stay mild indefinitely. Top-quality produce matures evenly but other cheeses develop strong flavours too early. The grader refers to these as 'moving on'; they are best sold quickly. It can be difficult to perceive the difference between a genuinely mature and an inferior strong cheese but experience teaches that they are not the same thing. Poorly made cheese rapidly becomes acidic and has a limited life; the acid level will continue to rise until it breaks down the protein. Over-acid

The Compleat Housewife (1729)

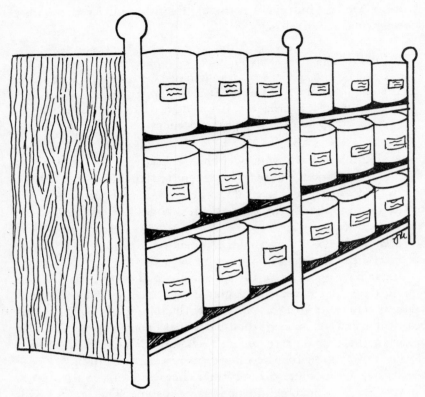

Traditional Cheddar maturing on racks.

cheeses have their *aficionados* – some people enjoy a sting to the palate – but well-made hard cheese should slowly improve in flavour over a year or so. Claims of extreme longevity are usually exaggerated, for cheese improves little after two years. Cheddar merely becomes harder and drier until it assumes a stony texture, from which point it may last indefinitely. On 3 January 1887, a letter-writer in *The Times* reported: 'I have a piece of Cheddar cheese lying under a glass on my hall table. It was made 41 years ago. It is hard now but it is quite sweet.'

Professional cheese graders use a *cheese iron* to inspect the interior of a cheese. The outer surface may carry salt, so the inner cheese must be checked or a false impression might be gained. The grader bores the iron, a stainless-steel gouge about 6 in (15

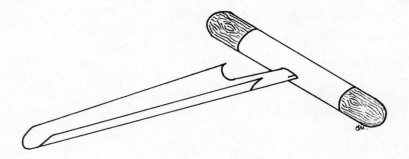

*A cheese iron. This is the cheese grader's essential tool, enabling a
bore to be sampled from within the cheese.*

cm) long, into the cheese and turns it once. Any lack of resistance
indicates a soft cheese, whilst with very hard cheese, it requires an
effort to extract the iron at all. The plug is withdrawn and held to
the nose at once to detect volatile smells (evidence of taint), as
these fade very quickly. The way the cheese fills the iron indicates
whether the sample is firm (*good bodied*) or *weak bodied* with an
unwanted tendency to crumble.

A close inspection of the sample is made to check the fat
content, colour and texture. An open texture might mean a *sweet*
or badly pressed cheeese. Finally, the cheese may be tasted to
check for bitterness. This must not be done too often, as the
grader examines many cheeses in a day. The plug of cheese is then
replaced, the block re-sealed and the grader marks down his
results.

Cheesemakers are proud of their skills and welcome an opportunity to display them. At shows around the country, examples of
the art compete against each other and are judged for body,
flavour, colour and finish. All types of cheese and cheesemakers
find their way to the show bench. Cups and rosettes in plenty are
awarded to traditional truckles, rindless blocks, farmers' wives
and promising newcomers. Each cheesemaking area has its own
show-place. Nantwich International Show, held each July since
1897, is a premier event, as is the Royal Bath and West Show, held
near Shepton Mallet each June. Not far away, the smaller but very
lively Frome Cheese Show has been running since 1877. The
Company of Scottish Cheese Makers run their own show where

the McLelland Championship Cup is the top award and, in Eire, cheesemakers attend the Dublin Spring Show.

THE FUTURE

During the 1980s, the cheese industry was preoccupied with excessive milk production, butter mountains and *quotas*, limitations on production imposed by the European Community to reduce the surplus of dairy products. Then the 1990s arrived and the picture changed, with cheesemakers finding themselves *short* of milk on occasions. The system of milk supply and distribution in the UK has radically altered as the Milk Marketing Board for England and Wales has lost its monopoly position and faces the future as Milk Marque, a public company. The MMB has served farmers well, but never again will there be central control of all aspects of milk distribution as there was between 1954 and 1992. Our membership of the EC has imposed new ground rules. Market forces, a phrase much loved by those shielded from the worst effects, will dictate the price and application of milk supplies. Market forces will similarly dictate what happens to Irish milk, which will go where the profit lies and not necessarily into cheesemaking. (There has long been more profit in bottling milk or making it into dairy desserts than in using it to make cheese.) As the price of milk rises, the price of dairy products must surely follow, but cheese will still represent astonishing value for money. The only danger is that the artisans and smaller farmhouse producers who find it difficult to recoup their increased costs may call it a day. If they go, we should all mourn their passing for without the specialist makers we shall increasingly be forced to accept bland, factory-produced cheese, lacking in character and individuality.

The cheese industry deserves to have a bright future in prospect. Penny for penny and pound for pound there is no protein food that is better value than cheese. The number of vegetarians is increasing and ewes and goats milk cheeses are finding a wider appreciation. British and Irish food stores are among the best in the world, yet many are guilty of neglecting cheese. The presentation of most prepacked cheese is appalling – there is nothing enticing about plastic bricks! A start might be made by improving the labels, drawing on the example provided by wine.

The label should first state the country of origin, then the name of the farm (as wine producers name the vineyard), followed by a description of the milk (pasteurised/unpasteurised, Jersey/ Guernsey). There should be a declaration as to whether the cheese is made on the farm using the farm's own milk, which would effectively provide a form of *appellation contrôllée*, and whether it is made traditionally (by hand). The fat content should be highlighted, as a wine declares its alcohol content.

TIME FOR CELEBRATION

There are those who say that cheese is not as good as it used to be. They have been saying it for many years and they are still wrong. The food of 50 or 100 years ago is best viewed through a telescope, and too much nostalgia makes you go blind. True, there may have been a superb cheese of recipe unknown which we are now denied, but there would also have been much rubbish which we are no longer forced to tolerate. It is easy to forget that the supposed charms of bygone days did not include the refrigeration and well-stocked shops that we now take for granted. This is a time for celebration. Never before have there been so many marvellous makers dedicated to their craft and so many excellent cheeses on offer. The combination of traditional manufacturing methods and modern process controls undoubtedly means that cheese is better made now than it has ever been. In addition to the interest in cheese shown by television and radio programmes, newspapers and magazines, cheese now has its own journal, *Fine Cheese* (Stanstead Publications), which is superbly colourful and informative.

For the buyer, the seller and the would-be expert there is now a professional qualification offered by the United Kingdom Cheese Guild in co-operation with Reaseheath College in Cheshire. The diploma course is interesting and inexpensive, well worthwhile for anyone interested in cheese, and based on excellent text books covering dairy science, cheese manufacture, selection, storage and counter skills. (Enquiries to the United Kingdom Cheese Guild, 58 High Street, Sutton, Surrey, SM1 1EZ.)

GOOD PLACES TO BUY CHEESE

The directory on pp. 95–201 lists over 1,000 cheeses, all at the mercy of the shops that sell them. What is a good place to buy cheese? We are now able to enjoy the vast array of merchandise offered by supermarkets and in less than 30 years most of us have changed from shopping over the counter to passing through the checkout. Retailers have become more organised and efficient, vying with each other to create veritable temples of shopping, equipped with the latest technology at considerable expense.

The war between 'big' shops and 'little' shops is over. The public voted with their feet long ago, choosing to make most of their purchases at supermarkets, but there is still a place for smaller retailers, especially those selling cheese. Some supermarkets have achieved a standard of excellence that even specialist retailers would find hard to emulate; there are good counters in some branches of almost all the major food retailers.

If staff have a sound working knowledge of what they sell, supermarkets can meet most routine needs, but it is in their dependence on prepacked cheese that they show their Achilles' heel. Such cheese is suited to mass retailing for it requires no skill to handle and display. It meets the needs of the less discriminating shopper and those in a hurry, and there its advantages end. Sealed in plastic and kept icy cold, cheese cannot develop but, worst of all, something that should be displayed in a glorious miscellany of shapes, colours, textures and smells is reduced to the conformity of house bricks. Even the labels are boring; do they design them that way? Good cheese is a living, breathing thing, giving off gas and moisture and altering with age. This does not suit the needs of the prepacker, who must select produce unlikely or unable to develop. It should also be remembered that prepacking does not come free. The process adds several pence per pound to the price of the product and, as prepacked cheese is frequently cheaper than cheese cut at the counter, one can only suspect that the prepacked product might be the inferior of the two.

Buying direct from the dairy (the directory indicates where this is possible) may present the opportunity to meet the maker and talk about cheese. Some dairies have farm shops offering a selection of products, others no more than a counter, and a few just sell from the doorstep, but whatever the size of the operation, you will be buying 'real' cheese.

WHAT TO LOOK FOR

It is good to know what one is buying, so I look for tickets that are clean and clear. Information should include the name of the cheese, its type, country of origin and the price. There should be advice, if needed, and the mark of good cheese retailing is that you are offered a taste before you buy. Cheese should be cut with a wire or two-handled knife, never with a knife that has been used for other foods. Rind can never be truly clean; therefore an expert always cuts outwards so as not to draw any soiling over the face of the cheese. Blue cheeses should be separated and cut on different cutting boards. As cheese is seldom cooked before being eaten, the highest standards of hygiene must prevail. Staff should wear hats and overalls, and serve cheese without touching the product. (An easy method is to use a plastic bag as a 'glove', pulling it off the hand and over the product before sealing.) Do not leave the cheese in the bag too long; that is not its purpose. Some cling films are also not appropriate for use with cheese. Different

*Clockwise from top: a cheese slicer, a cheese knife, a Dutch sampler,
a cheese iron and a Parmesan pick.*

cheeses should be wrapped separately and delicate varieties should be boxed, as you would box fancy cakes. I can never understand why two cream doughnuts (costing under £1) are presented in a semi-rigid box but soft, squashy cheese costing several pounds gets put in the ubiquitous plastic bag and never looks its best when I get home. Not before time, it is becoming obligatory for everyone involved in food handling to have an elementary knowledge of hygiene and to be trained in storing and serving food safely.

If, like me, you have an affection for cheese, then make a resolution to buy a different one every week for a year. It's not an expensive hobby; you need spend only a pound or two. Any reasonable cheese shop will provide 52 different cheeses. (Not all of them British, but I'm broad minded.) If you are sufficiently diligent, record your impressions of each purchase. At the end of the first week you will know more than you did before; at the end of the first month you will surely know more about cheese than your next-door neighbour; and at the end of the year, you'll know as much about cheese as anybody. Reading about cheese is one thing, but words are wasted until you have tasted.

And now to the cheeseboard!

15

The Cheeseboard: A Directory

What choice to choose, for delicacy best,
What order so contriv'd, as not to mix
Taste well join'd, inelegant, but bring
Taste after taste, upheld by kindliest change.
JOHN MILTON, *PARADISE LOST* (1667)

So many cheeses, so little time. There is a dazzling array of cheeses to choose from, but where can you find them? And when should you taste them? Any attempt to produce a complete list presents difficulties as many are made seasonally or distributed only within their own local area. I beg the reader's forgiveness for any that are omitted from the directory that follows.

On pp. 95–201 cheeses are listed by name with details of the milk, the maker, the type of product and a description of the cheese itself. Author's comments have generally given way to what the cheesemakers choose to say about themselves. Cheesemakers, like their products, come in all sizes. The largest are the creameries; farmhouse makers form the middle group, and the smaller specialists I have termed 'artisan' makers.

THE CREAMERIES

Creameries are operated by giant companies like St Ivel (Unigate PLC) or The Cheese Company in the UK, and Kerrygold in Ireland. They draw milk from a wide area to produce vast quantities of a standardised product. Some of the names may be unfamiliar, as they may be huge companies whose products appear under many guises. They have been included in the directory alongside the small-scale makers. Creameries can and do produce excellent cheese, regularly taking prizes at cheese shows to prove the point, but they have to conform to the requirements of a mass market, as defined by the multiple retailers.

THE FARMHOUSE MAKERS

Farmhouse producers form a diverse group, many having factories that rival the giant creameries for efficiency if not size. They work closer to the land, and often use only their own milk or milk drawn from near neighbours. A few, too few, have sufficient knowledge of their herds to continue using unpasteurised milk. Farmhouse makers control their raw material, enabling them to create a more individual cheese that reflects the character of the area from which it comes. A Cheshire cheese from Cheshire should surely be superior to one made in Lincolnshire. Farmhouse cheeses may be packed under supermarket brands but many are sold under their own name. This practice ought to become universal, as we have a right to know whence our cheese comes. The smallest farmhouse makers may sell only within their local area.

THE ARTISAN MAKERS

It is the small specialist makers who bring the most disparate group of products to our cheeseboards. Artisans vary in size, some being the equal of farmhouse makers. As might be expected, those using cows milk produce a far greater weight of product than those using goats or ewes milk. Such people work close to their herds or flocks, often using unpasteurised milk, experimenting with recipes and exploring possibilities. They may make only small quantities of cheese, but greater is our pleasure in seeking them out. Their products will vary, which is not to say that they are of inconsistent quality, but they will reflect the time and the season. Beware of any cheese that describes itself as 'consistent'. If you require your food to be unchanging then I recommend you buy Kelloggs cornflakes and Heinz baked beans, products unvarying in their excellence. However, if you require excitement in your diet, then take the trouble to seek out the artisan cheeses; there are hundreds to be found.

Makers who welcome visitors are clearly indicated in the directory that follows. Most, though not all, are able to supply the public with cheese, in some cases from a farm shop, in others 'at the door'. Please do not trouble them with too trivial an enquiry or too small a purchase; farms are busy places, not necessarily suitable for a family day out.

As there are strict food hygiene regulations, only in a limited number of cases is it possible to enter the dairy. Some farms have installed facilities for visitors to watch cheese being made, for which they make a modest charge. Check opening times in advance (especially in winter) and remember that cheesemaking starts early in the day. Smaller manufacturers may operate seasonally. Larger farms and creameries may accept parties of visitors by appointment, although some entertain only colleagues in the industry or serious students of cheesemaking. Always write first and enclose a stamped, addressed envelope with your enquiry.

NOTES ON THE CHEESEBOARD

The listings that follow contain the latest information available at the time of going to press. All makers will answer your enquiries but, if you are not a trade buyer, please write in the first instance.

Milk source and quality are of primary importance in cheesemaking. If you have yet to try ewes or goats milk cheeses then I recommend you rectify the omission by visiting a good cheese shop. Find out whether the cheese is made from raw or pasteurised milk, and decide for yourself which type provides the fuller flavour. Draconian regulations have forced some makers to change from raw to pasteurised milk against their better judgement. A number have already changed back, and others may do so.

I have indicated whether, in my opinion, a product is soft, semi-soft, semi-hard (a bit firmer) or hard-pressed. A cheese should be true to its type, although most grow harder with age. Similarly, my classifications 'full-fat' or 'low-fat' are made by palate, a method quite unrelated to what legally constitutes a 'full-fat' cheese. It is seldom possible for the fat content of every batch of cheese to be scientifically analysed.

Comments regarding taste have been kept brief. So many cheeses merit the description 'mild when young but matures to a fuller flavour' that I have sought to avoid repetition. Taste is subjective, so try the cheeses for yourself.

Vegetarians will applaud the movement towards the general use of non-animal rennet, which will probably continue. A number of cheesemakers are 'Registered Organic to the Standards of the Soil Association' whilst others, listed as 'organic' in the directory, also run their farms in sympathy with the ideas of natural soil management. Such people often treat their animals as pets.

At the time of going to press, uncertainties in the future pattern of milk supply have forced a small number of UK producers to withdraw from cheesemaking. Hopefully such suspensions of their activities will only be temporary and the entries in the Cheeseboard listing have been allowed to stand.

All suppliers are located in Great Britain unless otherwise stated. Weights and other measurements are approximate only.

A soft cheese coated with peppercorns.

ABBEY BLUE BRIE

Pat and Joan Hyland, Ballacola, Co. Laois, Republic of Ireland
Artisan maker
Type: Cows milk, semi-soft, full fat

Soft and creamy blue cheese, said to be the equal of Cambozola. The 4½ lb (2 kg) rounds are meticulously pierced by hand. The name is derived from Aghabo Abbey, which overlooks the fields of Ballacola and was founded by St Canice in the sixth century. Aghabo means 'the field of Canice's cows'.

ABBEYDALE

D. John Davidge, Ilchester Cheese Company, Ilchester, Somerset
Specialist diary making character cheeses
Type: Cows milk, hard-pressed, full fat

Double Gloucester cheese, its golden colour and mellow flavour enhanced by the tangy flavour of chopped onions and fresh garden chives. *See also* ILCHESTER.

ABBOTSDALE

Colin Brown, The Big Sheep, Abbotsham, Bideford, Devon
Artisan maker using the farm's own milk. Visitors welcome
Type: Ewes milk, hard-pressed, full fat, vegetarian

A re-creation of the original Wensleydale made by the monks of Fountains Abbey. Not as crumbly as the cows milk versions and will develop for 4–8 months to a rich maturity. Made in 7 lb (3 kg) discs. The Big Sheep is truly a showplace for sheep farming, and one of the most entertaining and instructive days out that you will find anywhere. If you've never seen sheep racing you've missed a treat! *See also* ASHLEIGH, FRIESLA.

ACID CURD CHEESE *see* CURD CHEESE

ACORN

Don and Karen Ross, Little Acorn Products, Mesen Fach Farm, Bethania, Llanon, Dyfed
Artisan maker. Visitors by appointment
Type: Unpasteurised ewes milk, hard-pressed, full fat, vegetarian

Firm, white cheese which has been likened to an old-fashioned Wensleydale and is inclined to blue on cutting. The first (modern) commercially produced ewes milk cheese from Wales, it has an ideal texture for soufflés, mousses, or soups and a superb aftertaste, good enough to win prizes at the London Cheese Show, the Royal Bath and West, Royal Welsh and Nantwich International shows. Mesen Fach means 'little acorn' in Welsh. The 5 lb (2.3 kg) truckles can be matured for up to six months. *See also* CAWS ABERAERON, LADY LLANOVER, MERLIN'S SANDWICH, MONKS OF STRATA, NOSON LAWEN, SKIRRID, TUDOR SMOKED.

ADMIRALS

D. John Davidge, Ilchester Cheese Company, Ilchester, Somerset
Specialist dairy making character cheeses
Type: Cows milk, hard-pressed, full fat

This combination of Cheddar cheese, ruby port and blue Stilton claims to be the perfect after-dinner cheese. It certainly contains a wealth of flavours. *See also* ILCHESTER.

AERON VALLEY FARM CHEESES

David J. Ellis, Aeron Valley Farm, Felinfach, Lampeter, Dyfed
Creamery

Type: Various cows milk cheeses, hard-pressed, full fat

A new creamery was opened at Aeron Valley Farm in the 1980s. Milk from local farms is used to produce a range of rindless cheeses, including Cheddar (matured up to 14 months), Double Gloucester, Cheshire, Monterey Jack, Munster and Colby.

ALLERDALE

Carolyn Fairbairn, Thornby Moor Dairy, Crofton Hall, Thursby, Carlisle, Cumbria
Artisan maker. Visitors welcome
Type: Unpasteurised goats milk, semi-hard, full fat, vegetarian

Creamy-sweet, moist cheese, organically produced, matured for 4–8 weeks. The 5 lb (2.3 kg), 2 lb (900 g) and 1 lb (450 g) waxed truckles are available plain or lightly smoked. *See also* CROFTON.

ANADL-Y-DDRAIG

Peter Sayer, Welsh Farmhouse Cheese, Maesllyn, Llandysul, Dyfed
Artisan maker using local milk. Visitors welcome
Type: Unpasteurised cows milk, hard-pressed, full fat, vegetarian

Anadl-y-ddraig means 'breath of the dragon' – no reflection, I'm sure, on the taste of this matured Welsh Cheddar with added port and green peppercorns. Sold in red-waxed 5 lb (2.3 kg) rounds or 1 lb (450 g) miniatures. *See also* ST EMELYN.

APPELDORE

Swarbrick's of Ormskirk, Preston Road, Longridge, Preston, Lancashire
Artisan maker
Type: Cows milk, hard-pressed, full fat

A unique blend of medium-mature, Lancashire cheese and flakes of real apple, coated in cinnamon. The flavours blend beautifully together. Invented in 1977 and still produced today by Mr Swarbrick himself. The 5 lb (2.3 kg) cheeses are presented ready for serving on a foil cutting board.

APPLEBY'S HAWKSTONE CHESHIRE

Edward and Christine Appleby, Broadhay, Lower Heath, Prees, Shropshire
Farmhouse maker using the farm's own milk. Visitors by appointment
Type: Unpasteurised cows milk, hard-pressed, full fat

The Appleby family have been making Cheshire cheese for nearly 50 years. The recipe has changed but little in the half-century, only the quality of the milk has improved, resulting in what many say is the best and possibly the last real Cheshire cheese. All are matured on the farm and presented in traditional cloth-bound rounds. Sizes:

ANCIENT CHEESE

A piece of cheese over 200 years old was auctioned by Sotheby's on 3 February 1993. It was already a century old when acquired by Henry Stumbles whilst on a tour of duty with the Tibetan Pioneer Mission in 1884–7. The buyer was Simon Perry of *What's Up Doc*, the children's television show, who paid £1,058 for the rock-like piece of cheese and a number of religious artefacts.

50 lb (22 kg), 18 lb (8 kg), 5 lb (2.3 kg) and 3 lb (1.4 kg). Naturally oak-smoked Cheshire is available in 5 lb (2.3 kg) wheels and 3 lb (1.4 kg) small truckles. Appleby's also produce a traditional Double Gloucester.

APPLEWOOD

D. John Davidge, Ilchester Cheese Company, Ilchester, Somerset
Specialist dairy making character cheeses
Type: Cows milk, hard-pressed, full fat

Applewood has become a best-seller. When launched in 1965, it was produced by gently smoking mature Cheddar over slowly burning apple-wood logs, but now a natural extract of wood smoke is employed. Smooth and close-textured, Applewood is sold in 5½ lb (2.5 kg) wheels, 7 oz (200 g) green-waxed truckles and 5 oz (150 g) wedges. *See also* ILCHESTER.

ARDRAHAN

Eugene and Mary Burns, Ardrahan House, Kanturk, Co. Cork, Republic of Ireland
Artisan maker using the farm's own milk. Visitors by appointment
Type: Unpasteurised cows milk, semi-soft, full fat

Highly praised in a survey conducted by the *Irish Times*. A soft, rind-washed cheese which ripens to a rich flavour. Made from the milk of a Friesian herd, the cheese has been compared to a Tomme or Havarti but such comparisons are invidious as the 1.1 lb (500 g) rounds of Ardrahan have a unique flavour.

ARRAN

Neil McLean, Torrylinn Creamery, Isle of Arran
Small creamery using milk from the island
Type: Cows milk, hard-pressed, full fat

There are only 12 dairy farms on Arran and less than 1,000 cows but, though small, the island provides superb grazing. The creamery uses only local milk to produce 250 tonnes each year of a Dunlop cheese which has gained high praise. Arran cheese is close textured, clean flavoured and normally matured for a minimum of nine months. Supplied in 5½ lb (2.5 kg) truckles, 4½ lb (2 kg) red-waxed rounds, 1 lb (450 g) miniatures and cut sizes.

ARRAN BLUE

Ian and Allison McChlery, Home Farm, Brodick, Isle of Arran, Strathclyde
Artisan maker using the farm's own milk. Visitors welcome
Type: Cows milk, semi-hard, full fat, vegetarian

ARTISTIC CHEESE

Cheese-carving is a popular sport in the United States. Contestants carve 60 lb (27 kg) cheeses into animals, buildings and all manner of fantastic shapes. As with so many things American, the idea has been copied in Britain. At the 1990 Scottish Cheese Show, students from Glasgow's School of Art displayed a chess set made of cheese. Michelle de Bruin, Alice Angus and Rhona Gemmel carved a full set of pieces from white and coloured Scottish Cheddar. These were displayed on a red and white chessboard – or was it a cheeseboard?

The quality of some of Scotland's blue cheeses is so high that they make Stilton producers look to their laurels. This is one such. Made by hand, unpressed, it develops a distinctive blue flavour. *See also* KILBRIDE.

ASCAIG

Kathy Biss, West Highland Dairy, Achmore, Stromeferry, By Kyle of Lochalsh, Wester Ross
Artisan maker using the farm's own and other local milk. Visitors welcome
Type: Goats milk, hard-pressed, full fat, vegetarian

Smooth and close-textured blue cheese. Has a fine, clean 'tang' without excessive saltiness, and a texture more buttery than most Stilton. The 4½ lb (2 kg) rounds are ripened for 6–8 weeks and develop a natural rind. *See also* CREAGMHOL, WEST HIGHLAND SOFT.

ASHDALE

Valerie Morris, Ashdale Cheese, Town Head Farm, Askwith, Otley, West Yorkshire
Artisan maker using the farm's own milk
Type: Unpasteurised goats milk, lightly pressed, full fat, vegetarian

Described as 'Wensleydale with a bit of a bite', Ashdale is made in 4 lb (1.8 kg) rounds and 10 oz (280 g) miniatures, both covered in bright sunshine-yellow wax. Ashdale Thistledown is for lighter palates. This is a soft and creamy goats cheese, mild in flavour, made in 1½ lb (700 g) rounds which are also yellow waxed. *See also* MATURE MEADOWS.

ASHDOWN CUMBERLAND SMOKED

Harry Fellows, Ashdown Smokers, Skellerah Farm, Corney, Cumbria
Specialist smoke house. Visitors by appointment
Type: Various, from small artisan makers

Not all cheese described as 'smoked' has been prepared in the same manner. Quick smoking at a high temperature, which seals the outside of the cheese, and the use of smoke 'extracts' are both commonplace. Ashdown Smokers are true specialists, smoking the product slowly over oak and beech chippings in a process which takes around 70 hours, adding a remarkable depth of flavour rather than a cosmetic finish. A range of English county cheeses are smoked, most of them hard-pressed and all supplied by smaller artisan makers. Examples include: Botton, Cheshire, Double and Single Gloucester, Lancashire, Nepicar, Ribblesdale, Staffordshire and Wensleydale.

Ashdown Cumberland Smoked is smoked young and then matured for at least six months. It is made in 10 lb (4.5 kg) flat discs. This product is also available unsmoked. The smokehouse can only be visited by prior appointment but it is possible to call and buy cheese direct. Telephone (01229) 718324 for details of opening times.

ASHES WENSLEYDALE

Chris and Iain Hill, Ribblesdale Cheesemakers, Ashes Farm, Horton in Ribblesdale, North Yorkshire
Artisan maker. Visitors by appointment
Type: Ewes milk, hard-pressed, full fat

Cheese has been made at Ashes Farm for generations. There used to be a slate cheese vat, and an old stone press is still on the site, but the craft was revived only in 1982. Initially a modest output of goats milk cheese was supplemented by cheese made from cows milk but now only ewes milk Wensleydale is made. Ashes Wensleydale is made in a 100 gallon (50 litre) vat, from a mixture of morning and evening milkings. Cheese is supplied in 4½ lb (2 kg) wheels and 1 lb (450 g) miniatures; both are waxed after ripening to ensure they keep well. *See also* RIBBLESDALE.

ASHLEIGH

Colin Brown, The Big Sheep, Abbotsham, Bideford, Devon
Artisan maker using the farm's own milk. Visitors welcome
Type: Ewes milk, hard-pressed, full fat, vegetarian

An unusual Mediterranean-type ewes cheese, which might have originated in Sardinia. Formed in 8 lb (3.6 kg) rounds, dry salted for a piquant flavour. This is a long-keeping cheese which develops an excellent granular texture after 12 months. *See also* ABBOTSDALE, FRIESLA.

ASHLEY CHASE FARMHOUSE CHEDDAR

Cedric Littman, Ashley Chase Estate, Parks Farm, Litton Cheney, Dorchester, Dorset
Farmhouse maker using the farm's own milk. Visitors by appointment
Type: Cows milk, hard-pressed, full fat

Kingston Russell Farm covers 2,750 acres. The 1,400 cows provide milk for the highly efficient modern dairy, which is the largest cheesemaker in Dorset. Traditional 60 lb (27 kg) round Cheddars, small truckles and rindless 40 lb (20 kg) blocks are made with meticulous attention to detail. Matured for nine months (or more), the cheese is highly respected in the trade. The production of English Gruyère has recently been introduced. Cheese can be bought from the farm but telephone (01308) 482580 before calling to check opening times.

ASH PYRAMID

Mary Holbrook, Sleight Farm House, Timsbury, Bath, Avon
Artisan maker using the farm's own milk.
Type: Unpasteurised goats milk, semi-soft, full fat

Ash-coated 8 oz (225 g) pyramids, smooth and creamy texture, nutty in taste without any unwanted 'goaty' flavours. A dusting of charcoal or wood ash was applied to the cheese in past generations to ward off flies (York hams were given the same treatment), but the ash is now used for more cosmetic purposes. *See also* MENDIP.

AUGHER CO-OPERATIVE CHEDDAR

Crossowen Road, Augher, Co. Tyrone, Northern Ireland
Creamery
Type: Cows milk, hard-pressed, full fat

A farmers' co-operative of 56 members, making 3,500 tonnes of rindless Cheddar each year.

AVONMORE FOODS

Avonmore Foods PLC, Ballyragget, Co. Kilkenny, Republic of Ireland
Major creamery proprietor manufacturing at several locations
Type: Cows milk, various

Although their name might be less than familiar to the consumer, Avonmore Foods are one of the giants of the dairy industry in the UK and Eire. At Ballyragget they produce about 12,000 tonnes of Cheddar and other cheeses. Their UK cheese interests are grouped as 'Golden Foods', making over 18,000 tonnes of cheese each year, including 10,000 tonnes of MOZZARELLA at Llangefni on Anglesey. Rindless Cheddar and a range of English territorial varieties are manufactured at Whitchurch in Shropshire. This creamery produces 5,000 tonnes of rindless cheese each year and achieved a notable success at the Nantwich Show, when it took a first prize for wheels of Double Gloucester, a second prize for Derby and a third prize for Double Gloucester, all in the same year.

BABY BRENDON

Alan and Kay Duffield, Exmoor Blue Cheese, Willett Farm, Lydeard St Lawrence, Somerset
Artisan maker using the farm's own milk. Visitors by appointment
Type: Unpasteurised goats milk, soft, full fat, vegetarian

Small rounds of soft, creamy cheese from Exmoor. *See also* QUANTOCK BLUE.

BAGBOROUGH FARMS CHEDDAR

R.J. Longman, Bagborough Farm, Pylle, Shepton Mallet, Somerset
Farmhouse maker using the farm's own milk
Type: Cows milk, hard-pressed, full fat

Producing about 400 tonnes of rindless Cheddar in 40 lb (20 kg) blocks each year.

BAKER'S KINGSTON FARM CHEDDAR

W.F. Baker, Leaze Farm, Haselbury Plunkett, Crewkerne, Somerset
Farmhouse maker using the farm's own milk
Type: Cows milk, hard-pressed, full fat

Producing about 700 tonnes of cheese each year, mainly rindless Cheddar in 40 lb (20 kg) blocks.

BALLINDALLOCH

Jane Heape, Corglass Farm, Ballindalloch, Grampian
Artisan maker using the farm's own milk
Type: Unpasteurised goats milk, hard-pressed, full fat, vegetarian

Just below the point where the river Avon joins the river Spey, the goats of Corglass Farm graze on Heather Hill. Their milk goes into a range of cheeses, all hand-made to a traditional Scottish recipe. Ballindalloch is a mature, full-flavoured hard cheese, brine dipped and matured for three months. It is allowed to form a natural rind before being sold. The cheese can be ordered with added green peppercorns or caraway seeds. Standard or vegetarian rennet is used according to buyer's requirements. Ballindalloch Mild is a younger cheese, slightly crumbly and fresh flavoured. All cheeses are made in 6 lb (2.7 kg) round truckles, 1 lb (450 g) boxed or 8 oz (225g) portion packs.

BALLYBLUE

Fivemiletown Co-op, Ballylurgan Road, Fivemiletown, Co. Tyrone, Northern Ireland
Creamery
Type: Cows milk, semi-soft, full fat

For those who prefer a milder taste, this smooth and creamy, mould-ripened (Brie-type), blue cheese will do nicely! Claimed to be the first mild blue cheese to be developed in Ireland it is certainly different to the ferocious blue cheeses made south of the border! Made in 4 lb (1.8 kg) flat discs. *See also* BALLYLURGAN CHEDDAR.

BALLYLURGAN CHEDDAR

Fivemiletown Co-op, Ballylurgan Road, Fivemiletown, Co. Tyrone, Northern Ireland

Creamery
Type: Cows milk, hard-pressed, full fat

The Fivemiletown and Brookboro' Co-op Agricultural and Dairy Society, to give it its full name, was established as a co-operative of dairy farmers in 1898 but started cheesemaking only in 1972. The creamery now produces around 3,000 tonnes of cheese each year. Mild and mature Cheddar in rindless 40 lb (20 kg) blocks, or in a range of cut sizes, accounts for the greater part of production but there are also smoked Cheddar wheels, Double Gloucester, Red Leicester and a selection of speciality cheeses. *See also* BALLYBLUE, COONEEN.

Ballyoak is a soft cheese from the same creamery. The successful smoking of a mould-ripened (Brie-type) cheese is not easily accomplished but this product is astonishingly good. The smoke from oak chippings is carried very slowly over the cheeses, imparting a deep and lasting flavour. Made in 4 lb (1.8 kg) flat discs.

BARBER, A.J. and R.G. *see* MARYLAND FARM

BARON'S TABLE CHEESES

Dramona Quality Foods, Antrim Road, Belfast, Northern Ireland
Creamery
Type: Cows milk, hard-pressed, full fat

The attractively presented Baron's Table range includes Cheddar with beer, garlic and parsley; Cheddar with smoked paprika; Double Gloucester with chives and onions; Red Leicester with walnuts. *See also* DRAMONA, SPELGA.

BASING

Maureen and Bill Browning, Lower Basing Farm, Cowden, Kent
Artisan maker using the farm's own milk. Visitors by appointment
Type: Unpasteurised goats milk, semi-hard, full fat, vegetarian

Mild flavoured, Caerphilly-type cheese. Organically made, with an open, creamy texture. Basing comes in 9 lb (4 kg) rounds, 3 lb (1.4 kg) truckles and cut wedges.

BATH

Graham and Gabrielle Padfield, Park Farm, Kelston, Bath, Avon
Artisan maker using the farm's own milk
Type: Unpasteurised cows milk, soft, full fat, vegetarian

Bath cheese, an easy-spreading cousin to Camembert, was thought to be lost for ever until Graham Padfield found an authentic recipe in an old textbook. It took many tries before the perfect companion to Bath Oliver biscuits was successfully re-created, but the thinly rinded 8 oz (225 g) squares are now available again, albeit in small quantities.

BAYDON HILL CHEESE

Joanna Hale, Eventide, Baydon Hill Farm, Aldbourne, Marlborough, Wiltshire
Artisan maker using the farm's own milk. Visitors by appointment
Type: Unpasteurised ewes milk, hard-pressed, full fat, vegetarian

Butter-coloured cheese, made using a long-lost North Wiltshire recipe which was traced only with the help of local historians and may date back to the twelfth century. The cheese has a close, creamy texture and is matured for 5–6 months until the flavour is sweet and rich. Sage is sometimes added. The 4 lb (1.8 kg) truckles and 1 lb (450 g) rounds are finished with a unique coating of natural beeswax. Mrs Hale also produces a full-fat, yellow cheese from unpasteurised cows milk. The recipe also comes from Wiltshire. This cheese is matured to five months and described as tangy-sharp; sage is sometimes added and the cheese is also available smoked. The 5 lb (2.3 kg) truckles and 1 lb (450 g) rounds have the same beeswax coating as the ewes milk cheese.

BAY LOUGH

Ann and Dick Keating, Bay Lough Farm, Clogheen, Co. Tipperary, Republic of Ireland
Artisan maker using the farm's own milk. Visitors welcome
Type: Cows milk, hard-pressed, full fat, vegetarian

Cheese with a nutty flavour, described as a cross between Derby and Cheshire. Bay Lough Farm is surrounded by forests and situated near the Vee, a scenic pass through the Knockmealdown mountains, where the pastures are full of wild herbs. Ann Keating is sure the herbs impart a special flavour to her cheese, which was awarded first prize at the prestigious Clones Show. The cheese is distributed in 10 lb (4.5 kg) and 3 lb (1.4 kg) rounds, or in a 14 oz (400 g) mini size and, in addition to plain Bay Lough, smoked, garlic and herb varieties are made. All cheeses are waxed.

BEAL

Kate Carmody, Beal Lodge Farm, Asdee, Listowel, Co. Kerry, Republic of Ireland
Artisan maker using the farm's own milk. Visitors welcome
Type: Unpasteurised cows milk, hard-pressed, reduced fat, vegetarian

From a family farm on the banks of the river Shannon, a hand-made cheese in three versions: low fat, full cream and full cream with garlic and herbs. All are carefully matured. The cheese is sold locally and can be bought from the farm. The farm is signposted off the North Kerry Coastal Drive and visitors are welcome to watch the cheesemaking. There are facilities for children, including pet pigs! Telephone (068) 41137 (local number) to check opening times.

BEAMISH

David Reed, Home Farm, Beamish Museum, Co. Durham
Artisan maker. Visitors welcome
Type: Cows milk, hard-pressed, full fat, vegetarian

Beamish was England's first open-air museum, its 200 acres filled with working exhibits which superbly illustrate the buildings, railways, farms and mines of the North Country. As part of the museum's activities, visitors are welcomed at the working home farm, where David Reed (see SWALEDALE) makes a mild and crumbly Dales-type cheese, said to have a hint of heather in the bouquet. The cheese is pressed in 5 lb (2.3 kg) discs and 1½ lb (700 g) rounds. Telephone (01207) 231811 for museum opening times.

BEAUCHAMP

Long Clawson Dairy, Melton Mowbray, Leicestershire
Creamery
Type: Cows milk, hard-pressed, full fat

Red Leicester cheese with added herbs and garlic. *See also* LONG CLAWSON.

BEENLEIGH BLUE

Robin Congdon, Ticklemore Cheese, Ticklemore Street, Totnes, Devon
Artisan maker using the farm's own milk. Visitors welcome

Type: Unpasteurised ewes milk, semi-hard, full fat

The two flocks of sheep that provide the milk for Beenleigh Blue graze the beautiful valley of the river Dart. The cheese is made by hand and matured for a minimum of four months in an underground store, by which time the 6 lb (2.7 kg) drums have developed a rich, robust flavour and a natural crust. Normally only available September to February. The shop in Totnes is a Mecca for lovers of cheese. *See also* TICKLEMORE.

BELLE D'ECOSSE

John and Christian Curtis, Easter Weens Farm, Bonchester Bridge, Hawick, Borders
Artisan maker using the farm's own milk. Visitors by appointment
Type: Unpasteurised cows milk, semi-soft, full fat

The milk of 24 Jersey cows is used to make this white, mould-ripened cheese with a French name meaning 'beauty of Scotland'. The 1 lb 4 oz (550 g) rounds, popular as a gift for visitors to take home, exhibit a fresh butteriness when young and ripen to a rich creamy flavour with a distinctive but pleasant tarry aftertaste. *See also* BONCHESTER.

BELLE TOUT

Terry and Pam Wigmore, Seven Sisters Sheep Centre, East Dean, West Sussex
Artisan maker using the farm's own milk. Visitors welcome
Type: Ewes milk, soft, full fat, vegetarian

Seven Sisters Sheep Centre is just inland from Beachy Head and the famous lighthouse. Here they produce soft cream cheese which is sold in tubs and comes in a variety of flavours: parsley, chives and garlic, dill, pepper-corns and hazelnut. Visitors are welcome to tour the sheep centre, which is a showplace for ewes milk dairying. Telephone (01323) 423207 to check opening times. *See also* CROWLINK, DUNWICK.

BELLSHIRE

Long Clawson Dairy, Melton Mowbray, Leicestershire
Creamery
Type: Cows milk, hard-pressed, full fat

Wensleydale with onions and chives. *See also* LONG CLAWSON.

BELSTONE

Rachel Stephens, Curworthy Cheese, Stockbeare Farm, Jacobstowe, Okehampton, Devon
Artisan maker using the farm's own milk
Type: Unpasteurised cows milk, hard-pressed, full fat, vegetarian

Made to the traditional Curworthy seventeenth-century recipe, but using non-animal rennet. Pressed in an old farmhouse press to form naturally rinded 5 lb (2.3 kg) and 2½ lb (1.1 kg) truckles which are described as 'slightly strong'. *See also* CURWORTHY.

BELTON CHEESE

Justin Beckett, Belton Cheese Ltd, Belton, Whitchurch, Shropshire
Farmhouse maker using the farm's own milk
Type: Cows milk, hard-pressed, full fat

Innovative cheesemaker producing around 2,500 tonnes per year of English territorials in rindless blocks, rindless wheels, or traditional form.

BELVOIR BLUE

Long Clawson Dairy, Melton Mowbray, Leicestershire
Creamery
Type: Cows milk, soft, full fat, vegetarian

William the Conqueror gave the mound on which Belvoir Castle stands, and all the land visible therefrom, to his standard-bearer Robert de Todeni, who named the castle 'Belvedere', now Belvoir, pronounced 'beever'. How appropriate that a name with French connections should be used for this surface-moulded, blue, Brie-type cheese, a prizewinner at Nantwich as soon as it was introduced. The 3 lb (1.4 kg) rounds are distributed at around four weeks and will ripen for a further month. *See also* LONG CLAWSON.

BERKSWELL

Stephen Fletcher, Ramhall Dairy Sheep, Berkswell, West Midlands
Artisan maker using the farm's own milk. Visitors by appointment
Type: Unpasteurised ewes milk, semi-hard, full fat, vegetarian

Firm flavoured, Manchego-type, hard cheese. Slightly salty, with a pleasing crumbly texture. The 6½ lb (3 kg) rounds are dry salted (not brine dipped) and dressed with a gold finish that dulls to a natural rind as the cheese matures. *See also* KELSEY, MARLOW.

BEWCASTLE

Carolyn Fairbairn, Thornby Moor Dairy, Crofton Hall, Thursby, Carlisle, Cumbria
Artisan maker. Visitors welcome
Type: Unpasteurised cows milk, soft, full fat

Jersey cows provide milk for this lightly pressed, lactic cheese. Organi-cally made and supplied plain, with garlic, or oak smoked, in 3 lb (1.4 kg) cylinders or 8 oz (225 g) rounds, waxed or with a rind. *See also* CROFTON.

BISHOP KENNEDY

Rosemary and Mike Marwick, Howgate Cheeses, Camperdown Creamery, Faraday Street, Dundee
Artisan maker
Type: Cows milk, semi-soft, full fat, vegetarian

An orange-red, crusted cheese washed in malt whisky from Scotland's smallest distillery. It ripens to a tempting, creamy, runny paste with a rich flavour. The crust of younger cheeses may be eaten and enjoyed. Pasteurised and raw-milk versions are available, in 3 lb (1.4 kg) rounds and 10 oz (280 g) miniatures. *See also* HOWGATE.

BLACKDOWN

Horlicks Farms and Dairies, Hort Bridge, Ilminster, Somerset
Creamery
Type: Cows milk, hard-pressed, full fat, vegetarian

Horlicks Farms and Dairies have been making cheese for 50 years so they know their Cheddar. The connoisseur's choice from their range must be this rindless Cheddar, aged around 9–10 months, normally supplied in 10 lb (4.5 kg) blocks. *See also* HORLICKS.

BLACKMORE VALE SOFT CHEESES

Blackmore Vale Farm Cream, Wincombe Lane, Shaftesbury, Dorset
Small creamery
Type: Cows milk, soft, vegetarian

A range of soft cheeses from the heart

of Dorset. The traditionally made cottage cheese is gently stirred by hand to ensure the large pieces of curd stay whole, then dressed with a creamy coating to add richness and flavour. The cream cheese is thick, rich and smooth (magnificent in cheesecakes), and the curd cheese, whilst lower in fat, retains the thick, smooth texture. All the cheeses are available in 7 oz (200 g) pots or larger packs.

BLADEN CHEDDAR

The Cheese Company, Keaton House, Widewater Place, Moorhall Road, South Harefield, Middlesex
Creamery
Type: Cows milk, hard-pressed, full fat

The Cheese Company dates back to 1864 when, as Express Dairy, it dealt in milk and cream. It is now a major cheese producer, with production points across the UK. The popular Bladen rindless Cheddar, sold from many cheese counters, is available mild or mature. *See also* THE CHEESE COMPANY.

BLEASDALE

Alan Riding, Singleton's Dairy, Mill Farm, Preston Road, Longridge, Preston, Lancashire
Creamery
Type: Cows milk, hard-pressed, full fat, vegetarian

Singleton's first started cheesemaking in the 1920s, drawing milk from the remote farms of Bleasdale. The company was acquired by the Riding family (still in control) in 1959, and a dairy was built at Longridge in 1961. It produces a range of cheeses; Lancashire, Cheshire, Cheddar, Leicester, Gloucester, Caerphilly and Wensleydale, many with added flavours, are made on the farm and exported all over the world. Bleasdale

itself is a unique product, a marbled Cheddar, slightly softer than traditional Cheddar and made from a mixture of plain and annatto-coloured curds. It is sold in rindless blocks for counter cutting. *See also* SINGLETON'S, TRUCKLEDOWN.

BLUE CHESHIRE *see* CHESHIRE (BLUE)

BLUE RATHGORE

Mr H. Webb, Woodford Dairy, Finaghy Road South, Belfast, Northern Ireland
Artisan maker
Type: Unpasteurised goats milk, hard-pressed, full fat

Highly praised Roquefort-type blue cheese. The delicate curd is produced using a *Penicillium* mould culture and animal rennet in a secret process. The young cheeses are cured in special ripening rooms, salt being rubbed manually into the surface of each cheese, and matured for four months before sale. Cheese made with vegetarian rennet is available to order.

BLUE VINNEY

Long Clawson Dairy, Melton Mowbray, Leicestershire
Creamery
Type: Cows milk, semi-hard, low fat

The fabled Blue Vinney is no longer used for cartwheels and grindstones. It is made from partly skimmed milk, providing a low-fat cheese with a drier texture than Stilton but sharing the same 'tang' in the blue vein. Available in 15 lb (7 kg) rounds. *See also* DORSET BLUE VINNEY.

BOILIE

Anne and John Brodie, Ryefield Farm,

Virginia, Co. Cavan, Republic of Ireland
Artisan maker using the farm's own milk
Type: Cows milk, soft, full fat, vegetarian

Soft and creamy cheese, made entirely by hand. The curd is gently rolled into balls and then sealed in 7 oz (200 g) glass jars with fresh garden herbs, garlic and sunflower oil. The makers recommend Boilie as a starter; serve it in a hollowed-out tomato or avocado pear. The oil makes a perfect dressing for the salad. *See also* RYEFIELD.

BONCHESTER

John and Christian Curtis, Easter Weens Farm, Bonchester Bridge, Hawick, Borders
Artisan maker using the farm's own milk
Type: Unpasteurised cows milk, soft, mould-ripened

A fresh cheese, made from the milk of Jersey cows in the lush valley of Rule. The Coulommier-type 10 oz (280 g) rounds develop a strong flavour and a Camembert-style coat, with a few freckles for good measure as the buttery curd mellows to a deep-yellow colour. Only available March to December, Bonchester takes its name from Bonchester Bridge, famous for the hill fort and the remains of circular stone-walled houses dating from the second century AD. *See also* BELLE D'ECOSSE, TEVIOTDALE.

BONNELL'S CHESHIRE

R.C. Bonnell, Town House Farm, Hankelow, Crewe, Cheshire
Farmhouse maker using the farm's own milk
Type: Unpasteurised cows milk, hard-pressed, full fat

Produces around 250 tonnes of traditional Cheshire cheese a year.

BONNET

Ann Dorward, Dunlop Dairy, West Clerkland, Stewarton, Strathclyde
Artisan maker using the farm's own milk
Type: Goats milk, soft, full fat

Bonnet is an appropriate name for a cheese from just north of Kilmarnock. This region was once famous for the manufacture of 'Tam o' Shanter' bonnets. Bonnet cheese is white and mild, described as 'moist Wensleydale with a subtle goat taste'. It was placed first in its class at Nantwich Show three years running. The 4 lb (1.8 kg) rounds are vacuum packed. *See also* DUNLOPPE.

BOSWORTH ASH

Hugh Lillingston, Innes Cheese, Highfields Dairy, Statfold, Tamworth, Staffordshire
Artisan maker using the farm's own milk
Type: Unpasteurised goats milk, soft, full fat, vegetarian

Bosworth has a light, lemon flavour. The 5 oz (150 g) rounds are made by hand, coated with ash or wrapped in leaves. Cheese can be bought from the dairy but telephone (01827) 830097 to check opening times. *See also* INNES.

BOURNE'S ORIGINAL CHESHIRE CHEESE

John Bourne, The Bank, Malpas, Cheshire
Artisan maker using the farm's own milk
Type: Cows milk, hard-pressed, full fat

The Bourne family have been making

fine Cheshire cheese since the 1930s, and are among the few makers still using the old methods to produce mature Cheshire for the connoisseur. Their cheese is rich and mellow in taste, firm but not hard bodied, with a free granular texture. Pasteurised and raw milk versions are available in 48 lb (21 kg), 20 lb (9 kg), 6 lb (2.7 kg) and 3½ lb (1.6 kg) cloth-bound and waxed rounds. Cheese can be bought from the farm but telephone (01948) 81214 before calling.

BOWLAND

Godfrey C. Williams, 9–11 The Square, Sandbach, Cheshire
Specialist retailer
Type: Cows milk, hard-pressed, full fat, with additives, vegetarian

A visit to Godfrey Williams's cheese shop is a delight, especially for anyone looking for the unusual. A small number of products are made on the premises. Bowland was an immediate success, taking first prize in its class at the Nantwich Show. It is a blend of mature (4-month) Lancashire cheese with apples, raisins and cinnamon. Made in 6½ lb (3 kg) flat rounds. Other products to be found in the shop include 'Red Hot Mex' (a Cheddar with Mexican Nacho chillies that is strictly for brave palates), rather cooler Cheshire cheese with mint, and a Double Gloucester with spring onion.

BRENDON BLUE

Alan and Kay Duffield, Exmoor Blue Cheese, Willett Farm, Lydeard St Lawrence, Somerset
Artisan maker using the farm's own milk. Visitors by appointment
Type: Unpasteurised goats milk, hard-pressed, full fat, vegetarian

Goats grazing on the hills of Exmoor

National Park provide the milk for Brendon Blue. The unpressed 4½ lb (2 kg) drums (and miniatures) are made by hand and have a blue mould imparted by *Penicillium roqueforti*. They are matured for 3–4 months. *See also* QUANTOCK BLUE.

BRIE *see* ABBEY BLUE BRIE, SHARPHAM BRIE, HOWGATE BRIE, SOMERSET BRIE

BRODICK BLUE

Ian and Allison McChlery, Home Farm, Brodick, Isle of Arran, Strathclyde
Artisan maker using the farm's own milk. Visitors welcome
Type: Ewes milk, semi-hard, full fat, vegetarian

The buttery-textured creaminess of a ewes milk cheese provides the natural complement to the tang of blue veining (hence the success of Roquefort) and Brodick Blue offers a flavour quite different to a cows milk 'blue' such as Stilton. The rounds develop a natural surface rind and carry a sweet aroma. *See also* KILBRIDE.

BURNDELL

Jenny Ferris, Malthouse Cottage Farm, Ashington, Pulborough, West Sussex
Artisan maker using the farm's own milk. Visitors by appointment
Type: Goats milk, hard-pressed, full fat, vegetarian

Clean flavoured cheese, sold in 3 lb (1.4 kg) cylinders, or 1 lb (450 g) 'smalls', both matured for three months to develop a mellow flavour and finished with a bright-yellow wax. Burndell is available smoked over Sussex oak logs and there is also a very special waxed Black Burndell, matured for 9–12 months. Certified organic to Soil Association standards. *See also* CHALK HILL BLUE, MALTHOUSE COTTAGE.

BUTLER'S FARMHOUSE LANCASHIRE

Jean Butler, Butler's Farmhouse Cheeses, Wilson Fields Farm, Inglewhite, Preston, Lancashire
Farmhouse maker using the farm's own milk
Type: Cows milk, hard-pressed, full fat, vegetarian

Jean Butler specialises in traditionally rinded cheeses, including a renowned Farmhouse Lancashire which secured a coveted first prize at the Nantwich Show. This product is also available smoked. The farm also produces Lancashire with garlic and chives, and Lancashire with sage, as well as traditionally rinded Double Gloucester and, a very rare commodity, a traditionally rinded Red Leicester. Total production is around 500 tonnes each year.

BUXTON BLUE

J.M. Nuttall, Hartington Creamery, Buxton, Derbyshire
Creamery
Type: Cows milk, semi-hard, full fat

Milder than the other English blue cheeses, Buxton Blue has a smooth texture, warm russet colour, delicate blue veining and 'honey' aftertaste. Made in 13 lb (6 kg) small truckles. *See also* DAIRY CREST.

CABOC

Reggie and Susannah Stone, Highland Fine Cheeses, Knockbreck, Tain, Highland
Artisan maker using local milk
Type: Cows milk, soft, full fat, rennet free, vegetarian

Rich, double-cream cheese, made without rennet and rolled in toasted pinhead oatmeal. Caboc is boxed in the Munro tartan of the Black Watch regiment which was raised by Reggie's Munro forbears. The recipe has been handed down from mother to daughter through Susannah's family, which can be traced back to the fifteenth century. Caboc is the oldest recorded Scottish cheese. *See also* CROWDIE.

CAERPHILLY

Type: Cows milk, hard or semi-hard, full fat, vegetarian

Traditional Caerphilly, the crumbly and light cheese that miners took down the pit in days gone by, almost vanished from the Welsh valleys during the last war as a result of milk shortages. Happily, cheesemaking has now returned to Wales, and the Principality's most famous cheese has returned home. Welsh artisan makers to look out for include CASTLE MEADOWS, CAWS CENARTH (unpasteurised), NANTYBWLA FARMHOUSE (unpasteurised), ST EMELYN (unpasteurised and smoked) and TEIFI (unpasteurised and smoked).

CAETHWAS

Peter Sayer, Welsh Farmhouse Cheese, Maesllyn, Llandysul, Dyfed
Artisan maker. Visitors welcome
Type: Unpasteurised cows milk, hard-pressed, full fat, vegetarian

This farm originated the idea of blending well-matured Cheddar with white wine, garlic and herbs. The recipe has been imitated but this is the original, made with Welsh Cheddar produced from local milk. Sold in black-waxed 5 lb (2.3 kg) rounds or 1 lb (450 g) miniatures. *See also* ST EMELYN.

CALEDONIA

Great Glen Fine Foods, Old Ferry Road,

North Ballachulish, Inverness, Highland
Specialist retailer
Type: Goats milk, hard-pressed, full fat

If you are ever in the region of Fort William, you must visit Douglas Locke's marvellous store, Great Glen Fine Foods. With a stunning array of over 1,000 Scottish delicacies, this is a gourmet's paradise. The 1 lb (450 g) drums of strong, well-matured Caledonia are just one of the good things on offer. *See also* GLENCOE.

CAMPBELTOWN TRUCKLES

Scottish Pride Creamery, Campbeltown, Strathclyde
Creamery
Type: Cows milk, hard-pressed, full fat

Campbeltown is a small seaport lying on the Kintyre peninsula, an area with a long tradition of cheesemaking in the far west of Scotland. The creamery is best known for its rindless Cheddar but is also noted for Campbeltown black-waxed truckles. A cheese of stunning appearance, it is matured for at least nine months and specially graded by the Company of Scottish Cheesemakers.

CAPRICORN

Lubborn Cheese, North Street, Crewkerne, Somerset
Artisan maker
Type: Pasteurised goats milk, soft, full fat, vegetarian

There was a cheese sold under the name of Capricorn in ancient Rome. It might well have been made from goats milk but it is most unlikely to have resembled the one made today! Capricorn is a white-coated cheese which ripens from the outside and has a very clean flavour. The makers liken it to French

chèvre but while this can vary considerably from very mild to ferociously pungent, the home-grown product is not so temperamental. Sold in 4 oz (100 g) logs, with a 2½ lb (1.1 kg) brick for delicatessen counters. *See also* SOMERSET BRIE.

CAPRINI

Lyn and Jenny Jenner, Nut Knowle Farm, World's End, Gun Hill, Horam, East Sussex
Artisan maker using the farm's own milk
Type: Goats milk, various, vegetarian

Nut Knowle Farm produces a highly praised range of traditional goats cheeses: soft, mould ripened, hard-pressed and the delicately flavoured ash-coated pyramids. Caprini is made from slices of the soft cheese, marinated in oil and fresh herbs, wild nettle and garlic, or spicy peppers. It is excellent as a starter. Chabis is a range of firmer goats cheeses, individually waxed, in four flavours. Cremet is a distinctive, mould-ripened variety, flavoured with herbs and garlic and topped with parsley. It is sold in 5 oz (150 g) rounds. *See also* ST GEORGE, ST MAURE, SUSSEX YEOMAN.

CARNEVALE MOZZARELLA

Carnevale House, Blundell Street, London N7
Creamery
Type: Cows milk, soft, full fat, vegetarian

You may not see the name Carnevale in the shops but if the pizza you had last night was particularly good it may have been this Mozzarella that made the difference. The two production points (London and Huddersfield) make around 800 tonnes each year of this soft, white, pasta filata cheese, most of which goes to Italian restaurants.

CAROLINA

Harold Woolley, British Sheep Dairy Products, Nepicar Farm, Wrotham Heath, Kent
Artisan maker using the farm's own milk. Visitors by appointment
Type: Unpasteurised ewes milk, semi-hard, full fat, vegetarian

How appropriate that ewes milk cheese is made by a Mr Woolley. Carolina can be traced back to a twelfth-century Dales recipe. Sold in 6 lb (2.7 kg) or 1 lb (450 g) rounds. *See also* NEPICAR.

CARRAIG GOAT CHEESE

Lieke and Aart Versloot, Carraig Cheese, Ballingeary, Co. Cork, Republic of Ireland
Artisan maker using the farm's own milk
Type: Unpasteurised goats milk, hard-pressed, full fat

Leike and Aart, originally from Holland, now make cheese on their farm close to the source of the river Lee in Gougane Barra. The land is managed by organic methods. Their 50 goats are milked by hand and the cheese is also hand-made to a Gouda recipe. It is kept for 6–8 weeks before sale but can be matured for much longer.

CARRIGALINE

Anne and Patrick Farrell, Leacht Cross, Carrigaline, Co. Cork, Republic of Ireland
Artisan maker
Type: Cows milk, semi-soft, full fat

A mild Gouda-type cheese, made in 14 oz (400 g) rounds, sometimes flavoured with garlic and herbs. Milk from a Friesian herd, grazing natural limestone pasture, is used.

CARRON LODGE

Mr R. Rhodes, Rhodes Cheese, Park Head Farm, Inglewhite, Preston, Lancashire
Farmhouse maker using the farm's own milk
Type: Cows milk, hard-pressed, full fat

A range of cheese from the Forest of Bowland: creamy and crumbly Lancashire, Red Leicester, Cheshire and Cheddar. Regular winners at the Great Eccleston Show. There is an innovative selection of 'additive' cheeses: Double Gloucester with chives, Lancashire with blackberry and apple, Cheddar with elderberry port, Lancashire with garlic and – an unusual presentation – Lancashire with sage (the herbs in a delightful flower pattern). Some of the cheeses are available oak-smoked, usually in 12 in (30 cm) discs. I particularly admired the range presented at the Nantwich Show, when cheeses were pressed in the shape of red roses, in various sizes.

CASHEL BLUE and CASHEL WHITE

Jane and Louis Grubb, Beechmount Farm, Fethard, Co. Tipperary, Republic of Ireland
Farmhouse maker using the farm's own milk. Visitors by appointment
Type: Cows milk, semi-hard, full fat

The best known of Ireland's 'fancy' cheeses, made using milk from the farm's herd of 100 Friesian cows. Only 50 tonnes per year of Cashel Blue are made but this has not stopped the cheese from earning itself an international reputation. Cashel Blue is made in the same way as Roquefort, although it is a little softer, moister and less salty. As the blue veins turn to green, the cheese develops a ferocious flavour that could cross the Irish Sea without a ferry ticket. Cashel White was introduced in 1990 and succeeded in winning first prize for Jane Grubb in a Dublin 'new cheeses' competition. The cheese is delightfully curdy and crumbly, best eaten whilst young and firm. The gold-wrapped cheeses are available in 3 lb (1.5 kg), 12 oz (350 g) and 6 oz (170 g) sizes.

CASTLE DAIRIES CHEDDAR

John Lloyd, Castle Dairy, Pontygwindy Industrial Estate, Caerphilly, Mid Glamorgan
Creamery
Type: Cows milk, hard-pressed, full fat

Manufacturer of rindless 40 lb (20 kg) Cheddar and English territorial cheeses. Total production is around 3,000 tonnes per year.

CASTLEFARM GOATS CHEESE

Catherine Corkery, Castlefarm Goats Cheese, Hospital, Co. Limerick, Republic of Ireland
Artisan maker using the farm's own milk
Type: Goats milk cheeses, various, organic

The village of Hospital is so called because it was at one time in the possession of the Knights Hospitallers. The goats enjoy the rich pasture of the Golden Vale, and an old family recipe is used to make a cheese that has found favour with many chefs in the area. Castlefarm cheese is sold traditionally hard-pressed (usually in a bright-red wax) or semi-hard. Catherine also makes a soft, fresh cheese and a cottage cheese. All the range is organically made and vegetarian cheeses are available.

CASTLE MEADOWS CAERPHILLY

Bryson Craske, Abergavenny Fine Foods, Castle Meadows Park, Abergavenny, Gwent
Artisan maker. Visitors welcome
Type: Cows milk, hard-pressed, full fat

Traditional Caerphilly, made near the castle from which the cheese takes its name, using a recipe developed after months of research in the former mining communities. Hand-made by methods which date back to the 1890s, this re-created cheese is moist and slightly crumbly, with a clean fresh flavour. Visitors are welcome to buy cheese at the dairy but telephone (01873) 850001 first to check opening times. *See also* CHEVELLES, GLAMORGAN SAUSAGES, PANT-YS-GAWN, ST DAVID, WELSH RAREBIT, Y-FENNI.

CATHEDRAL CITY MATURE CHEDDAR

Mendip Foods, North Parade, Frome, Somerset
Cheese packers
Type: Cows milk, hard-pressed, full fat

It is the job of expert graders to select well-aged Cheddar with a consistently strong flavour to be packed as Cathedral City. This is one of the few cheeses to build a 'brand image' through television advertising, making it a star performer in the cheese trade. Mendip Foods also markets the products of several Farmhouse cheese makers from their famous cheese store at Wells, and operates a cheesepacking facility at Frome capable of handling 20,000 tonnes per year. Rindless Cheddar is also sold under other brand names, including Mendip Hills, Bishop's Reserve and Joseph Harding.

CAWS ABERAERON

Don and Karen Ross, Little Acorn

Products, Mesen Fach Farm, Bethania, Llanon, Dyfed
Artisan maker. Visitors by appointment
Type: Cows milk, hard-pressed, full fat, vegetarian

Caws Aberaeron Applemint is one of the most innovative additive cheeses you are likely to find: Welsh Cheddar mellowed with fine slithers of apple, enlivened with a touch of warming mustard and cooled with the freshness of mint. What a mouthful! Try it crumbled over a green salad or layer it with Welsh lamb in a shepherd's pie. Caws Aberaeron Hot Tomato is enriched with the deep colour and rich flavour of sun-dried tomatoes. Both cheeses are made in 6 lb (2.7 kg) waxed wheels for cutting and in waxed miniatures.

CAWS CENARTH CAERFFILI

Gwynfor and Thelma Adams, Fferm Glyneithinog, Pontseli, Boncath, Dyfed
Artisan maker using the farm's own milk. Visitors welcome
Type: Unpasteurised cows milk, hard-pressed, full fat, vegetarian

Gwynfor and Thelma Adams have been farming since the early 1960s, building up a herd of pedigree British Holstein/Friesian dairy cattle. The cattle feed on grass from the lush pastures of the Cych Valley. In a beautifully restored barn the Adams family makes the award-winning Caws Cenarth, which a *Good Food Guide* jury decided was one of the finest examples of British cheese. It is made in 10 lb (4.5 kg) wheels, 2 lb (900 g) truckles and 1 lb (450 g) miniatures, available smoked over oak wood or with added herbs. The herb and spice version is known as Caws Cenarth Antiphebi. The miniatures, in presentation wooden drums bearing the Caws Cenarth logo, make an ideal gift.
    A new range of cheeses are also available: with peach and pear liqueur (my favourite); fresh peppers and white wine; garlic, peppers and white wine; and sun-dried tomatoes and white wine. The Adams family are a fine advert for Welsh cheesemaking. They are keen conservationists and open their Dyfed farm for the public to see traditional cheesemaking. All the Adamses can run a half-marathon (strong stuff, Welsh cheese) and they find time to breed Corgis! (The father of the Queen's first Corgi came from their kennels.) Cheese can be bought at the farm and visitors can watch the cheesemaking from a viewing gallery but telephone (01239) 710432 first to check opening times. *See also* CHRISTMAS PUDDING CHEESE.

CAWS TARRON

Peter Sayer, Welsh Farmhouse Cheese, Maesllyn, Llandysul, Dyfed
Artisan maker. Visitors welcome
Type: Unpasteurised cows milk, hard-pressed, full fat, vegetarian

Caerphilly cheese, traditionally made by hand using local milk, but with the addition of orange and tarragon. Available in yellow-waxed 5 lb (2.3 kg) rounds or 1 lb (450 g) miniatures. *See also* ST EMELYN.

CECELIA

Harold Woolley, British Sheep Dairy Products, Nepicar Farm, Wrotham Heath, Kent
Artisan maker using the farm's own milk. Visitors by appointment
Type: Unpasteurised ewes milk, hard-pressed, full fat, vegetarian

Named after the maker's mother (nice thought), this cheese is made with a hint of the Kentish hops on which it has been matured. Sometimes available smoked. Sold in 6 lb (2.7 kg) or 1 lb (450 g) rounds. *See also* NEPICAR.

CERNEY

Lady Angus, Cerney House, North Cerney, Cirencester, Gloucestershire
Artisan maker using the farm's own milk. Visitors welcome
Type: Unpasteurised goats milk, soft, full fat, vegetarian

After being in commercial production for only three years this pyramid-shaped cheese from the Cotswolds won an award at the London International Cheese Show. The unpressed cheeses are white and mild, weigh about 8 oz (225 g) and are covered with black ash and sea-salt mix. They are also available smoked or flavoured with orange. A miniature size is sold as Cerney Starter. Cheese can be bought direct from the dairy. The informal, romantic gardens of Cerney House are open to the public and well worth a visit. (A small charge is made for entry.) Telephone (01285) 831300 for details of opening times.

CHABIS

Kevin and Alison Blunt, Greenacres Farm, Whitesmith, Lewes, East Sussex
Artisan maker using the farm's own milk. Visitors welcome
Type: Unpasteurised goats milk, soft, full fat, vegetarian

Creamy cheese, made in 3 oz (85 g) conical cylinders. The flavour is pleasantly tart, with just a hint of sharpness and a rich finish. *See also* FLOWER MARIE, GOLDEN CROSS.

CHALK HILL BLUE

Jenny Ferris, Malthouse Cottage Farm, Ashington, Pulborough, West Sussex
Artisan maker using the farm's own milk. Visitors by appointment
Type: Pasteurised goats milk, semi-hard, full fat, vegetarian

Malthouse Cottage Farm holds the Soil Association's symbol for organic dairy products. This calls for a lot more than mere sympathy with organic farming methods. Animals have to be fed on naturally grown herbage, so their pastures are organically managed. No spraying with herbicides is allowed. The routine use of antibiotics, hormones and steroids is also banned, and even the use of conventional medicines is strictly controlled. The organic farmer has to accept that his land will support fewer animals per acre. Chalk Hill Blue is made in the Roquefort style, but is less crumbly in texture. It is presented in 3 lb (1.4 kg) rounds, which develop a natural rind.

Chancton, from the same maker, is a soft, creamy cheese with a white, mould-ripened crust. It is made by hand, in 10 oz (280 g) rounds and packed in Camembert-style boxes. Free from colouring, emulsifiers and preservatives, the cheese is made using pure sea-salt. *See also* BURNDELL.

CHARNWOOD

Long Clawson Dairy, Melton Mowbray, Leicestershire
Creamery
Type: Cows milk, hard-pressed, full fat

Mellow Cheddar cheese with a smoked flavour, surface-coated with paprika to add colour. *See also* LONG CLAWSON.

CHAVANNES

Nachi Elkin, Gedi Enterprises, Plumridge Farm, Stagg Hill, Barnet, Hertfordshire
Artisan maker using the farm's own milk. Visitors welcome
Type: Goats milk, semi-soft, full fat, vegetarian

Nachi Elkin bluntly admits that he is out to beat the French at their own game, and a string of show awards confirms his successes. Using pasteurised milk, from the farm's herd of 400 goats, he has created goat products especially for the British palate – milder in flavour, perhaps, but with a character to rival their French counterparts. From the delicate to the fiery, from ash coated to immersed in oil, all Gedi cheeses are exciting. Likened to Camembert in taste and appearance, Chavannes is made in 4½ oz (125 g) rounds with a downy crust and mild smooth interior that develops with age. Visitors are welcome to buy cheese at the farm but telephone (0181) 449 0695 first to check opening times. *See also* CORINNA, CROTTIN, JOUVENET, MOILLON, ROUBILIAC, VELDE.

CHEDDAR GORGE CHEDDAR

Cheddar Gorge Cheese Co., The Cliffs, Cheddar Gorge, Cheddar, Somerset
Artisan maker using local milk. Visitors welcome
Type: Cows milk, hard-pressed, full fat

Cheddar cheese might be made here, there and everywhere but only one Cheddar is actually made at the foot of the Gorge! Traditional 60 lb (27 kg) drums of Cheddar cheese are manufactured on most days and this working demonstration of cheese manufacture has deservedly become a popular tourist attraction. The display is set in a colourful re-creation of a 1920s village and is suitable for all the family. Cheese can be bought in the shop. Open all year. For further information telephone (01934) 742810.

CHEDDAR (MATURE, RINDLESS)

Type: Cows milk, hard-pressed, full fat

The cheese that we call Cheddar comes from many different sources and varies widely in quality. The source of the milk, style of manufacture, maturing time and even the way the product is handled and packed all affect the final outcome. Cheddar begins to develop a fuller flavour at five to six months and then slowly improves for a year or longer. Top-quality rindless mature Cheddar is there to be found, but only by customers who pay a fair price and go to those retailers who take a genuine interest in what they sell. Cheese described as strong is not necessarily well-aged and certainly not always the best. Look for a rich, clean flavour with a full, rounded 'nutty' aftertaste. See entries for: ASHLEY CHASE, BAGBOROUGH FARMS, BAKER'S KINGSTON FARM, CLAPPS CHEDDAR, CLOTHIER'S CHEDDAR, CRICKET MALHERBIE CHEDDAR, DENHAY TRADITIONAL, FORD FARM, HAWKRIDGE FARMHOUSE, ISLE OF ATHELNEY, LONGMAN'S CHEDDAR, LOVINGTON FARMERS, LYE CROSS, MARYLAND FARM, PARKHAM FARM, TY'N GRUG, WARREN FARM.

CHEDDAR (MATURE) WITH RICH FRUIT CAKE

Long Clawson Dairy, Melton Mowbray, Leicestershire
Creamery
Type: Cows milk, hard-pressed, full fat

It has long been the custom to eat cheese and fruit cake together. In this cheese, pieces of rich fruit cake are added to the curd, imparting a fruity sweetness. Supplied in 3 lb (1.4 kg) triangular packs for cutting. The same dairy's mature Cheddar with sweet pickle promises a different spicy taste, whilst a Cheddar with asparagus and leek provides an intriguing combination of flavours. *See also* LONG CLAWSON.

CHEDDAR (MILD)

Type: Cows milk, hard-pressed, full fat

'Mild cheese is mild cheese and all that matters is the price.' Don't believe it!

The cheapest is seldom the best to buy. Cheddar is inedible before four weeks, scarcely palatable before six, indifferent at eight, begins to develop character at 12, but is better still at 14–16. Mild Cheddar is made all over the world and the flavour inevitably varies with the quality of the milk and the skill of the cheesemaker. More than most cheeses, it suffers from being offered for sale too young. Prepacked cheese is more likely to disappoint than cheese sold loose from a counter but, ultimately, quality depends on the probity of the retailer and the interest of the consumer. Try to taste before you buy.

CHEDDAR (TASTY)

Type: Cows milk, hard-pressed, full fat

You have to seek out good tasty Cheddar. It is the favourite cheese of many consumers in the west of England. Maturing cheese can develop spots of moisture within its fissures (graders term this 'showing moisture on the iron'), accompanied by a strident tangy flavour. Such cheese has a limited life, as the acid level rises very quickly. This is a great shame, for tasty Cheddar can be excellent cheese. Taste before you buy is the best recommendation. Labels to look out for include Mathews & Skailles Tasty Cheddar (packed by Adams Foods, Leek, Cheshire) and WESTWAY DAIRY 'Red Label' Tasty Cheddar.

CHEDDAR (TRADITIONAL, WITH RIND)

Type: Cows milk, hard-pressed, full fat

There is a unique character to Cheddar that is larded and cloth-bound in the traditional manner. Most comes from smaller makers whose cheese is likely to have an individual flavour and to be made from unpasteurised milk. The natural surface drying of traditionals may lead to a slight mould intrusion, forming fine threads of blue veining. This is praised, not rejected, by those who know good cheese, and some would say that 'blue vinnied' Cheddar is the best cheese on earth. It requires an experienced cheesemonger to handle any rind-on cheese to best advantage; a little cutting waste is inevitable but the flavour makes it well worth the small extra cost. Makers who still use unpasteurised milk include KEEN'S UNPASTEURISED CHEDDAR, MONTGOMERY'S UNPASTEURISED CHEDDAR, TIMES PAST, TY'N GRUG FARMHOUSE CHEDDAR. West Country makers using pasteurised milk include ASHLEY CHASE, CHEDDAR GORGE CHEDDAR, CHEWTON, DAIRY CREST, DENHAY TRADITIONAL CHEDDAR, GOULD'S TRADITIONAL CHEDDAR, GREEN'S TRADITIONAL CHEDDAR, LONGMAN'S CHEDDAR, QUICKE'S TRADITIONAL CHEDDAR and TOWER FARMS CHEDDAR.

CHEESE COMPANY, THE

Keaton House, Widewater Place, Moorhall Road, South Harefield, Middlesex
Major creamery proprietor manufacturing at several locations

The Cheese Company is one of the giants of the dairy industry, producing 60,000 tonnes of cheese each year, mainly rindless Cheddar, some 20% of the UK total. Its cheese is made in large creameries and widely sold under supermarket own-labels. The biggest creamery, at North Tawton in Devon, produces 25,000 tonnes of rindless Cheddar and English territorial cheeses per year. At Appleby in Cumbria, the creamery makes 13,000 tonnes of rindless Cheddar a year, whilst the production facility at Oswestry, Shropshire, is responsible for speciality cheeses and houses the largest prepacking facility in the UK. In Scotland,

LOCKERBIE Creamery, Dumfries and Galloway, produces 15,000 tonnes of rindless Cheddar and other cheeses per year. In Northern Ireland, cheese and butter are made at Magheralin, Co. Armagh. The Cheese Company also owns TUXFORD AND TEBBUTT, the biggest Stilton manufacturer (producing around 2,000 tonnes a year), and REECE'S Creamery of Malpas, Cheshire, where 5,000 tonnes of Cheshire and other cheeses are made annually. The Cheese Company has recently introduced an innovative Bio-Cheddar, containing special cultures which are said to make the cheese more easily digestible. *See also* BLADEN, CHURNTON.

CHESHIRE

Type: Cows milk, hard-pressed, full fat

Cheshire is England's oldest cheese, delicious with fresh fruit and rich fruit cake. Unfortunately, poor, plastic-wrapped imitations of the genuine article are frequently all that can be found. The preferred texture is loose and crumbly, with a mild and slightly salty flavour which is said to emanate from the salt deposits beneath the meadows around Nantwich. Cheshire is best eaten within three months of manufacture; if kept too long it can turn acid and bitter in flavour. The cheese is often coloured red with annatto, a harmless vegetable dye. Distinguished makers (see individual entries) include: APPLEBY'S OF HAWKSTONE (unpasteurised traditional), BELTON CHEESE, R.C. BONNELL, BOURNE'S ORIGINAL CHESHIRE (traditional), HANKELOW MANOR FARM, V.J. HARES (traditional and rindless), JOSEPH HELER (traditional and rindless), P.J. HUNTBACH (traditional and rindless), KNOLTON FARMHOUSE (traditional and rindless), W.J. and T.E. WINDSOR (traditional).

CHESHIRE (BLUE)

Long Clawson Dairy, Melton Mowbray, Leicestershire
Creamery
Type: Cows milk, semi-hard, full fat

Lost to its home county, a blue Cheshire cheese is made by Long Clawson Dairy of Long Clawson in Leicestershire. The dark-blue veins contrast sharply with the annatto-coloured cheese and the flavour is superb. The cheese is sold in 13 lb (6 kg) drums which form a natural crust. Blue Cheshire has always been a rarity amongst cheeses, even in its home county. The blue vein or 'green fade', as it was called, resulted from a spontaneous intrusion of bacteria rather than the deliberate introduction of *Penicillium roqueforti*. Such cheeses used to be rejected, or applied as an ointment to treat ear-ache or skin infections (a subject worthy of research by medical historians). It was not until the twentieth century that cheeses were deliberately pierced to encourage mould intrusion, and the care and control employed in modern dairies means that a fortuitous accidental blueing is a thing of the past.

CHETWYND BLUE

Gerry Beechinor, Castlewhite House, Waterfall, Co. Cork, Republic of Ireland
Artisan maker. Visitors by appointment
Type: Cows milk, soft, full fat

An excellent Roquefort-style cheese, creamy textured, mild and attractively foil-wrapped. When fully matured, it is said to be even stronger than CASHEL BLUE.

CHEVELLES

Bryson Craske, Abergavenny Fine

Foods, Castle Meadows Park, Abergavenny, Gwent
Artisan maker. Visitors welcome
Type: Unpasteurised goats milk, semi-
soft, full fat, vegetarian

Chevelles is made at Pant-ys-Gawn
Farm, Mamhilad, a remote sixteenth-
century hill farm buried deep in the
Brecon Beacons National Park. The
product is a mild, goats milk cheese
formed into small rounds with a crispy-
crunch coating of toasted crumbs. The
cheese is additive free and designed to
be grilled or fried in the manner of the
little French Camembert cheeses that
are often served fried in breadcrumbs.
Chevelles is delicious served with cran-
berry or redcurrant sauce. *See also*
CASTLE MEADOWS CAERPHILLY.

CHEWTON CHEDDAR

*Nigel Pooley, Chewton Dairy, Priory
Farm, Chewton Mendip, Somerset*
Small creamery. Vistors welcome
Type: Cows milk, hard-pressed, full
fat

Chewton Dairy belongs to Viscount
Chewton, heir to Earl Waldegrave,
whose ancestor Sir Edward Waldegrave
was given the land around Chewton
Mendip by Mary I in 1553. There was
once a Benedictine abbey on the site of
the present farm; this was replaced by a
large Gothic-style house called
Chewton Priory. It may have been the
medieval monks who introduced
cheesemaking here; parts of their
outbuildings are now incorporated in
the farm shop and a building adjacent
to the dairy, where around 400 tonnes
of cheese are made each year. There is
an excellent viewing gallery and a
pleasant restaurant overlooking the
cheese room. A modest charge is made
for entry. Chewton Dairy is an ideal
place to view cheesemaking. (Coach
parties by prior notice only.) Telephone
(01761) 241666 first to check opening
times.

CHRISTMAS PUDDING CHEESE

*Gwynfor and Thelma Adams, Fferm
Glyneithinog, Pontseli, Boncath, Dyfed*
Artisan maker using the farm's own
milk. Visitors welcome
Type: Unpasteurised cows milk, hard-
pressed, full fat, vegetarian

Not a cheese with added ingredients
but a natural Caerphilly delightfully
waxed to resemble an old-fashioned
Christmas pudding. A rare touch of
humour, and one of the most innovative Christmas products I've seen. *See
also* CAWS CENARTH.

CHURNTON

*The Cheese Company, Hampton,
Malpas, Cheshire*
Creamery
Type: Cows milk, hard-pressed, full fat

Churnton is described as a
Cheddar–Cheshire cross. The recipe is
a new one, the details remaining a
closely guarded secret. The end
product is mild and fresh tasting,
similar to mild Cheddar but with a
little more flavour. *See also* THE CHEESE
COMPANY.

CLAPPS CHEDDAR

*R.L. Clapp and Son, West Town House,
Baltonsborough, Somerset*
Farmhouse maker using the farm's own
milk. Visitors by appointment
Type: Cows milk, hard-pressed, full fat

R.L. Clapp and Son farm land with a
story to tell that goes back to the very
foundations of British history. Two
thousand years ago the place would
have been an island amid marshes and
lakes, for there was water covering the
peaty areas we now call the Somerset
Levels. The remains of primitive lake
villages have been discovered nearby.
This may have been the cradle of

British agriculture, with early farmers taking advantage of the fertile soil as the waters receded and progressively learning to drain the land for themselves. There is still good soil in these parts, producing top-quality milk for the Clapps' excellent Cheddar cheese. Production is around 700 tonnes of rindless 40 lb (20 kg) blocks a year.

CLAYMORE CHEDDAR

Claymore Creamery, Kirkwall, Orkney

Type: Cows milk, hard-pressed, full fat

Most of the cheese made in Scotland (14% of UK production) never leaves the country, but the northernmost creamery at Kirkwall, in the Orkney Islands, produces Cheddar for export to England and elsewhere. The cheese has won many show awards.

CLIFTON ASH, CLIFTON LEAF

Hugh Lillingston, Innes Cheese, High-fields Dairy, Statfold, Tamworth, Staffordshire
Artisan maker
Type: Unpasteurised goats milk, semi-soft, full fat, vegetarian

Distinctive mould-ripened cheese, goaty and slightly salty. The 2½ oz (70 g) rounds are finished with an ash coating or wrapped in leaves. *See also* INNES.

CLOISTERS

Charles Martell & Son, Laurel Farm, Dymock, Gloucestershire
Artisan maker using the farm's own milk
Type: Cows milk, semi-hard, full fat, vegetarian

Laurel Farm is thought to form part of the lost Manor of Ryelands in Dymock, land that would have been farmed by Cistercian monks in the thirteenth century. After many years' research, Charles Martell has re-created a peppery cheese of the type the monks might have made. Produced in 5 lb (2.3 kg) rounds with an annatto washed rind. *See also* SINGLE GLOUCESTER.

CLOTHIER'S CHEDDAR

H.W. Clothier, Milton Westcombe Farms, Evercreech, Shepton Mallet, Somerset
Farmhouse maker using the farm's own milk
Type: Cows milk, hard-pressed, full fat

Highly respected producer of top-quality rindless 40 lb (20 kg) Cheddar, making around 1,000 tonnes per year. This is a good, long-keeping product, a credit to Somerset cheesemaking. It has a distinctive flavour, a firm frontal 'bite' and a superb long, dry finish on the palate.

COACHMAN

Long Clawson Dairy, Melton Mowbray, Leicestershire
Creamery
Type: Cows milk, semi-hard, full fat

Not just one cheese, but a range of flavours presented in a hand-made roll, just ready for slicing. A smooth roll of Red Leicester surrounds centres of Wensleydale with apple and celery or Wensleydale with garlic. *See also* LONG CLAWSON.

COLBY

South Caernarfon Creameries, Chwilog, Pwllheli, Gwynedd
Creamery
Type: Cows milk, hard-pressed, full fat

A variant of Cheddar, named after the small town in Wisconsin where it was developed by a family named Steinward in the 1890s. The cheese is made by the washed-curd method; it is softer, sweeter and moister than Cheddar and has proved so popular that it has been produced throughout North America and Australasia and, more recently, in Wales.

COLEFORD BLUE

Alan and Kay Duffield, Exmoor Blue Cheese, Willett Farm, Lydeard St Lawrence, Somerset
Artisan maker using the farm's own milk. Visitors by apppointment
Type: Unpasteurised ewes milk, semi-soft, full fat, vegetarian

Made by hand, using milk from local flocks. *Penicillium roqueforti* is employed to 'blue' the chesse. The blue tang is quite mild in the creamy, young cheese but becomes decidedly stronger with age. The 4½ lb (2 kg) drums are unpressed and matured for 2–4 months. Coleford Blue won a first prize for ewes milk cheese at the Royal Bath and West Show. There is also a Coleford Mild, made without the blue mould. *See also* QUANTOCK BLUE.

COLERAINE

Golden Cow Dairies, Artabrackagh Road, Portadown, Co. Armagh, Northern Ireland
Creamery
Type: Cows milk, hard-pressed, full fat

Golden Vale/Dairy Produce Packers are major suppliers of processed and rindless cheese from Northern Ireland. Rindless Cheddar and other English territorial cheese are packed under the Coleraine and Golden Cow brands. *See also* SALMON LEAP.

COLESPARK CHEESES

Margaret Cruft, Fore Street, Morchard Bishop, Crediton, Devon
Artisan maker
Type: Unpasteurised goats milk, soft, medium fat, vegetarian

Unripened fresh cheeses, made from the milk of a single small goat herd using the Coulommier recipe. There are five flavours: plain; with garlic and wrapped in vine leaves; coated in black peppercorns; with toasted sesame seeds; or with dill seeds. Two hard cheeses are also made, a Wensleydale-type and a washed-rind cheese that is matured for 2–4 months.

COLOURED CHEESES

It has been common practice for thousands of years to enhance the colour of some foods. The use of saffron, which entails the collection of a quarter of a million crocus stamens for each pound of dye, goes back to the time of the Phoenicians. Saffron was frequently added to cheese and butter in the Middle Ages but, when it became harder to obtain, other colourings such as carrot juice were tried. The degree of colour produced by carrot juice was unpredictable and it was progressively replaced by annatto during the eighteenth century. Annatto is extracted from the red berries of a tree that grows in the West Indies, *Bixa orelana*. It has no effect on the taste of the cheese, and is commonly used in 'red' Cheddar, coloured Cheshire, Red Leicester and other cheeses. Government legislation requires that all cheese containing annatto must bear a label stating 'Added ingredient: annatto. E160 (b)'.

COLSTON BASSETT STILTON

Colston Bassett and District Dairy, Colston Bassett, Nottinghamshire

Small creamery
Type: Cows milk, semi-hard, full fat

A co-operative of five farmers making around 200 tonnes of Stilton each year.

COMPSEY CREAMERY SOFT CHEESES

Compsey Creamery, Mullinahone, Co. Tipperary, Republic of Ireland
Creamery
Type: Cows milk, soft, low to full fat, vegetarian

Compsey Creamery was opened in 1985 by Mullinahone Co-op, the oldest working co-operative in Ireland. It has since gained an international reputation for the excellence of its soft cheeses, winning a string of awards at cheese shows. Cottage cheese, crème fraiche, soft cheese and cream cheese are produced, most in high-fat or low-fat versions. Some products are available with added herbs and spices, garlic and pepper, orange or pineapple. The Orange Cream Cheese has been particularly applauded. The products are usually distributed in 4½ lb (2 kg) tubs for sale from delicatessen counters.

COOLBAWN

Donal Hayes, Liathmore Cheese, Two-mile-borris, Thurles, Co. Tipperary, Republic of Ireland
Artisan maker using the farm's own milk
Type: Cows milk, soft, full fat, vegetarian

The farm's herd of 160 cows provide the milk for this natural cream cheese, made without rennet, preservative or stabiliser. Soft, white, ideal spreading cheese, supplied plain or with garlic. Packed in 4½ oz (125 g) tubs, and larger sizes for delicatessen counters. *See also* TWO CHURCHES.

COOLEA

Helene and Dick Willems, Coolea Farmhouse Cheese, Coolea, Macroom, Co. Cork, Republic of Ireland
Artisan maker using the farm's own milk. Visitors by appointment
Type: Unpasteurised cows milk, hard-pressed, full fat

Yellow-waxed, Gouda-type cheese. Creamy and mild at 3–10 weeks, when the cheese is only semi-hard. This cheese is available plain, with nettles, or with herbs and a touch of garlic. The harder matured cheese, over six months old, might only be available seasonally but you can, if you're lucky, find Coolea aged for up to two years. Coolea has been Supreme Champion at the Dublin Show and judged the Best Irish Farmhouse Cheese. John McKenna in *The Bridgestone Irish Food Guide* described the taste as 'an astonishing clout of butter, butter on butter on butter... stored up sunshine'.

COOLEENEY FARMHOUSE CAMEMBERT

Breda Maher, Cooleeney Farmhouse Cheese, Moyne, Thurles, Co. Tipperary, Republic of Ireland
Artisan maker using the farm's own milk. Visitors by appointment
Type: Unpasteurised cows milk, soft, full fat

Breda Maher's 90 cows graze the pastures of the river Suir. The cheese is soft and creamy in texture and full flavoured when ripe. It won first prize in the soft cheese section at the Cheese Festival of London and was first in its class at the International Foods Exhibition. The *Irish Times* awarded it three stars in a survey. Packed in 7 oz (200 g) portions and 3 lb (1.5 kg) wheels.

COONEEN

Fivemiletown Co-op, Ballylurgan Road, Fivemiletown, Co. Tyrone, Northern Ireland
Creamery
Type: Goats milk, semi-soft, full fat

Only local goats milk is used in the production of this mould-ripened cheese. The recipe has been developed over many years, resulting in a very mild cheese, without the 'goaty' flavours that are not to everyone's taste. If you haven't tried (or liked) goats cheese before, this one might surprise you! Made in 3½ lb (1.7 kg) flat Brie-type discs. *See also* BALLY-LURGAN CHEDDAR.

CO-OP CHEDDAR

Associated Co-op Creameries/C.W.S., Llandyrnog, Clwyd
Creamery
Type: Cows milk, hard-pressed, full fat

The Co-op movement stands alone amongst retailers in the UK in that it is also a major cheese producer. At Llandyrnog they maintain a highly efficient creamery which produces around 12,000 tonnes of cheese each year. This is mainly Cheddar in 40 lb (20 kg) rindless blocks. The cheese was good enough to take the 'Best UK Cheddar' award at the Nantwich Show.

COQUETDALE

Mark Robertson, Northumberland Cheese Company, Soppitt Farm, Otter-burn, Northumberland
Artisan maker using the farm's own milk. Visitors welcome
Type: Cows milk, semi-soft, medium fat, vegetarian

Mould-ripened cheese (one of few from the northern counties) made by hand in the style of a French Tomme. The 4½ lb (2 kg) flat discs and 1½ lb (625 g) miniatures have a natural grey rind and soften when ripe. *See also* NORTHUMBERLAND.

CORINNA

Nachi Elkin, Gedi Enterprises, Plum-ridge Farm, Stagg Hill, Barnet, Hertfordshire
Artisan maker using the farm's own milk. Visitors welcome
Type: Goats milk, soft, full fat, vegetarian

Silky soft cheese, gently flavoured, preserved in virgin olive oil. Ideal for eating with a fresh green salad. *See also* CHAVANNES.

CORLEGGY

Silke Cropp, Corleggy, Belturbet, Co. Cavan, Republic of Ireland
Artisan maker using the farm's own milk. Visitors by appointment
Type: Goats milk, soft or hard-pressed, full fat, vegetarian

Recommended by *The Bridgestone Irish Food Guide*. Made by organic methods, the young, 1 lb (450 g) rounds are clean and sharp. The larger 2 lb (900 g) wheels are allowed to mature to a stronger flavour, developing a natural rind in the process. *See also* DRUMLIN, QUIVVY.

CORNISH SOFT CHEESE

Michael and Margaret Horrell, Lynher Valley Dairy, Upton Cross, Liskeard, Cornwall
Artisan maker using the farm's own milk. Vistors welcome
Type: Cows milk, soft, full fat, vegetarian

The river Lynher runs from Bodmin

Moor to join the Tamar at Plymouth. The Horrell family have farmed this part of the Duchy of Cornwall estate since 1905, building up their pedigree Holstein-Friesian herd. The soft spreading cheeses have won prizes at the Nantwich Show. There are two varieties: one mixed with six herbs and garlic and then rolled in parsley, the other coated with cracked black peppercorns. Sold in 1lb (450 g) or 2 lb (900 g) rounds, and 3½ oz (100 g) tubs. Visitors are welcomed during the summer months to a new 'interpretation centre' and cheese is sold at the farm, but telephone (01579) 62244 first to check opening times. *See also* YARG.

COTHERSTONE

Joan Cross, Teesdale, Barnard Castle, Co. Durham
Artisan maker
Type: Unpasteurised cows milk, semi-soft, full fat

Soft, crumbly and moist, this open-textured cheese has a refreshing and buttery flavour. Usually eaten at 2–3 weeks, although they can be ripened for up to three months, the 2 lb (900 g) or 5 lb (2.3 kg) rounds form a soft, golden crust. Highly praised by food writers and, for some reason I cannot discover, popular with drinkers of heavy stout. Cotherstone has been made for many generations, being mentioned in the *Teesdale Mercury* over 100 years ago. It has found fame today amongst gourmets all over the UK.

COTSWOLD

Long Clawson Dairy, Melton Mowbray, Leicestershire
Creamery
Type: Cows milk, hard-pressed, full fat

Double Gloucester flavoured with onions and chives. *See also* LONG CLAWSON.

COTTAGE CHEESE

Type: Cows milk, soft, fat content variable

Cottage cheese is one of the oldest foods known. In past centuries it was made in homes all over the country, to avoid waste after the cream had been skimmed off the milk. The skimmed milk was soured and the resulting curd drained. Today, the curd is cut into small cubes with wire 'knives' before being washed and rinsed thoroughly, so there is little fat in the curd or lactose (milk sugar) in the whey. This makes cottage cheese a favourite with slimmers. It contains barely 4% fat (even lower fat varieties are available) against 30–40% fat in other cheeses. Makers (see entries) include: BLACKMORE VALE, COMPSEY CREAMERY, J.E. Dickenson (see LONGLEY FARM), DRAMONA, LONG CLAWSON DAIRY, MOORE CHEESE, RAINES DAIRY, RACHEL'S DAIRY, UNIGATE (ST IVEL) and WEST ULSTER FARMERS.

COULOMMIER

Type: Various milks, medium-fat, surface ripened

Coulommier is a small version of Brie. It takes its name from the town in the Seine et Marne region of France where it is produced. In Britain Coulommier-type cheeses are made by numerous small artisan makers, many of whom supply only locally or on a seasonal basis. Suppliers (see entries) include: HOWGATE CHEESES (cows), MALTHOUSE COTTAGE FARM (goats), SHARPHAM CREAMERY (cows), SHEPHERDS PURSE (ewes), and WEST HIGHLAND DAIRY (cows, ewes, goats).

COVERDALE

Fountains Dairy Products, Kirkby Malzeard, Ripon, North Yorkshire
Creamery

Type: Cows milk, semi-hard, full fat

In 1987 Kirkby Malzeard creamery was scheduled for closure, ending 900 years of cheesemaking in lower Wensleydale, but a group of employees bought the dairy and are now busy reviving old recipes like Coverdale, which had not been made since the 1930s. The 13 lb (6 kg) cylinders are made by hand using local milk. They are ready for eating after about a month. Smaller sizes include 4½ lb (2 kg) truckles and 1 lb (450 g) miniatures. Also made with added chives. *See also* FOUNTAINS DAIRY.

CRATLOE HILLS

Sean and Deirdre Fitzgerald, Brickhill, Cratloe, Co. Clare, Republic of Ireland
Artisan maker using the farm's own milk. Visitors by appointment
Type: Ewes milk, semi-hard, full fat

From the pioneers of modern ewes milk cheesemaking in Ireland, a unique cheese, moulded in the shape of a Celtic cross. Around 4 lb (1.8 kg) in size. There is also Cratloe Gold, a well-aged round version of the cheese waxed in a caramel colour.

CREAGMHOL

Kathy Biss, West Highland Dairy, Achmore, Stromeferry, By Kyle of Lochalsh, Wester Ross
Artisan maker using the farm's own and other local milk. Visitors welcome
Type: Pasteurised, various milks and cheese types, vegetarian

Anyone wishing to try their hand at practical cheesemaking would do well to read Kathy Biss's book of that name, full of clear and comprehensive instruction (sadly out of print but copies can be found). Kathy now puts her skilled hands to making a range of Creagmhol cheeses. Ewes milk is used to make a semi-hard and full-fat Dales-type cheese. Moist but closer textured than Wensleydale, it ripens slowly to a delicate flavour. The 4½ lb (2 kg) rounds are black-waxed. Cows milk is used to make a similarly presented cheese which, surprisingly, is inclined to be slightly more creamy than the ewes milk version. Local goats milk is used to make a closer textured cheese, ripened for 3–4 months but still mellow, without the ferocious character of some goat products. This is also available in 4½ lb (2 kg) black-waxed rounds. Curd and Coulommier-type cheeses are made from all three milks. Visitors are

---

CREAM CHEESE

The diverse nature of products retailed as cream cheese renders general classification almost useless but cream cheeses have existed for many centuries. Wiltshire farms once excelled in their manufacture but varieties such as New Forest, Guildford and Little Welshie disappeared long ago and the name is now wrongly applied to processed and blended imitations. A real cream cheese would have been made without rennet. Rich, unpasteurised cream was allowed to solidify, then hung in fine muslin and allowed to drain. More cream might be worked into the curd to create double-cream or even triple-cream cheese. There are good cream cheeses to be found today, but most are made with rennet and a gelling agent to ensure a consistent product. Makers (see entries) include: BLACKMORE VALE, COMPSEY CREAMERY, DAN DAIRIES, Liathmore Cheese (see COOLBAWN), LONG CLAWSON, MOORE CHEESE and RAINES DAIRY.

welcome to buy cheese at the farm; the shop is open all year, and the dairy can be viewed by prior arrangement. For those who wish to try cheesemaking for the first time, or to sharpen up their skills, Kathy runs short courses which can be combined with a delightful holiday in this part of Scotland. Telephone (01599) 577203 for details. *See also* ASCAIG, WEST HIGHLAND SOFT.

CRICKET MALHERBIE CHEDDAR

Graham Fry, Cricket Malherbie Farms, Nether Stowey, Bridgwater, Somerset
Farmhouse maker using the farm's own and other local milk. Visitors welcome
Type: Cows milk, hard-pressed, full fat, vegetarian

It was Lord Beaverbrook who brought cheesemaking to Nether Stowey in 1948. The Jeanes family purchased Cricket Malherbie Ltd in 1978, since when the farm has made the famous Cricketers Cheddar, 'Fit for Lord's' and consistently a favourite in Somerset. The cheese is noted for its good firm 'bite' when mature. Total production is over 1,000 tonnes per year. The dairy also produces a vegetarian cheese from another local farm's pasteurised ewes milk. This is sold in red-waxed miniatures. Visitors are welcome to view the cheesemaking from a gallery above the dairy, but telephone (01278) 732084 first to confirm opening times. There is an excellent farm shop. *See also* NANNY'S GOAT CHEDDAR.

CROFTON

Carolyn Fairbairn, Thornby Moor Dairy, Crofton Hall, Thursby, Carlisle, Cumbria
Artisan maker. Visitors welcome
Type: Unpasteurised milk, hard-pressed, full fat, vegetarian

Organic cheese with a distinctive flavour, made from a mixture of cows and goats milk. Pressed in 5 lb (2.3 kg) and 2 lb (900 g) discs which develop a natural rind. Cheesemaking can be viewed through a glass panel in the farm shop but telephone (01697) 345555 first to check opening times. *See also* ALLERDALE, BEWCASTLE, CUMBERLAND.

CROGHAM

Luc and Ann van Kampen, Ballyna-drishoge, Blackwater, Enniscorthy, Co. Wexford, Republic of Ireland
Artisan maker using the farm's own milk
Type: Goats milk, semi-hard, full fat

Mellow-flavoured Reblochon-type cheese which matures well. Highly praised as one of Ireland's most distinctive goats cheeses, winning many premier awards. Soft cheeses are sometimes made by the same dairy, dusted with peppercorns and herbs.

CROPWELL BISHOP STILTON

David Skailles, Somerset Creameries Ltd, Nottingham Road, Cropwell Bishop, Nottinghamshire
Small creamery. Visitors by appointment
Type: Cows milk, hard-pressed, full fat, vegetarian

The origins of Somerset Creameries date back to 1847 and since 1912 the name of Cropwell Bishop has been synonymous with white and blue Stilton. A new creamery at Cropwell Bishop was opened in 1986 and now makes around 2,000 tonnes of Stilton, Shropshire Blue, Cheddar and other English cheeses each year, all of them attractively presented. The famous blue Stilton is made in 17 lb (8 kg) rounds; various cut sizes and presentation jars are also available. *See also* SHROPSHIRE BLUE.

CROSSELLE

J.J. Saunders, Emborough Farm Foods, Old Down Farm, Emborough, Somerset
Farmhouse maker
Type: Cows milk, semi-hard, full fat, vegetarian

Cheese with garlic and mixed herbs. Normally sold ready-grated.

CROTTIN

Nachi Elkin, Gedi Enterprises, Plumridge Farm, Stagg Hill, Barnet, Hertfordshire
Artisan maker using the farm's own milk. Visitors welcome
Type: Goats milk, semi-soft, full fat, vegetarian

The French *crottin* might be literally translated as 'horse-dropping'. The English version shows considerably more delicacy in name and flavour! Round 2½ oz (70 g) cheeses, with a thin white crust, fully matured until the cheese becomes 'nutty' with age. Ideal for grilling. *See also* CHAVANNES.

CROWDIE

Reggie and Susannah Stone, Highland Fine Cheeses, Knockbreck, Tain, Highland
Artisan maker using local milk
Type: Cows milk, soft, fresh, low fat, rennet free, vegetarian

Crowdie (*Gruth* in the Gaelic) is one of the oldest cheeses in the world and may have been brought to Scotland by the Vikings. This is the definitive Scottish fresh cheese, sometimes soft and spreading, sometimes crumbly and lemon tasting. It was traditionally eaten on oatcakes and in Easter Ross it remains popular before a ceilidh, as it is said to limit the effects of prolonged whisky drinking! As a practical way of using up surplus milk it was widely made by thrifty Scots into 'porridge cheese' for breakfast but virtually died out until revived by Susannah Stone. In 1962 Reggie Stone asked his new wife to make some cheese 'like mother used to make', and the first batch was strained over the bath, through a pillow case. This fresh, unpressed cheese has since had a new lease of life. Mrs Stone produces her Crowdie from skimmed milk with a little added fresh cream and, on occasion, fresh or dried herbs. It is slightly crumbly and has a faint lemon taste. Its texture makes it ideal for cheesecakes and salad dips. *See also* CABOC, GALIC, GRUTH DHU, HRAMSA and HIGHLAND SOFT.

CROWLINK

Terry and Pam Wigmore, Seven Sisters Sheep Centre, East Dean, West Sussex
Artisan maker using the farm's own milk. Visitors welcome
Type: Ewes milk, hard-pressed, full fat, vegetarian

Crumbly, Wensleydale-type cheese which retains the natural sweetness of ewes milk. *See also* BELLE TOUT.

CUMBERLAND

Carolyn Fairbairn, Thornby Moor Dairy, Crofton Hall, Thursby, Carlisle, Cumbria
Artisan maker. Visitors welcome
Type: Unpasteurised cows milk, hard-pressed, full fat

Organic cheese, produced from the milk of shorthorn cows. It has a mature, creamy flavour and is made in cloth-bound or waxed cylinders and truckles, ranging from 1 lb (450 g) to 20 lb (9 kg). Available plain, or with garlic, sage, dill or fennel. There is also an oak-smoked version. *See also* CROFTON.

CURD CHEESE

Type: Various milks, fresh, low or medium fat, vegetarian

For centuries, curd cheese was made from sour, unpasteurised milk which was allowed to separate naturally into curds without the action of rennet. Now it is made either by the natural coagulation of soured milk or, more commonly, with a special culture medium. After separation, the curd is drained and blended with a little salt. In the seventeenth century curd cheese was often coloured and flavoured with marigold, spinach, or sage juice and may have been set in a mould, like a blancmange. Curd cheese is made in soft or pressed varieties, characterised by a mild, slightly acidic flavour and a soft spreadable texture. Makers (see entries) include: BLACKMORE VALE (cows), HIGHLAND SOFT (cows), MOORE CHEESE (cows), WEST HIGHLAND DAIRY (cows, ewes, goats).

CURWORTHY

Rachel Stephens, Curworthy Cheese, Stockbeare Farm, Jacobstowe, Okehampton, Devon
Artisan maker using the farm's own milk
Type: Cows milk, semi-hard, full fat

The 90 acres of Stockbeare Farm, on the edge of Dartmoor, support 70 Friesian cows. Their milk is used in a traditional seventeenth-century recipe, and the cheese is made by hand each day. The milk is pasteurised or not depending on the buyer's requirements. It is creamy white, light and buttery tasting when young, developing into a full-flavoured mellowness when aged. Available in naturally rinded 5 lb (2.3 kg) or 2½ lb (1.1 kg) truckles and waxed miniatures. *See also* BELSTONE, DEVON OKE, MELDON, VERGIN.

CWMTAWE PECORINO

Giovanni Irranca, Ty Gwyn Farm, Ystalyfera, West Glamorgan
Artisan maker using the farm's own milk
Type: Ewes milk, semi-hard, full fat, vegetarian

Pecorino is a cheese of great antiquity, mentioned by the Roman writer Columella in his *De Re Rustica* 2,000 years ago. Cwmtawe lies in the foothills of the Brecon Beacons, where the sheep graze on wild grasses and natural herbs. The result is a rich cheese, high in protein, made to an old Italian recipe and pressed in 9 lb (4 kg) or 1½ lb (800 g) rounds. Pecorino has been nicknamed 'the vegetarian bacon' as it can be fried with eggs in place of bacon.

DAIRY CREST CHEESES

Dairy Crest, Dairy Crest House, Portsmouth Road, Surbiton, Surrey
Major creamery proprietor manufacturing at several locations

Dairy Crest is a major force in the cheese industry, responsible for over 20% of UK production. The cheese is sold either as Dairy Crest, Davidstow, Trencherman and other labels, or retailed under supermarket own-brands. The range is vast, including Cheddar and all the English territorials, Stilton and soft cheeses. Davidstow Creamery, near Camelford in Cornwall, is Dairy Crest's largest creamery, drawing milk from 1,000 Cornish farms and capable of making over 100 tonnes of rindless Cheddar or Red Leicester each day. Davidstow Cheddar has gained respect for its consistent quality. Aspatria Creamery in Cumbria draws milk from 775 farms and is capable of making 70 tonnes of rindless Cheddar or Double Gloucester each day. Curds and whey pass through a Cheddarmaster production process in under 2½ hours, by which time the whey has been separated and the curd salted and 'cheddared' to form cheese ready for maturing. Up to 5,000 tonnes of cheese are held in store. The Creamery has gained the 'Champion Cheese' award at the Scottish Cheese Show. Hartington Creamery, near Buxton in Derbyshire, produces Stilton and other specialist cheeses (see BUXTON BLUE, DOVEDALE, NUTTALL'S, WENSLEYDALE BLUE). The creamery at Sturminster Newton in Dorset draws milk from 50 farms around the Blackmore Vale and is Dairy Crest's centre for traditional Cheddar production, making around 30 tonnes each week of traditional Cheddar (see STURMINSTER OAK SMOKED). Smaller quantities of regional cheeses are produced at Scalford in Leicestershire. Many of Dairy Crest's speciality cheeses are marketed under the J.M. NUTTALL brand name.

DALES PRIDE CHEESES

British Creameries Limited, West Marton, North Yorkshire
Creamery
Type: Cows milk, hard-pressed, full fat

The brand name for a range of cheeses produced at West Marton Creamery, including Cheddar, Cheshire, Wensleydale, Lancashire, Caerphilly, Leicester, Double Gloucester and Derby. The creamery has frequently won awards at Nantwich and other cheese shows.

DALLOW BRIDGE CHEESES

Central Midlands Co-op Society, Dallow Bridge Creamery, Burton-upon-Trent, Staffordshire
Creamery
Type: Cows milk, hard-pressed, full fat

Your local Co-op can be an excellent place to buy cheese. Central Midlands Co-op have their own creamery, where, amongst a range of cheeses, they produce Cheddar and Red Leicester marbled with the famous Marmite spread. Just the thing if you were a Marmite baby! They also produce a range of Cheddar cheeses flavoured with Schwartz spices: *herbes de Provence*, shallot and herb, garlic pepper, and celery and basil. *See also* CO-OP CHEDDAR.

DAN DAIRIES SOFT CHEESE

Dan Dairies, Leeds, West Yorkshire
Creamery
Type: Cows milk, soft, full fat

Prizewinners at the Nantwich Show. Range includes: plain, with chives, with garlic and with smoked salmon.

DANSCO TOLONA MOZZARELLA

Don Morris, Priorswood Place, East Pimbo, Skelmersdale, Lancashire
Creamery
Type: Cows milk, soft, full fat

Specialist manufacturers of Italian-style Mozzarella for pizza toppings (they manufacture the bases as well), with production points at Edinburgh and Newcastle Emlyn in South Wales. Current output is around 12,000 tonnes per year, a third of the UK total.

DENHAY TRADITIONAL CHEDDAR

Amanda Streatfeild, Streatfeild Hood & Co., Denhay Farm, Broadoak, Bridport, Dorset
Farmhouse maker using the farm's own milk. Visitors by appointment
Type: Cows milk, hard-pressed, full fat

Streatfeild Hood have been making traditional Cheddar for over 30 years. Using milk from their own cows, grazing in the Marshwood Vale, deep in Thomas Hardy country and only a few miles from the coast, they make around 2,000 tonnes each year. After maturing for up to 12 months, the cheese is checked by an independent grader and only the best is selected to be Denhay Cheddar. Streatfeild's attention to detail has paid dividends, for they have won four trophies for Farmhouse Cheddar at the Royal Bath and West Show in one year (1987) and many other awards since. Very popular with visitors to the West Country, their 'Dorset Drums' are miniature truckles of around 4½ lb (2 kg).

DEPWADE

Susan Moore, Cranes Watering Farm, Starston, Harleston, Norfolk
Artisan maker using the farm's own milk. Visitors by appointment
Type: Cows milk, semi-soft, full fat, vegetarian

Famous cows provide the milk for this cheese. The Depwade Jersey herd, established in 1951, included Depwade Happy Dahlia, who produced 15 calves and held both the World Jersey Butterfat and the European Lifetime Yield records. Sadly, Happy Dahlia passed on in 1975 but her descendants still provide the milk for this Norfolk cheese. It is slightly salted and the 9 oz (250 g) rounds are rolled in mixed herbs. *See also* MOORE CHEESE.

DERBY

Type: Cows milk, hard-pressed, full fat

Derby cheese was never kept to a great age: 'Sell your cheese often and marry your daughter young' was the old Derbyshire axiom. Derby was the first English cheese to be made in a factory, an idea which came from the USA after Jesse Williams of Rome, New York State, persuaded other farmers to sell

excess milk to him instead of making their own cheese, in the 1850s. His cheese was derided as 'store cheese' or even 'rat cheese' but the factory prospered. In 1870 a factory was opened by the Derbyshire Agricultural Society at Longford. To encourage local farmers to participate in the scheme a guarantee fund of £5,000 was collected and farmers were promised at least 6½d for each gallon of milk delivered to the factory. Cheesemaking began on 8 April 1870 under the management of two Americans, Levi and Cornelius Schermerhorn. Seventeen farms participated in the scheme, and an equal amount had to be turned away. The accounts for 1873 show that 86 tons of cheese were made, providing the farmers with a return of 7½d per gallon. At first only one factory was planned but the experiment attracted thousands of visitors, and similar projects were launched throughout Derbyshire, Cheshire and Somerset. By 1876 there were five factories in Derbyshire but enthusiasm faltered as cheese prices were depressed by a flood of cheap foreign imports. In addition, the Longford factory failed to produce a consistent product due to failures in its own management and the poor quality of milk delivered by unscrupulous or careless farmers. Despite these unhappy beginnings, those Derbyshire factories pointed the way for cheesemaking in the twentieth century. In the process, however, much cheese was robbed of its local character. Until recently, Derby has been little more than a mild, waxy Cheddar, although better makers are now trying to recapture the sweetness that should be characteristic of this cheese. It is best eaten after only four weeks but can be matured for up to six months, remaining similar in texture to Cheddar but with a darker honey colour and a full, tangy flavour followed by a sweet aftertaste. A good cheese to eat with apples, pears or grapes. Makers include: CARRON LODGE, Fowlers of Earlswood (see

LITTLE DERBY), Golden Foods (see AVONMORE) and KNOLTON FARM-HOUSE. *See also* SAGE DERBY.

DESMOND

Sean Ferry and Bill Hogan, West Cork Natural Cheese, Dereenatra, Schull, Co. Cork, Republic of Ireland
Artisan maker using the farm's own milk
Type: Unpasteurised cows milk, hard-pressed, medium fat

Made only during the summer months with milk from four small farms, this very hard Swiss-style cheese has a fine, grainy texture and a piquant flavour followed by a prolonged sharp after-taste. The cheese has a natural, golden-yellow, crusted rind (produced by a mixture of bacterial and yeast cultures) which requires no wax or plastic coating. Sold in 50 lb (25 kg) and 10 lb (4.5 kg) wheels. *See also* GABRIEL, MIZEN.

DEVON BLUE

Robin Congdon, Ticklemore Cheese, Ticklemore Street, Totnes, Devon
Artisan maker using the farm's own milk. Visitors welcome
Type: Unpasteurised cows milk, semi-soft, full fat

Milk from the single herd of Ayrshires is used to make this stunning, blue-veined cheese. Firm bodied with a deep, mellow flavour that really lingers. The 5 lb (2.3 kg) drums are matured for over six months and wrapped in an attractive gold foil. *See also* TICKLE-MORE.

DEVON COUNTRY

Elize Jungheim, Trehill Farm, Sampford Courtnay, Okehampton, Devon
Artisan maker. Visitors welcome

Type: Unpasteurised cows milk, hard-pressed, full fat, vegetarian

Rustic, country cheese with a natural 'knobbly' rind and a taste so rich that it has been described as 'clotted cream in a cheese'. Sadly the 5 lb (2.3 kg) truckles are only available seasonally but they can be ordered by post. *See also* TREHILL.

DEVON OKE

Rachel Stephens, Curworthy Cheese, Stockbeare Farm, Jacobstowe, Oke-hampton, Devon
Artisan maker using the farm's own milk
Type: Cows milk, semi-hard, full fat

Made to the seventeenth-century CURWORTHY recipe at a dairy near the river Oke. Milk is pasteurised or not according to buyer's requirements. Naturally rinded 5 lb (2.3 kg) and 2½ lb (1.1 kg) truckles, matured for six months.

DEVON RUSTIC

Robin Congdon, Ticklemore Cheese, Ticklemore Street, Totnes, Devon
Artisan maker using the farm's own milk. Visitors welcome
Type: Unpasteurised cows milk, semi-soft, full fat, vegetarian

Hand-made cheese, moist and creamy with the tang of chives and garlic. The same farm produces Devon Herb and Garlic, a pressed curd cheese with Provençal herbs and garlic, but this is presently only available in its home county. *See also* TICKLEMORE.

DEW-LAY LANCASHIRE CHEESE

Ian Coggin, Dew-Lay Products, Green Lane West, Garstang, Lancashire
Farmhouse maker using the farm's own milk

Type: Cows milk, semi-hard, full fat

The Kenyon family have been making Lancashire cheese for nearly 40 years. Milk from their own farm and 20 others around the Forest of Bowland is used to make an extra-creamy cheese with a crumbly texture and a clean, rich, mellow flavour. The 40 lb (20 kg) rounds are cloth-bound and waxed; there are also vacuum-packed smaller sizes. Also available is a Lancashire with garlic, and Lancashire with chives and sage. A regular prizewinner at the country's top cheese shows, Dew-Lay production is around 1,000 tonnes each year. *See also* GRACEFIELD SELECT.

DINGBELL

David Reed, Home Farm, Beamish Museum, Beamish, Co. Durham
Artisan maker. Visitors welcome
Type: Cows milk, soft, full fat, vegetarian

The working dairy at Beamish open-air industrial museum (see BEAMISH) chose this resounding name for their washed-rind cheese. Made in 3 lb (1.4 kg) rounds.

DORSET BLUE VINNEY

Mike Davies, Woodbridge Farm, Stock Gaylard, Sturminster Newton, Dorset
Artisan maker using the farm's own milk. Visitors by appointment
Type: Unpasteurised cows milk, unpressed, medium fat, vegetarian

Vinney is a dialect word for 'veiny'. Dorset buttermakers used their residual buttermilk to make a low-fat cheese, adding 'a dram of rennet, an ounce or two of salt and a pinch of flour to help it turn blue'. Natural mould spores in the dairy produced the blueing, although legend infers that boot straps and old harnesses were dunked in the milk to aid the process.

The cheese was legendary for its hardness; axes were said to be honed on its surface. Farmer Ian Bailey of Motcombe, who knows a story or two, told me his grandfather used to take Blue Vinney to London as 'They were the only ones daft enough to buy it.' Any unsold stock was used as wheels on the cart to save wear on the iron tyres. There was apparently plenty of tread on four hard and dry Blue Vinney cheeses for the journey back to Dorset! Elihu Burritt, a visiting American farmer, reported in 1868 that 'softer missiles have been fired from cannons'. Whatever the truth of the tales regarding 'old' Blue Vinney, the invention of the skimming machine left too little fat in the milk for its manufacture. It had almost disappeared by 1930 and became extinct during the Second World War, but the continuing interest of cheese-lovers led to demands for its revival. For a period, second-grade Stilton was passed off as Blue Vinney but the manufacture of the genuine article has happily returned to Dorset. Mike Davies's product is a delightful creamy cheese with a unique blue tang, and guaranteed not to damage your cutlery. It is made in 14 lb (6.5 kg) cylinders.

DOUBLE BERKELEY

Charles Martell and Son, Laurel Farm, Dymock, Gloucestershire
Artisan maker using the farm's own milk
Type: Cows milk, semi-hard, full fat, vegetarian

From a farm famous for Gloucester cheese comes a stablemate by the name of Double Berkeley. In 1984 Charles Martell revived an ancient recipe, re-milling white and coloured curds, then putting them back in the press, to produce cheese with a marbled appearance. Mild in flavour, made in 8 lb (3.6 kg) wheels. *See also* SINGLE GLOUCESTER.

DOUBLE GLOUCESTER

Type: Cows milk, hard-pressed, full fat

Although Gloucester is an ancient cheese, it only became popular at the beginning of the eighteenth century. The traditional Double Gloucester was made in discs about 20 in (50 cm) round and 5 in (13 cm) thick but, for less affluent customers, a 'single' Gloucester was made with thinner milk in a thinner size so that customers could see at a glance which they were getting. As the larger variety had better keeping qualities, Single Gloucester fell out of favour. True Gloucester cheese is hard to find, much of the creamery-produced cheese bearing scant resemblance to the real thing. It should be orange-red with a buttery, open texture and a light creamy flavour. Only Diana Smart of Birdwood (see SMART'S GLOUCESTER CHEESE) still produces the cheese in its home county, making unpasteurised Single and Double Gloucester. Other makers include APPLEBY'S OF HAWKSTONE and TIMES PAST DAIRY. Both use unpasteurised milk.

DOUBLE GLOUCESTER WITH ONIONS AND CHIVES

Millway Foods, Harby, Leicestershire
Creamery
Type: Cows milk, hard-pressed, full fat

Double Gloucester with extra ingredients.

DOUBLE WORCESTER

Alyson Anstey, Anstey's of Worcester, Broomhall Farm, Worcester
Farmhouse maker using the farm's own milk. Visitors welcome
Type: Unpasteurised cows milk, hard-pressed, full fat, vegetarian

Broomhall Farm, two miles south of the city of Worcester, has been farmed by the Anstey family for four generations. In truly traditional style, cheese is made by the farmer's wife from the milk of their own Friesian cows. Double Worcester is a tasty cheese, matured to a rich golden colour and a worthy fellow to Double Gloucester. Available in calico bandaged 7 lb (3 kg) truckles, and smaller sizes. *See also* OLD WORCESTER WHITE.

DOVEDALE

J.M. Nuttall, Hartington Creamery, Buxton, Derbyshire
Creamery
Type: Cows milk, soft, full fat

Soft, creamy cheese with a mild blue flavour. The 5½ lb (2.5 kg) discs are brine dipped, instead of being dry salted, and foil-wrapped. *See also* DAIRY CREST.

DRAMONA CHEDDAR

Dramona Quality Foods, Antrim Road, Belfast, Northern Ireland
Creamery
Type: Cows milk, hard-pressed, full fat

Dramona Quality Foods, part of the Milk Marketing Board for Northern Ireland, produce 5,000 tonnes of cheese per year at their plant at Dunman, near Cookstown. Mainly mild, medium and mature rindless Cheddar with smaller quantities of speciality cheeses. *See also* BARON'S TABLE, SPELGA.

DRUIDALE

Ellan Vannin Farms, Isle of Man Milk Marketing Association, Tremode, Isle of Man
Creamery using local milk
Type: Cows milk, hard-pressed, full fat, vegetarian

Ellan Vannin is the Manx name for the Isle of Man. The island has a long history of cheesemaking and its own particular custom. On New Year's Day youngsters would go from house to house singing a song of good wishes which went: 'May you of potatoes and herrings have plenty/With butter and cheese and each other dainty.' Druidale came into existence after a long search during the 1980s for a truly Manx cheese. The result is a light, crumbly, clean-tasting cheese which has been praised for its distinctive sharp bite. *See also* TYNWALDE.

DRUMLEISH

Rothesay Creamery, Townhead, Rothesay, Isle of Bute, Strathclyde
Creamery using local milk
Type: Cows milk, hard-pressed, full fat

A new creamery was opened on the Isle of Bute in May 1992 to make a range of 'village' cheeses using milk from local producers. Drumleish is rindless but traditionally made, the curd being dry-stirred rather than cut and turned in the Cheddar manner. The cheese has a slightly acidic taste and a soft, crumbly texture.

DRUMLIN

Silke Cropp, Corleggy, Belturbet, Co. Cavan, Republic of Ireland
Artisan maker using the farm's own milk. Visitors by appointment
Type: Cows milk, hard-pressed, full fat, vegetarian

A range of close-textured cheeses in two sizes, 1 lb (450 g) and 2 lb (900 g); traditional (plain), garlic and red pepper, green peppercorns and cumin seeds. *See also* CORLEGGY, QUIVVY.

DUCKETT'S CAERPHILLY

R.A. Duckett, Walnut Tree Farm, Wedmore, Somerset
Farmhouse maker using the farm's own milk. Visitors by appointment
Type: Unpasteurised cows milk, hard-pressed, full fat, vegetarian

Continuing a tradition that began in the 1800s, when Caerphilly cheese was first made in Somerset to feed the teeming population of the Welsh mining valleys, the renowned Duckett's Caerphilly has won so many prizes that it has to be acknowledged as the best. Slightly crumbly, fresh and light on the palate and pleasantly salty, it really is a product of exceptional quality. The 2 lb (900 g) and 7 lb (3.2 kg) wheels are sometimes held back to develop a fuller flavour and sold as mature Caerphilly. *See also* WEDMORE.

DUDDLESWELL

Mark Hardy, Sussex High Weald Dairy, Putlands Farm, Duddleswell, Uckfield, East Sussex
Artisan maker using the farm's own milk. Visitors by appointment
Type: Unpasteurised ewes milk, hard-pressed, full fat, vegetarian

Duddleswell lies in the heart of Ashdown Forest, part of the hunting grounds of the kings of England since 1382. Putlands Farm dates back 200 years but there is a brand-new dairy where yoghurt and a range of cheeses are made. Duddleswell is a Dales-type cheese. It has a natural rind, a light creamy flavour and is matured for a minimum of three months. The 4½ lb (2 kg) truckles are sold plain, with chives, or with crushed peppercorns. Putlands Farm derives its name from a 'put', or seventeenth-century countryman, what we might call a bumpkin. *See also* FETA, HALLOUMI, RICOTTA, SUSSEX SLIPCOTE.

DUNLOP – THE SCOTTISH CHEDDAR

Type: Cows milk, hard-pressed, full fat

The art and secrets of cheesemaking have long been passed down from mother to daughter, and it was Barbara Gilmour who carried the recipe for Dunlop cheese from Ireland to Scotland in the seventeenth century. Her family settled near Dunlop in Ayrshire and made a hard cheese, quite different to the Crowdie common in the area. Within 100 years the manufacture of Dunlop had become a Scottish tradition. Dunlop cheese is said to be slightly sweeter than Cheddar and some claim that it has better toasting and melting properties. Makers include the creameries at Kirkwall (see ORKNEY), Lockerbie (see THE CHEESE COMPANY) and Torrylinn (see ARRAN).

DUNLOPPE

Ann Dorward, Dunlop Dairy, West Clerkland, Stewarton, Strathclyde
Artisan maker
Type: Cows milk, hard-pressed, full fat

The old spelling of the village name is used for this example of Scotland's national cheese. The 4½ lb (2 kg) rounds are made to a local recipe and matured for up to 12 months, developing the characteristic sweet and nutty flavour. A younger cheese, named ANNICK after a local brook, is also made to order. *See also* BONNET, SWINZIE.

DUNSYRE BLUE

H.J. Errington and Co., Walston Braehead, Ogscastle, Carnwath, Strathclyde
Artisan maker
Type: Unpasteurised cows milk, semi-hard, full fat, vegetarian

The uplands of the Dunsyre countryside, 1,000 ft (330 m) above sea level, are often cold and windswept but the light loam soils produce good swards of clover, timothy and other hardy grasses. Milk from the Ayrshire cows of Strathbogie Farm, Elsrickle, is used to make Dunsyre Blue. This milk is particularly suitable for cheesemaking as it has the finely distributed fat globules of Old Gloucester cows milk. The cheese is made in 3 lb (1.5 kg) cylinders which are matured for three months to develop a superb 'herby' Gorgonzola flavour. *See also* LANARK BLUE.

DUNWICK

Terry and Pam Wigmore, Seven Sisters Sheep Centre, East Dean, West Sussex
Artisan maker using the farm's own milk. Visitors welcome
Type: Ewes milk, semi-soft, full fat, vegetarian

Dunwick Barn is over 300 years old, replete with flint and ships' timbers, providing the name for this Coulommier-type cheese. Made in small 3½ in (9 cm) rounds which are sold young and fresh. Also available with garlic and chives, herbs and garlic, and dill and black peppers. Seven Sisters Sheep Centre is just inland from Beachy Head and the walks along the chalk cliffs are exhilarating. *See also* BELLE TOUT.

DURRUS

Jeffa Gill, Coomkeen, Durrus, Bantry, Co. Cork, Republic of Ireland
Artisan maker using the farm's own milk. Visitors by appointment
Type: Unpasteurised cows milk, semi-soft, full fat, vegetarian

Invented and made by Jeffa Gill, Durrus is a surface-ripened cheese with a smooth, silky texture and fresh taste. It has been compared to the French *Tomme de Savoie*, with *The*

Bridgestone Irish Food Guide adding: 'Durrus is one of the best cheeses you can find in Ireland'. Jeffa Gill uses only untreated morning milk from a top-quality Friesian herd and does her cheesemaking by hand. Durrus is mild when young, normally sold at five weeks, but becomes earthy and full flavoured at three months, by which time it has developed a natural dark rind. Sold in 14 oz (400 g) and 3 lb (1.5 kg) rounds.

ELGAR

Nick Hodgetts, Malvern Cheesewrights, Manor House, Lower Wick, Worcester
Farmhouse maker using the farm's own milk
Type: Unpasteurised cows milk, semi-hard, full fat, vegetarian

Made at Lightwood Farm in the Teme Valley, Elgar has a mild taste. The 4 lb (1.8 kg) rounds are finished with a distinctive gold wax; there is also a 1 lb (450 g) miniature, sold in a souvenir box. After 6–7 months the cheese develops a mellow, nutty flavour and is sold as Elgar Mature. These cheeses are traditionally bound in calico. *See also* MALVERN.

ELSDON

Mark Robertson, Northumberland Cheese Company, Soppitt Farm, Otter-burn, Northumberland
Artisan maker using the farm's own milk. Visitors welcome
Type: Goats milk, soft, full fat, vegetarian

Full, rich cheese with a light, salty taste. Softens with age and warmth, developing a clean, goat flavour but no 'off' smell. The 1½ lb (740 g) and 6½ lb (3 kg) truckles are lightly brined. *See also* NORTHUMBERLAND.

EMBOROUGH FARM FOODS *see* SAUNDERS

EMLETT

Mary Holbrook, Sleight Farm House, Timsbury, Bath, Avon
Artisan maker using the farm's own milk
Type: Unpasteurised ewes milk, semi-soft, full fat

Brie-type cheese with a creamy delicate flavour. The 5 oz (150 g) rounds are supplied fresh and slightly acid, or ripened to a nutty finish in the farm's own cellars. *See also* MENDIP.

ENGLAND'S CHOICE

Long Clawson Dairy, Melton Mowbray, Leicestershire
Creamery
Type: Cows milk, hard-pressed, full fat

A masterpiece of cheesemaking technology: natural cheese with layers of white and coloured Cheddar, Wensleydale, Double Gloucester and Red Leicester. *See also* LONG CLAWSON.

ETTRICK

Rosemary and Mike Marwick, Howgate Cheeses, Camperdown Creamery, Faraday Street, Dundee
Artisan maker
Type: Cows milk, hard-pressed, full fat, vegetarian

Traditionally cloth-bound cheese, intensely flavoured and nutty but with a light and slightly crumbly texture, quite unlike Cheddar. The 3 lb (1.4 kg) and 10 lb (4.5 kg) truckles are sometimes coloured with annatto. Sold when six months old. Pasteurised and raw milk versions are made but only in limited quantities. White Ettrick, a soft, white, surface-moulded cheese, is sometimes available. This matures slowly over four months or longer to become strong and firm with a crusted rind. Pasteurised and raw milk versions are made, in 3½ lb (1.6 kg) truckles and 4½ lb (2 kg) balls, but only in limited quantities. *See also* HOWGATE.

EXMOOR GOATS CHEESE IN OIL

Alan and Kay Duffield, Exmoor Blue Cheese, Willett Farm, Lydeard St Lawrence, Somerset
Artisan maker using the farm's own milk. Visitors by appointment
Type: Goats milk, semi-hard, full fat, vegetarian

Goats cheese, moulded in small balls and marinated in oil, herbs and garlic. *See also* QUANTOCK BLUE.

FAIRFIELD CHEESE

Brenda Esdaile, Fairfield Opportunity Farm, Dilton Marsh, Westbury, Wiltshire
Artisan maker using the farm's own milk
Type: Unpasteurised cows milk, soft, low to full fat

Fairfield Opportunity Farm is a registered charity, training mentally handicapped young adults in a variety of land-based industries. With only four Friesians and one Jersey cow, milk supplies are limited but the farm produces a very palatable Coulommier-type soft cheese. Finished in 4 in (10 cm) rounds. Telephone (01373) 823028 for details of where to buy.

FARMHOUSE CHEESEMAKERS LTD

David Johnson, Farmhouse Cheese-makers Ltd, Union Street, Wells, Somerset
Farmhouse makers mainly using their farm's own milk
Type: Cows milk, mainly hard-pressed Cheddar or territorials

The word 'Farmhouse' originally referred to products made and marketed under a scheme set up by the Farmhouse Cheesemakers Federation. For the purposes of this book, 'Farmhouse' is applied to on-farm makers principally using their own milk. Members' cheese was carefully graded and this led to a steady improvement in quality, not least because it enabled the better producers to command a premium price for their goods. The scheme was incorported as Farmhouse Cheesemakers Ltd in 1982. A range of attractively packed cheeses under the Farmhouse Cheesemakers brand name is available from many supermarkets.

FARNDALE CHEESES

Peter and Kath Wright, Farndale Dairy Goats, Oak House Farm, Farndale, North Yorkshire
Artisan maker using the farm's own milk. Visitors welcome
Type: Unpasteurised goats milk, soft, full fat, vegetarian

Although the Wrights have only been making cheese since 1988, their farmhouse has seen it all before. In the

---

FAST CHEESE

Students at Brackenhurst Agricultural College in Nottinghamshire entered the record books in 1990 when they converted milk into cheese (from milking the cow to the final pressing) in less than seven hours. They produced five Derby cheeses flavoured with sage, chives and red wine. Three were eaten on the same day at a Ploughman's Supper.

eighteenth century it was actually called Cheeseman's House. Farndale Dairy cheeses were first exhibited at the 1991 Great Yorkshire Show, and today a very wide range of cheeses is produced from the milk of the farm's British Toggenburg goats, albeit only in small quantities. There is a plain, soft curd cheese; waxed rounds with apple-mint and Calvados; a garlic cheese; a heart-shaped and whisky-flavoured cheese rolled in oatmeal; a herb roll; and a small herb cheese marinated in cold-pressed olive oil, said to be especially delicious melted over pasta. Visitors are welcome to buy cheese at the farm shop but telephone (01751) 433053 before calling to check opening times.

FERMANAGH CHEDDAR

Fermanagh Creamery, Lisnaskea, Co. Fermanagh, Northern Ireland
Creamery
Type: Cows milk, hard-pressed, full fat

Producer of Cheddar cheese in rindless 40 lb (20 kg) blocks.

FETA

Type: Ewes milk, semi-hard, low fat

Formerly regarded as a Greek cheese, appearing in various forms all over the Balkans, Feta is the cheese of the Arab world and vast quantities are supplied to Middle Eastern countries every year. True Feta is a soft, white, ewes or goats milk cheese, supposedly developed by shepherds in the mountains outside Athens. Most Feta is now made from cows milk, although both sorts are produced in Britain. The original Feta is made from naturally curdled milk, heated until the casein and albumen protein solidifies. It should have a refreshingly sharp and salty taste, being pickled and matured in a brine solution. Feta is normally sold moist as a curdy mass, and frequently packed with brine. Ripened for at least a month but generally no longer than six weeks, it has a flavour that can vary from very pronounced to mildly salty. It is best to rinse the surface of Feta with fresh water just before serving; if the cheese is found to be too sharp and salty, soak it in milk to soften the flavour. The Big Sheep at Abbotsham, Bideford, Devon (see ASHLEIGH), makes an excellent Feta from pasteurised milk. Artisan makers using their own unpasteurised milk include: Mary Holbrook (see MENDIP), MENALLACK FARMHOUSE, Shepherds Purse (see YORKSHIRE BLUE), and Putlands Farm (see SUSSEX SLIPCOTE).

FIFIELD

Diana Coad, Altarnum, Fifield, Shipton-under-Wychwood, Oxfordshire
Artisan maker using the farm's own milk. Visitors welcome
Type: Unpasteurised goats milk, hard, full fat, vegetarian

Diana Coad has been producing cheese from the milk of her Anglo-Nubian goats since the late 1980s. Fifield is available plain or peppered. The 5 lb (2.3 kg) rounds are finished with a Manchego-type rind, ripened for a minimum of three months and waxed before sale. Other soft cheeses are made to order and include Coulommier, Halloumi, Ricotta and Anari. Cheese can be bought at the farm but telephone (01993) 830518 before calling to check opening times.

FIVE COUNTIES

D. John Davidge, Ilchester Cheese Company, Ilchester, Somerset
Specialist dairy making character cheeses
Type: Cows milk, hard-pressed, full fat, vegetarian

As exciting to look at as it is to eat; a combination of Cheddar, Double Gloucester, Leicester, Cheshire and Derby. Supplied in 4 lb (1.8 kg) wheels. *See also* ILCHESTER.

FLOWER MARIE

Kevin and Alison Blunt, Greenacres Farm, Whitesmith, Lewes, East Sussex
Artisan maker. Visitors welcome
Type: Unpasteurised ewes milk, semi-soft, full fat, vegetarian

Mould-ripened cheese, hand-made and finished in 7 oz (200 g) squares. Can be ripened for up to six weeks. *See also* CHABIS, GOLDEN CROSS, LAUGHTON.

FORD FARM CHEDDAR

Pullin Brothers, Ford Farm, Chewton Mendip, Somerset
Farmhouse maker using the farm's own milk
Type: Cows milk, hard-pressed, full fat

An ideal gift at Christmas (or any time of the year!) these cloth-bound truckles of hand-made Cheddar are available in 14 oz (400 g), 1½ lb (750 g) and 4½ lb (2 kg) sizes. The farm also makes a range of 8 oz (225 g) miniature cheeses which are individually moulded: Cheddar, Cheddar with garlic and herbs, and a delicious Cheddar with mustard and white wine. Produced in small quantities, Cheddar 'rabbits' are a speciality of this farm. Cast in a beautifully carved hardwood mould, they are about 15 in (38 cm) long, weigh around 5 lb (2.3 kg) and provide a unique centre-piece for a buffet table.

FOREST OF BOWLAND

Tim Procter, Procter's Cheeses, Saunders Raike, Chipping, Preston, Lancashire
Small creamery
Type: Cows milk, hard-pressed, full fat

Best known for their traditional Lancashire cheese, Procter's also pack a range of carefully selected rindless cheeses, in 10 lb (4.5 kg) blocks for counter cutting: mild, mature and extra-mature Cheddar, Double Gloucester, Red Leicester, Wensleydale and Cheshire.

FOUNTAINS DAIRY CHEESES

Fountains Dairy Products, Kirkby Malzeard, Ripon, North Yorkshire
Creamery
Type: Cows milk, hard-pressed, full fat

Fountains Dairy is a specialist cheese-maker producing around 2,000 tonnes of cheese each year. Wensleydale, made by hand using local milk, accounts for 20% of the total, sold in 4½ lb (2 kg) or 13 lb (6 kg) truckles, 1 lb (450 g) miniatures and a range of rind-less packs. There is also a Wensleydale with sliced ginger, a smoked Wensley-dale and a most unusual blue Wensleydale which is well worth trying. A full range of English territo-rial cheeses is also made. Fountains Gold, from the same creamery, was revived from an old recipe in 1992. This cheese is made from full cream Gold Top Jersey and Guernsey milk. It has a moist texture, a distinctive buttery flavour and an unusual 'toasted wheat' rind. Sold in 4½ lb (2 kg) half wheels. *See also* COVERDALE, WENSLEYDALE BLUE.

FRIESLA

Colin Brown, The Big Sheep, Abbot-sham, Bideford, Devon
Artisan maker using the farm's own milk. Visitors welcome
Type: Ewes milk, hard, full fat, vege-tarian

An unpressed hard cheese, similar to

Gouda but less waxy in texture. Formed into 8 lb (3.6 kg) rounds which will mature for 4–8 months. The farm produces a number of ewes milk cheeses, including Feta and Halloumi. There are also cottage cheeses, available salted or unsalted, with garlic and chives, with peppers, celery and herbs, and as a Christmas speciality, with whisky and almonds. All the cheeses can be ordered by post or bought at the farm. The Big Sheep provides an entertaining day out for all the family. Telephone (01237) 472366 for details. *See also* ABBOTSDALE, ASHLEIGH.

FRUIT CAKE CHEDDAR *see* CHEDDAR (MATURE) WITH RICH FRUIT CAKE

GABRIEL

Sean Ferry and Bill Hogan, West Cork Natural Cheese, Dereenatra, Schull, Co. Cork, Republic of Ireland
Artisan maker using local milk
Type: Unpasteruised cows milk, hard-pressed, medium fat

Only four small farms provide the milk for this very hard, Swiss-style, mellow cheese, with a hidden bloom that leads to a noticeably prolonged aftertaste, subtle and full bodied at once. The natural rind protects the cheese for many months, even years, after pressing. Sold in 13 lb (6 kg) and 66 lb (30 kg) rounds. *See also* DESMOND, MIZEN.

GALIC

Reggie and Susannah Stone, Highland Fine Cheeses, Knockbreck, Tain, Highland
Artisan maker using the farm's own milk
Type: Unpasteurised cows milk, soft, medium fat

Natural soft cheese, mixed with the chopped fresh leaves of locally picked 'all-healing' wild garlic. The magic herb imparts a spring-like flavour, light in comparison with continental garlic, that leaves no aftertaste. The 4 oz (100 g) cheeses are rolled in crumbled and flaked toasted nuts before being packed in heather-coloured Culloden tartan boxes. *See also* CROWDIE.

GALLOWAY CHEDDAR

Galloway Creamery, Stoneykirk Road, Stranraer, Dumfries and Galloway
Creamery
Type: Cows milk, hard-pressed, full fat

One of the largest makers of rindless Cheddar in Scotland. Production of mild and mature Cheddar in 40 lb (20 kg) rindless blocks is around 10,000 tonnes each year.

GALLOWAY FARMHOUSE CHEESE

Alan Brown, Galloway Farmhouse Cheese, Millaires, Newton Stewart, Dumfries and Galloway
Artisan maker using the farm's own milk. Visitors welcome
Type: Unpasteurised ewes milk, soft or hard-pressed, full fat, vegetarian

The farm's flock of 300 ewes, mainly Friesland cross, provide the milk for four cheeses. The full-fat, hard cheese is sweet and nutty, matured for at least six months, and comes waxed in various sizes from 6 oz (170 g) wedges to 5 lb (2.3 kg) rounds. The same cheese is available with green peppercorns, in a green wax, or smoked in the Galloway Smokehouse at Carluith and then coated in yellow wax. Galloway Farmhouse Mature is held back for around 12 months, by which time the 5 lb (2.3 kg) rounds develop a natural rind. I love their slogan 'From Ewe to You': very neatly put. Cheese can be bought at the farm, and cheesemaking holiday breaks are available. Telephone (01988) 850224 for details.

GALLOWAY GOATS CHEESE

Gordon and Dorothy Walling, California Farm, Whithorn, Newton Stewart, Dumfries and Galloway
Artisan maker using the farm's own milk
Type: Goats milk, soft or hard-pressed, medium fat, vegetarian

Fresh, soft cheese. The 4 oz (100 g) rounds are rolled in herbs or a mixture of oatmeal and whisky before being packed in wooden boxes. Small balls of the same cheese are marinaded in virgin olive oil with herbs and garlic and packed in 12 oz (350 g) jars. A hard cheese is also made; the 2½ lb (1.1 kg) waxed rounds are available smoked or plain.

GARLIC CHEDDAR

Dairy Crest, Dairy Crest House, Portsmouth Road, Surbiton, Surrey
Creamery
Type: Cows milk, hard-pressed, full fat

Cheddar with fresh garlic, also available smoked. Comes in 6½ lb (3 kg) rounds. *See also* DAIRY CREST.

GIGHA FRUITS

David Easton, Inverloch Cheeses, Leim Farm, Isle of Gigha, Strathclyde
Artisan maker
Type: Cows milk cheeses, hard-pressed, full fat

Unique miniature Cheddars delightfully shaped and waxed to resemble fruits and add colour to the cheeseboard. Each weighs around 7 oz (200 g). Red Apples contain mature Cheddar with garlic; Green Apples,

mature Cheddar and cream cheese; Brown Apples, mature Cheddar with chives; Maroon Apples, mature Cheddar with Scottish liqueur; Oranges, mature Cheddar with Grand Marnier; Pears, mature Cheddar with Schnapps. *See also* INVERLOCH CHEESE.

GLAMORGAN SAUSAGES

Bryson Craske, Abergavenny Fine Foods, Castle Meadows Park, Abergavenny, Gwent
Artisan maker. Visitors welcome
Type: Cows milk cheeses, hard-pressed with other ingredients, full fat, vegetarian

Glamorgan sausages, *Selsig Sir Forganwwg* in Welsh, used to be made with Glamorgan cheese. Alas, Glamorgan cheese is now extinct, as are the white Gwent cattle which provided the milk. This recipe combines Cheddar and Caerphilly, blended with leeks and spices and then rolled in toasted crumbs ready for grilling or frying. *See also* CASTLE MEADOWS CAERPHILLY.

GLASGWM

Peter Sayer, Welsh Farmhouse Cheese, Maesllyn, Llandysul, Dyfed
Artisan maker using the farm's own milk. Visitors welcome
Type: Unpasteurised cows milk, hard-pressed, full fat, vegetarian

Matured Welsh Cheddar, made using local milk, with added chives, hazelnuts and whisky. Sold in green-waxed 5 lb (2.3 kg) rounds or 1 lb (450 g) miniatures. *See also* ST EMELYN.

GLENCOE

Great Glen Fine Foods, Old Ferry Road, North Ballachulish, Inverness, Highland
Specialist retailer. Visitors welcome
Type: Goats milk, semi-soft, full fat

Made near Loch Leven, Glencoe is available in 3½ oz (100 g) rounds, either plain or with garlic and herbs. Douglas Locke's excellent Scottish Speciality Food Shop, on Old Ferry Road, stocks a vast range of local cheeses. It is open all year, except January, and cheese can be ordered by post at any time. Telephone (01855) 821277 for details. *See also* CALEDONIA.

GLEN O'SHEEN

Mathew and Margaret O'Brien, Ballinacourty, Glenroe, Kilmallock, Co. Limerick, Republic of Ireland
Artisan maker
Type: Unpasteurised cows milk, hard-pressed, full fat

Kilmallock, just north of the Ballyhoura Hills, is set in an exceedingly fertile part of Ireland called the Golden Vale, an ideal venue to produce this Cheddar-type cheese. Matured for up to six months, it is made in 8–30 lb (4–13 kg) truckles, bandaged and waxed.

GLENPHILLY

D. John Davidge, Ilchester Cheese Company, Ilchester, Somerset
Specialist dairy making character cheeses
Type: Cows milk, hard-pressed, full fat

Cheddar with whisky, adding a golden glow in colour and taste. Sold in 5 lb (2.3 kg) rounds and miniatures of various sizes. *See also* ILCHESTER.

GOATFELL

Ian and Allison McChlery, Home Farm, Brodick, Isle of Arran, Strathclyde
Artisan maker using the farm's own milk. Visitors welcome

Type: Goats milk, semi-hard, full fat, vegetarian

Soft, white cheese, available smoked or plain. One of a range of cream cheeses, with oatmeal, garlic and herbs, or pepper and oatmeal. Glenshant, from the same farm, is an unpressed, blue-veined cheese. *See also* KILBRIDE.

GOLDEN CROSS

Kevin and Alison Blunt, Greenacres Farm, Whitesmith, Lewes, East Sussex
Artisan maker using the farm's own milk. Visitors welcome
Type: Unpasteurised goats milk, semi-soft, full fat, vegetarian

Kevin Blunt's goats graze natural pasture and the milk is used fresh to make this log-shaped cheese, to a traditional Sainte-Maure recipe. The 8 oz (225 g) cheeses are dusted with charcoal before being left to mature for 4–5 weeks, when they develop a velvety-white coat, a creamy texture and tart flavour. Praised in *Good Cheese* magazine as 'one of the finest natural-rind goats cheeses on the market'. Cheese can be bought in the farm shop but telephone (01825) 872380 to check opening times. *See also* LAUGHTON, FLOWER MARIE.

GOLDEN FOODS *see* AVONMORE

GOLD TOP BLUE

Alan and Kay Duffield, Exmoor Blue Cheese, Willett Farm, Lydeard St Lawrence, Somerset
Artisan maker. Visitors by appointment only
Type: Unpasteurised cows milk, hard-pressed, full fat, vegetarian

The best milk is Gold Top and this candidate for best new blue cheese also deserves high honours. Produced at

Willett Farm under licence from Quality Milk Producers Ltd, it has a wonderful flavour and aroma and an attractive natural crust. *See also* QUANTOCK BLUE.

GOUDA PATRICE *see* TEIFI FARMHOUSE CHEESE

GOULD'S TRADITIONAL CHEDDAR

E.F.J. Gould, Batch Farm, East Pennard, Shepton Mallet, Somerset
Farmhouse maker using the farm's own milk
Type: Cows milk, hard-pressed, full fat

One of the few makers still producing traditional cloth-bound Cheddars in 60 lb (27 kg) rounds. Production is about 400 tonnes per year.

GOWRIE

Derek and Ann Brow, The Ingle Smokehouses, Arran Place, Perth, Tayside
Artisan maker
Type: Cows milk, semi-hard, full fat

Firm, cream-coloured, Cheddar-type cheese with a slightly open texture and fresh taste. Made by hand, using a recipe that has been in the same family for three generations, it is cloth-wrapped and ripened on raw wood slats. Locally grown herbs (chives, basil or nettles) are sometimes added. Cheesemaking started at Ingle Smokehouses in 1987; now they use 500 gallons (2,300 litres) of local Friesian cows milk each day. *See also* SCOTTISH OAK SMOKED CHEDDAR.

GRACEFIELD SELECT LANCASHIRE CHEESE

Ian Coggin, Dew-Lay Products, Green Lane West, Garstang, Lancashire

Farmhouse maker using local milk
Type: Unpasteurised cows milk, semi-hard, full fat, vegetarian

Genuine traditional Lancashire cheese is hard to find; even rarer is one made from unpasteurised milk. However, customers' demands for a richer flavoured Lancashire have led to the introduction of Gracefield by one of the most experienced makers. The 40 lb (18 kg) rounds are cloth-bound and waxed; there are vacuum packed smaller sizes. *See also* DEW-LAY.

GRANT'S TRADITIONAL CHEDDAR

H. and E.J. Grant, Hamwood Farm, Trull, Taunton, Somerset
Farmhouse maker using the farm's own milk. Visitors by appointment
Type: Cows milk, hard-pressed, full fat

The Grant family have been making Cheddar at Hamwood Farm since 1953 and have consistently won prizes for their product. Regrettably, fewer and fewer farms are prepared to undertake the making of traditionally rinded cheese; the extra labour and cost involved have turned many farms over to rindless Cheddar, but the Grant family remain committed to the manufacture of 'real' Cheddar. Their cheese is rich and strong, and carries a unique flavour, the result of good milk, skilled making and many months of careful turning in the store. Supplies are limited (only around 120 tonnes are produced each year) but the Cheddar is much sought after in Somerset where locals in the know demand cheese from Grant's of Trull.

GREENFIELDS DAIRY LANCASHIRE CHEESE

Peter Procter, Greenfields Dairy Products, Goosnargh, Preston, Lancashire
Creamery

Type: Cows milk, hard-pressed, full fat, vegetarian

A prizewinner at agricultural shows such as Longridge and Goosnargh, and Great Eccleston, this smaller creamery uses local milk to make Lancashire cheese, Lancashire with garlic and other English territorial varieties in 13 lb (6 kg) and 22 lb (10 kg) rounds, as well as rindless 40 lb (18 kg) blocks. There is also an innovative range of cheeses in 9 lb (4 kg) wheels, including Cheddar with onion, Double Gloucester with chives and onion, Red Leicester with herbs, and Red Leicester with walnuts. Cheese can be bought direct from the dairy but telephone (01995) 640312 before calling to check opening times.

GREEN'S TRADITIONAL CHEDDAR

H.G. Green, Newtown Farm, Redlake Dairy, West Pennard, Somerset
Farmhouse maker using the farm's own milk
Type: Cows milk, hard-pressed, full fat, vegetarian

Three generations of the Green family have been making cheese since 1917 and their prizewinning products have found fame on more than one occasion. It was Newtown Farm which produced the cheeses for the Silver Jubilee of H.M. Queen Elizabeth II. A traditional 90 lb (40 kg) cloth-bound Cheddar, flanked by two 9 lb (4 kg) truckles, was placed in a specially made basket and presented to Her Majesty. All three were pressed in an iron press, made during the 1800s and still in daily use. When a giant Cheddar cheese was required for the 1989 Food and Farming Year celebrations it was the Green family who were called upon to re-create the monster cheese presented to Victoria and Albert to mark their betrothal 150 years before. On 3 March 1989, 1,200 gallons (5,500 litres) of milk were collected from local farms, and Green's head cheesemaker David Higgon used the 1839 recipe to make a Cheddar cheese 3 ft (1 m) in diameter, weighing 1,200 lb (550 kg). A huge mould and special equipment had to be built and, after 24 days in the press, the cheese required six strong men to lift it and lace it into a calico 'corset'. The farm now produces around 500 tonnes each year of traditional rind-on Cheddar in 60 lb (27 kg) rounds.

GROVEHILL

Susan Moore, Cranes Watering Farm, Starston, Harleston, Norfolk
Artisan maker using the farm's own milk. Visitors by appointment
Type: Unpasteurised cows milk, semi-soft, full fat, vegetarian

A Norfolk milk cheese, made from the milk of Jersey and Guernsey cows. Slightly salted, the 9 oz (250 g) rounds are topped with walnuts. *See also* MOORE CHEESE.

GRUTH DHU

Reggie and Susannah Stone, Highland Fine Cheeses, Knockbreck, Tain, Highland
Artisan maker using local milk
Type: Cows milk, soft, fresh, low fat, rennet free, vegetarian

Light, soft Crowdie, with its 'oatmeal' flavour, is absolutely stunning when presented in Susannah Stone's crunchy coating of crushed peppercorns (one of my personal favourites). Gruth Dhu is Gaelic for 'black Crowdie'. *See also* CROWDIE.

GUBBEEN

Giana Ferguson, Gubbeen House, Schull, Co. Cork, Republic of Ireland

Artisan maker using the farm's own milk. Visitors by appointment
Type: Unpasteurised cows milk, semi-soft, full fat, vegetarian

Milk from Friesian and Jersey cows is used to make this rind-washed, pale-yellow cheese, nutty in taste and soft and creamy in texture. Sold in 1 lb (450 g) or 2 lb (900 g) rounds. Normally sold at three weeks, this low-salt cheese can be held back for three months, by which time it has a distinctive taste and a pink bloom. Praised by Michael Bateman for its aroma 'of ripe vegetables with a bitter chicory finish'. Also available oak-smoked.

GUERNSEY CHEESE

The States Dairy, St Martins, Guernsey, Channel Islands
Small creamery using local milk
Type: Cows milk, hard-pressed, full fat, vegetarian

Guernsey milk and cream is synonymous with high quality and famous all over the world, but the island's cheese remains a well-kept secret. If there ever were any indigenous cheeses they have disappeared and it was only in 1979 that the States Dairy started to bring Guernsey cheese to a wider public. Production is mainly in rindless 40 lb (18 kg) blocks, although traditional round cheeses have been made. The cheese has a character reminiscent of a Scottish Dunlop, but develops a fuller flavour at quite an early age – doubtless the influence of the creamy Guernsey milk. The smoked version is particularly good, one of the pleasures of a holiday on the island.

HALLOUMI

Type: Ewes milk, soft, full fat, vegetarian

Halloumi (or Halloumy) originated in Cyprus but is made all around the Mediterranean. Like Feta, it is a 'pickled' cheese, matured in brine. In appearance, Halloumi is a firmish putty-like mass, creamy white in colour and with a stringy texture. The curd is dipped in hot whey, kneaded, rolled out and folded with mint leaves or herbs between the layers. Halloumi is delicious diced or grated into salads, and especially tasty grilled or dry fried in thin slices to a golden brown, when it has a flavour similar to that of bacon. Halloumi, eggs and Glamorgan sausages would provide a full vegetarian breakfast! Ewes milk Halloumi is made by The Big Sheep (see FRIESLA) and Sussex High Weald Dairy, and cows milk Halloumi by CRICKET MALHERBIE Farms and HERITAGE Cheeses.

HANKELOW MANOR FARM CHEESES

Paul Smith-Palmer, Hankelow Foods, Hankelow Manor Farm, Nantwich, Cheshire
Creamery
Type: Cows milk, hard-pressed, full fat, vegetarian

Producers of traditional territorial cheeses: Cheshire, Caerphilly, Double Gloucester, Lancashire, Red Leicester and Wensleydale, making around 400 tonnes each year. Sizes include large and small truckles and 9 lb (4 kg) wheels.

HARBOURNE BLUE

Robin Congdon, Ticklemore Cheese, Ticklemore Street, Totnes, Devon
Artisan maker. Visitors welcome
Type: Unpasteurised goats milk, semi-soft, full fat

Made by hand, using only local milk, this cheese is very aromatic and has a distinctive flavour. The 6 lb (2.7 kg) rounds are matured for 2½ months. *See also* TICKLEMORE.

HARES CHESHIRE CHEESE

V.J. Hares and Son, Millenheath, Higher Heath, Whitchurch, Shropshire
Farmhouse maker using the farm's own and other local milk
Type: Cows milk, hard-pressed, full fat, vegetarian

Makers of traditional Cheshire cheese in 20 lb (9 kg) and 40 lb (20 kg) cylindricals. Consistently amongst the prizewinners at cheese shows, having produced the Supreme Champion at the Nantwich Show for two consecutive years, 1993 and 1994. Their success is due to good management of the Friesian herd, careful feeding of the stock (mainly grass silage) and, above all, the skill of Geoffrey Roberts, who has been head cheesemaker since 1959. Geoffrey is rightly regarded as a perfectionist! Production is around 250 tonnes each year, mainly Cheshire cheese (white and coloured) or other English territorials. The farm has had particular success with Double Gloucester and Caerphilly. Cheese can be bought at the farm but telephone (01948) 840288 before calling to check opening times.

HAWES WENSLEYDALE *see* WENSLEYDALE (COWS MILK)

HAWKRIDGE FARMHOUSE CHEDDAR

Frank and Dinah Beer, Hawkridge Farm, Coldridge, Crediton, Devon
Farmhouse maker using the farm's own and other local milk
Type: Cows milk, hard-pressed, full fat, vegetarian

The Beer family began making cheese in the Taw Valley, between Dartmoor and Exmoor, in the 1960s. Their cheeses regularly win prizes at the Royal Bath and West and other shows, a tribute to the consistent quality of their product. They use milk from their own herd of 300 Holsteins and other local farms whom they know well. Production is around 1,000 tonnes per year, mainly rindless 40 lb (20 kg) blocks of Cheddar and Double Gloucester.

HELER, JOSEPH *see* LAURELS FARM

HEREFORD HOP

Charles Martell and Son, Laurel Farm, Dymock, Gloucestershire
Artisan maker using the farm's own milk
Type: Cows milk, hard-pressed, full fat, vegetarian

Re-created by Charles Martell in 1988, this is a rustic cheese of the type that would have been common on the Herefordshire border a century ago. The crust of dried hops imparts an unusual savoury flavour to the taste of the maturing cheese and in former times would have helped to prevent unwanted surface mould. Available in 5 lb (2.3 kg) wheels. *See also* SINGLE GLOUCESTER.

HEREFORD RED

Nick Hodgetts, Malvern Cheesewrights, Manor House, Lower Wick, Worcester
Artisan maker using the farm's own milk
Type: Unpasteurised cows milk, semi-hard, full fat, vegetarian

Richly flavoured and silky textured cheese, made with milk from the Lower Wick Friesian herd. Coloured with annatto and matured in 7 lb (3 kg) rounds, which develop a natural rind. The farm also produces its own HEREFORD HOP, a creamy and 'lemony' version with a coating of toasted hops adding their unusual savoury flavour. Available in 3½ lb (1.6 kg) wheels, 3 lb

(1.3 kg) truckles and 14 oz (400 g) miniatures. *See also* MALVERN.

HERITAGE

Heritage Cheeses, The Creamery, Glan-Yr-Afon Estate, Aberystwyth, Dyfed
Creamery
Type: Cows milk, various, vegetarian

Each day Heritage produce around 15 tonnes of hard-pressed cheeses, including Cheddar, Mozzarella and Monterey Jack. Indian Paneer, Italian, Greek and various Spanish-style cheeses are also made, and specialist curd cheeses are available. *See also* HALLOUMI, KEFOLOTYRI, PROVOLONE.

HERRIOT FARMHOUSE

Judy Bell, Shepherds Purse, Leachfield Grange, Bellfields, Newsham, Thirsk, North Yorkshire
Artisan maker
Type: Ewes milk, semi-hard, full fat, vegetarian

Did a certain vet inspire the name Herriot? Judy Bell's ewes graze mature pastures, mainly clover, giving a local flavour to a cheese which is made to a nineteenth-century recipe. Finished with a cloth wrap and ripened for three months to develop a nutty flavour and natural grey rind, it is sold in 3 lb (1.4 kg) and 7 lb (3.2 kg) truckles. *See also* SHEPHERDS PURSE.

HEYDALE

Cameron Baines, Chamberhouse Urban Farm, Rochdale Road East, Heywood, Lancashire
Artisan maker using the farm's own milk. Visitors welcome
Type: Unpasteurised ewes milk, soft and hard-pressed, full fat

Chamberhouse Farm is one of the few remaining city farms. Owned by Rochdale Corporation, it is a working farm but opens to the public free of charge and is a popular venue for school visits. The 66 acres support 12 Jersey cows and 60 Friesland milking sheep. The ewes milk is used for two rind-washed hard cheeses, Heydale Mellow and Mature, and a low-fat soft cheese, supplied plain or with herbs. All are sold in the farm shop. Telephone (01706) 48710 for details of opening times.

HIGHLAND CHOICE

Long Clawson Dairy, Melton Mowbray, Leicestershire
Creamery
Type: Cows milk, hard-pressed, full fat

Dunlop cheese blended with Drambuie and flaked almonds. Drambuie is made from whisky, honey and herbs to a recipe given to a Mr Mackinnon by Bonnie Prince Charlie in 1745. Highland Herb, from the same creamery, is a blend of Dunlop, Innimore mustard and herbs, and makes a delightful sauce. *See also* LONG CLAWSON.

HIGHLAND SOFT

Reggie and Susannah Stone, Highland Fine Cheeses, Knockbreck, Tain, Highland
Artisan maker using local milk
Type: Cows milk, soft, full fat, vegetarian

Once made in the Lowlands and called Ayrshire Soft, this is one of the few cheeses still made in pails. Very smooth, mild and slightly sweet, Highland Soft is ideal for cheesecakes. *See also* CROWDIE.

HORLICKS FARMS AND DAIRIES CHEDDAR

Horlicks Farms and Dairies, Hort Bridge, Ilminster, Somerset
Creamery
Type: Cows milk, hard-pressed, full fat

Horlicks Farms and Dairies are rightly proud of their mature and extra-mature rindless Cheddar. Around 5,000 tonnes of cheese are made each year, using milk supplied by farms in the Taunton Vale and Blackdown Hills. The creamery has a fascinating history, connected with many famous names in the grocery trade. It was originally run by Kraft, was taken over by Horlicks (makers of the famous bedtime drink) in the 1940s and absorbed into the Beecham group in 1968. The company is now owned by the Dairygold Co-operative Society of Mitchelstown in Ireland, and the manufacture of fine Cheddar continues. The cheese is packed in 10 lb (4.5 kg) blocks, and vacuum-packed wedges. It is sold by several large supermarket groups. *See also* BLACKDOWN.

HOWGATE SOFT CHEESES

Rosemary and Mike Marwick, Howgate Cheeses, Camperdown Creamery, Faraday Street, Dundee
Artisan maker
Type: Cows milk, soft, full fat, vegetarian

A range of hand-made, bloomy-rinded cheeses which ripen to a rich creamy

---

HOME-MADE CHEESE

Home cheesemaking is not difficult and, for soft cheeses, no special equipment other than a yard or two of cheesecloth is required. Books (now out of print) containing recipes include *Making Cheeses* by Susan Ogilvy (Batsford, 1976), *The Home Dairying Book*, edited by Katie Thear (Broad Leys, 1978) and *Practical Cheesemaking* by Kathy Biss (Crowood Press, 1988). Kathy takes the reader through each stage of the process and her book is suitable both for home use and for those making cheese on a small-scale commercial basis. She also offers short cheesemaking courses on her farm (see the entry for CREAGMHOL on p. 123). Colleges offering cheesemaking courses include Brackenhurst College at Southwell in Nottinghamshire, Lackham College at Chippenham in Wiltshire and Reaseheath College near Nantwich in Cheshire. (Expect to pay around £100.) Equipment and materials, including commercial starter, can be obtained from Fulwood Ltd, Grange Road, Ellesmere, Shropshire, SY12 9DF (telephone 01691 622391). Fulwoods also supply helpful books on cheesemaking. Commercial rennet can be obtained from Hansen's Laboratory, 476 Basingstoke Road, Reading, Berkshire (telephone 01734 861056); Stratton Sales, Charlton Industrial Estate, Shepton Mallet, Somerset (telephone 01749 344071); and Moorlands Goats Cheese, Blackwood Hill, Rushton Spencer, Macclesfield, Cheshire (telephone 01260 226336).

Beginners anxious to try their hand at simple cheesemaking might like to try the following recipe. Boil four pints of Gold Top milk, take off the heat and add four tablespoons of vinegar and one teaspoon of cumin. Do not stir. When cool, strain off the whey and pile the curd in a clean tea towel. Twist the cloth firmly then press under a weight for two hours. The result will be a cheese with an intriguing spicy flavour as served as a side-course in the more authentic Indian restaurants.

flavour. Howgate Scottish Brie is available in 3 lb (1.4 kg) and 6 oz (175 g) rounds, Howgate Coulommier in 10 oz (300 g) rounds, and Howgate Camembert in 2 lb (900 g) and 10 oz (300 g) rounds. Howgate Blue is a blue-veined soft cheese. Made in 3½ lb (1.6 kg) rounds and matured for 3 months until it becomes soft and creamy, it has a strong and salty, blue tang. Pasteurised and raw milk versions are available. *See also* BISHOP KENNEDY, ETTRICK, PENTLAND, ST ANDREWS, STRATHKINNESS.

HRAMSA

Reggie and Susannah Stone, Highland Fine Cheeses, Knockbreck, Tain, Highland
Artisan maker using local milk
Type: Cows milk, soft, fresh, medium fat, rennet free, vegetarian

Cottage cheese made with fresh cream. Also available with leaves of fresh, wild Highland garlic and in a low-fat version. Sold in 5 oz (150 g) tubs. *See also* CROWDIE.

HUNDALEE

Liddy Hall, Hundalee Cottars Farm, Jedburgh, Borders
Artisan maker using the farm's own milk. Visitors welcome

Type: Goats milk, soft and hard-pressed, full fat, vegetarian

Hundalee Soft Cheeses are made from the milk of 50 pedigree goats grazing organic pasture. They are sold young, in 4 oz (110 g) wooden boxes, natural or with garlic. Also available in 5 oz (150 g) ash pyramids. Hundalee Cream Cheese in 2.2 lb (1 kg) tubs and the semi-pressed Hundalee Nouvelle in 1–2 lb (450–900 g) rounds are luxury products for unashamed gourmet palates. Hundalee Hard Pressed Cheeses, young and mild or fully matured, have been widely praised. The plain and smoked varieties are finished in 4 lb (1.8 kg) waxed rounds and 4–6 oz (110–170 g) miniatures. Cheese may sometimes be bought at the farm but telephone (01835) 862064 before calling. *See also* PANEER.

HUNTBACH'S CHESHIRE CHEESE

P.J. Huntbach, Hayfield Farm, Audlem, Crewe, Cheshire
Farmhouse maker using the farm's own milk. Visitors by appointment
Type: Cows milk, hard-pressed, full fat, vegetarian

Makers of 40 lb (20 kg) and 20 lb (9 kg) traditional round Cheshire cheeses, as well as rindless (40 lb/ 20 kg) blocks of

---

HUGE CHEESE

There has long been a practice of making giant cheeses for special occasions. In 1825 the city of Chester presented the Duke of York (who went up the hill and down again) with a Cheshire cheese weighing 150 lb (70 kg). In 1908 the winner of the Gold Medal and Challenge Cup at Chester was a cheese of 200 lb (90 kg), which was subsequently presented to Edward VII. The largest recorded Cheshire cheese, weighing 1,200 lb (544 kg), was presented to Thomas Jefferson, third President of the USA. It was made, appropriately, by the town of Cheshire, Massachusetts. The current holder of the title 'The World's Largest Cheese' is a leviathan Cheddar manufactured in March 1988 by Simon's Speciality Cheese of Little Chute, Wisconsin. It weighed 40,060 lb, just over 18 tonnes.

Cheshire and Cheddar. Total production is around 500 tonnes per year.

HUNTSMAN

Long Clawson Dairy, Melton Mowbray, Leicestershire
Creamery
Type: Cows milk, two-layer, full fat

A long-established and popular sandwich of mild Stilton between two layers od Double Gloucester cheese. *See also* LONG CLAWSON.

ILCHESTER

D. John Davidge, Ilchester Cheese Company, Ilchester, Somerset
Specialist dairy making character cheeses
Type: Cows milk, hard-pressed, full fat, vegetarian

The advertising campaign for LYMESWOLD in the 1980s, proclaiming it 'the first new cheese for generations', rather forgot Ilchester cheese, which was born in the kitchen of a local hotel in 1963. Oddments of Cheddar blended with beer were served as a bar snack and met with such acclaim that a whole new generation of blended cheeses came into being. Now the original Ilchester cheese is available again, made in a brand-new factory, but still a smooth blend of Cheddar, strong Fuller's ale, piquant spices and chives. The Ilchester Cheese Company is England's largest exporter of table cheeses to the US and Japan and deserves credit for proving that the British can make a variety of products every bit as exciting as their competitors in Europe. *See also* ABBEYDALE, ADMIRALS, APPLEWOOD, FIVE COUNTIES, GLENPHILLY, ROMANY, SOMERTON, VINTAGE, WALDORF, YEOMAN.

INNES FRESH CHEESE

Hugh Lillingston, Innes Cheese, Highfields Dairy, Statfold, Tamworth, Staffordshire
Artisan maker using the farm's own milk
Type: Unpasteurised goats milk, soft, medium fat, vegetarian

A range of soft cheeses, entirely handmade, best eaten fresh and wet before any rind has formed. Available plain, coated with ash, or rolled in mixed herbs, and in three sizes: Buttons (1½ oz/40 g), Clifton (3 oz/90 g) and Bosworth (12½ oz/350 g). Cheese can be bought from the dairy but telephone (01827) 830097 before calling to check opening times. *See also* BOSWORTH ASH.

INVERLOCH CHEESE

David Easton, Inverloch Cheese, Leim Farm, Isle of Gigha, Strathclyde
Artisan maker using the farm's own milk
Type: Cows and goats milk, speciality cheeses

Proof again, if proof were needed, that innovative cheeses come from smaller makers. David Easton's cheeses regularly take awards at cheese shows. His farm produces around 25 tonnes per year of Cheddar cheese, using Guernsey milk, plus a range of soft, goats milk cheeses. The Cheddar cheese is presented in 7 oz (200 g) miniatures with a range of extra ingredients: Laird's Mustard, made with Scottish mustard, is yellow-waxed; Poacher's Choice with garlic is red-waxed; Lazy Ploughmans with pickle is clear-waxed; and a Cheddar with chives is green-waxed. *See also* GIGHA FRUITS.

IRTHINGSPA

Jayne Burrough and Diane Gerrard,

Irthingspa Dairy Goats, Holme View, Gilsland, Cumbria
Artisan maker using the farm's own milk. Visitors by appointment
Type: Goats milk, semi-soft or hard, full fat, vegetarian

The clear waters of the river Irthing, the windswept grassland around Hadrian's Wall, and a Roman spa are all suggested in the name of this cheese. The close-textured, hard version is also available smoked. The moist, fresh and lemony soft cheese is made in 1–5 lb (450 g–2.3 kg) rounds and is available plain, with crushed peppers or with herbs. Cheese can be bought on the farm and tours of the dairy can sometimes be arranged but telephone (01697) 747481 first for details of opening times. *See also* TYNEDALE SPA.

ISLE OF ATHELNEY

David Gillard, Westway Dairy Company, Westway Farm, Bishop Sutton, Avon
Farmhouse Cheddar specialist
Type: Cows milk, hard-pressed, full fat, vegetarian

An intermingling of Arthurian legend and the real-life history of Saxon kings surrounds the low-lying land around Glastonbury Tor that we know as the Somerset Levels. The peaty Levels were once covered by the sea to form a series of islands; one of the largest of these, about seven miles from Taunton, was the Isle of Athelney. The name means 'Island of Princes' and here King Alfred founded a great abbey to commemorate his victory over the Danes in 879. Nothing remains of the abbey, but the Isle of Athelney has become the brand name for a superb and distinctive extra-mature Cheddar, the *grand cru* of vintage cheeses. The cheese is cut and turned (in the cheddaring process) by hand, then salted and turned again, on open tables. After being carefully graded to maintain the

highest standards, the cheese is held on the farm to mature like a fine wine for up to 15 months. The result proves just how good a rindless cheese can be. Normally sold in 6½ lb (3 kg) rindless blocks for counter cutting. *See also* CHEDDAR (TASTY), WESTWAY DAIRY.

ISLE OF MULL

Jeffrey Reade, Sgriob-ruadh Farm, Tobermory, Isle of Mull, Strathclyde
Artisan maker using the farm's own milk. Visitors welcome
Type: Unpasteurised cows milk, hard-pressed, full fat

Jeffrey Reade's herd of 120 Friesians, with an odd Ayrshire, Jersey or even a shaggy Highlander in their ancestry, graze land bounded by forest on one side and the Sound of Mull on the other. Isle of Mull is a Cheddar-type, made by hand, cloth bound and matured at Tobermory Distillery. The 5 lb (2.3 kg), 10 lb (4.5 kg) and 50 lb (22 kg) rounds are hard and firm, with a powerful spicy flavour. The name of the farm (pronounced 'Skribrooah') is Gaelic for 'red furrow'. Isle of Mull Flavells, made from the same cheese, are available in 7 oz (200 g) rounds, plain or smoked and with additions such as mixed herbs, cracked black peppers, caraway seeds or Mull mustard. There is a visitor centre and farm shop; telephone (01688) 2235 before calling to check opening times. *See also* TOBERMORY TRUCKLES.

JACANTI

J.J. Saunders, Emborough Farm Foods, Old Down Farm, Emborough, Somerset
Farmhouse maker using the farm's own milk
Type: Cows milk, semi-hard, full fat

Two new presentations of Cheddar cheese with additives: a 'pizza cheese' (ideal for toppings) and Cheddar with spring onion and tomato. *See also* SAUNDERS' CHEDDAR.

JERSEY BLUE

Alan and Kay Duffield, Exmoor Blue Cheese, Willett Farm, Lydeard St Lawrence, Somerset
Artisan maker using the farm's own milk. Visitors by appointment
Type: Unpasteurised cows milk, semisoft, full fat, vegetarian

Absolutely delicious herby, blue-veined cheese from the milk of a single Jersey herd. Made in 3 lb (1.5 kg) rounds, the cheese rapidly develops a strong and tangy flavour. *See also* QUANTOCK BLUE.

JOSEPH HELER *see* LAURELS FARM

JOUVENET

Nachi Elkin, Gedi Enterprises, Plumridge Farm, Stagg Hill, Barnet, Hertfordshire
Artisan maker using the farm's own milk. Visitors welcome
Type: Goats milk, semi-soft, full fat, vegetarian

Although the Gedi herd was established by Israeli cheesemaker Nachi Elkin as recently as 1989, Plumridge Farm is now one of the largest goats cheese producers in Britain. The success of the range was confirmed when Nachi Elkin won second prize (out of 1,100 entries) at the New York Fancy Food Show in May 1992. Jouvenet has the rough texture of a provincial French cheese, but also a rich palate and a creamy aftertaste. Served in 4 oz (110 g) small rounds. *See also* CHAVANNES.

JUMBLIE

Peter Pugson, Cliff House, Terrace Road, Buxton, Derbyshire
Specialist retailer
Type: Goats milk, hard-pressed, full fat, vegetarian

Buxton, set in the Derbyshire Dales, was once a notable spa town; indeed, it is one of the oldest spas in the country. Amongst its tourist attractions must surely rate Peter Pugson's cheese shop, for he is a master cheesemonger. Jumblie Farm, near Buxton, makes cheese from the milk of a single herd of Anglo-Nubian goats.

KEEN'S UNPASTEURISED CHEDDAR

S.H. and G.H. Keen & Sons, Moorhayes Farm, Verrington Lane, Wincanton, Somerset
Farmhouse maker using the farm's own milk. Visitors by appointment
Type: Unpasteurised cows milk, hard-pressed, full fat

Behind the beautiful Tudor farmhouse occupied by the Keen family an old barn conceals an outstanding new dairy where cheesemaking goes on every day of the year. They have been making it since 1899 and the matured 60 lb (27 kg) cloth-bound cylindricals have a flavour rarely found today. With its fresh grassy tang and even a hint of licorice, this is the strong cheese for which Somerset is famous. In his book *The Feast of Christmas* Paul Levy described this Cheddar as the best he had ever tasted. More recently, Keen's Cheddar was selected as the Supreme Champion at the Royal Bath and West Show of 1994. The farm's 180 Friesian cows, grazing land between the Blackmore Vale and Mere Downs, provide milk for around 100 tonnes of Cheddar each year, mainly in 60 lb (27 kg) rounds; small truckles of 3–7 lb (1.5–3 kg) are sometimes available.

KEFOLOTYRI

Heritage Cheeses, The Creamery, Glan-Yr-Afon Estate, Aberystwyth, Dyfed
Creamery
Type: Cows milk, hard-pressed, full fat, vegetarian

Authentic Greek-style, mealy and oily cheese with a hard rind. Takes its name from its shape, which is supposed to resemble a Greek hat. Lightly salted and tangy, it is often used for grating and cooking. *See also* HERITAGE.

KELSAE

Brenda Leddy, Garden Cottage Farm, Stichill, Kelso, Borders
Artisan maker using the farm's own milk
Type: Unpasteurised cows milk, semi-hard, full fat

The pedigree Stichill Jersey herd provides the milk for Mrs Leddy and her daughter to make Kelsae. They use natural yoghurt (made on the same farm) as a starter, which gives a unique flavour. Kelsae is not unlike Wensleydale, but much creamier on the palate. Vegetarian or animal rennet is used to meet buyer's requirements. *See also* STICHILL.

KELSEY

Stephen Fletcher, Ramhall Dairy Sheep, Ram Hall, Berkswell, West Midlands
Artisan maker using the farm's own milk
Type: Unpasteurised ewes milk, semi-hard, full fat, vegetarian

Produced at the aptly named Ram Hall, Kelsey is made in 14 oz (400 g) flat rounds. Several varieties are available: plain, with fresh garlic and chives, and with tarragon. *See also* BERKSWELL.

KERRYGOLD CHEDDAR

Kerrygold/An Bord Baine, Grattan House, Lower Mount Street, Dublin, Republic of Ireland
Major creamery proprietor manufacturing at several locations

Kerrygold is a subsidiary of the Irish Dairy Board, one of Ireland's major exporters with annual sales approaching £1 billion. Their range of dairy products includes Kerrygold mild and mature rindless Cheddar. Kerrygold's packing facility at Leek in Staffordshire handles 35,000 tonnes each year, making it the third biggest cheese company in the UK.

KILBRIDE

Ian and Allison McChlery, Home Farm, Brodick, Isle of Arran, Strathclyde
Artisan maker using the farm's own milk. Visitors welcome
Type: Cows milk, hard-pressed, full fat, vegetarian

Scottish island Cheddar, attractively presented with a range of added ingredients: Balmoral with claret; Hamilton's Choice with chives; Hebridean Herb with herbs; Islander with whisky; another with mustard; and an oak-smoked version presented in red wax. All available in 12 oz (330 g) rounds. Visitors welcome but telephone (01770) 2788 before calling to check opening times. *See also* ARRAN BLUE, BRODICK BLUE, GOAT FELL.

KINGDOM CHEESE

Kingdom Cheese, Glenfield Industrial Estate, Cowdenbeath, Fife
Creamery
Type: Cows milk, semi-hard, full fat

Produces around 1,500 tonnes of

Mozzarella and smaller quantities of cottage cheese and cream cheeses each year.

KIRKHAM'S TRADITIONAL LANCASHIRE

J.J. Kirkham, Beesley Farm, Mill Lane, Goosnargh, Lancashire
Artisan maker using the farm's own milk
Type: Unpasteurised cows milk, hard-pressed, full fat

Ruth Kirkham only started making Lancashire cheese in the 1970s, following the example set by her mother and grandmother, but whilst they made cheese for a local market, Ruth has succeeded in establishing herself as one of England's premier makers of rich and crumbly Lancashire cheese. Each cheese has an individual flavour, drawing its character from the natural, unpasteurised milk. Ruth totally rejects any idea of using pasteurised milk. Farming 30 acres with husband John (they have 40 cows), she makes about half a ton (500 kg) of cheese each week with most of the work done by hand. It's hard work but healthy, and Ruth has never has as much as a cold in 30 years. Cheeses are finished with a natural rind and available in 40 lb (20 kg) cloth-bound rounds as well as in smaller sizes.

KNOCKALARA

Wolfgang and Agnes Schliebitz, Cappoquin, Co. Waterford, Republic of Ireland
Artisan maker using the farm's own milk
Type: Ewes milk, semi-soft, full fat, vegetarian

Fresh cheese with a mild, lemony flavour. Limited availability.

KNOCKANORE

Patricia and Eamonn Lonergan, Ballyneety, Knockanore, Co. Waterford, Republic of Ireland
Artisan maker using the farm's own milk
Type: Cows milk, semi-soft, full fat

Made by hand in a valley between Tallow and Youghal, this cheese has been likened to Port Salut. Sold in waxed 5 lb (2.5 kg) wheels.

KNOLTON FARMHOUSE SUPREME CHESHIRE CHEESE

Jonathan and Russ Latham, Knolton Farmhouse, Overton-on-Dee, Wrexham, Clwyd
Farmhouse maker using local milk
Type: Cows milk, hard-pressed, full fat, vegetarian

The Latham family have been cheese-makers for four generations and the farm dates back to 1775 when cheeses were sent to London by the Shropshire Union Canal. Cheesemaking is still very much a family business although, over the last ten years, the dairy has been greatly extended and modernised. Milk from 18 local farms is collected to make 3,000 tonnes of cheese each year, principally Cheshire (traditional and rindless), although Wensleydale, Leicester, Double Gloucester and Caerphilly are all made regularly.

KNOWLE LOG

Lyn and Jenny Jenner, Nut Knowle Farm, World's End, Gun Hill, Horam, East Sussex
Artisan maker using the farm's own milk
Type: Goats milk, soft, full fat, vegetarian

Mould-ripened cheese with a light creamy flavour and superb texture.

Made in the manner of Camembert but sold in 2.2 lb (1 kg) logs for cutting. *See also* CAPRINI.

LACTIC CURD CHEESE

David Williams, Plas Dairy Farm, Llanfaelog, Ty Croes, Anglesey, Gwynedd
Artisan maker using the farm's own milk
Type: Cows and goats milk, soft, low to medium fat, vegetarian

Lactic, or acid curd, cheeses are made without rennet. The milk is set by natural bacteriological action when raw milk is used, or by the addition of a starter to pasteurised milk. The earliest cheeses were probably formed this way in prehistoric times. David Williams's cows and goats graze the clover-rich swards just a mile from the coast and produce the milk used to make a range of low-fat (9½%) and medium-fat (18%) soft cheeses. Prizewinners at the Nantwich Show, the cheeses have a distinctive, refreshing, lactic taste. The cows milk variety is available plain, with freshly crushed garlic and herbs, with chives and fresh herbs, or with freshly ground pepper. The medium-fat, goats milk cheese is supplied plain or with added garlic and herbs. All cheeses are supplied in 4 oz (120 g) tubs. They are ideal for spreading. *See also* LOCH ARTHUR FARMHOUSE CHEESE, VULSCOMBE.

LADY LLANOVER

Don and Karen Ross, Little Acorn Products, Mesen Fach Farm, Bethania, Llanon, Dyfed
Artisan maker. Visitors by appointment
Type: Unpasteurised ewes milk, hard-pressed, full fat, vegetarian

The only cheese I have discovered which is rind-washed with saffron, a process which imparts a distinctive colour to the rind. Combines the rich smoothness of a ewes milk cheese with tangy 'bite'. The 5 lb (2.3 kg) rounds mature for up to four months. *See also* ACORN.

LANARK BLUE

H.J. Errington and Co., Walston Braehead, Ogscastle, Carnwath, Strathclyde
Artisan maker using the farm's own milk
Type: Unpasteurised ewes milk, semi-hard, mould ripened

It may have been Humphrey Errington's knowledge of history (he read the subject at Cambridge) which inspired him to lead a revival of Scottish ewes milk cheeses, but it was modern invention that turned Lanark Blue from a dream to a reality. The 400 sheep, grazing pastures 1,000 ft (300 m) above sea level overlooking the valley of the upper Clyde, are split into two flocks. These lamb at different times of the year, March and October, thus extending the milking period. The farm has Britain's first rotary milking-parlour for sheep, a model of efficiency, but from that point on everything is done by hand. A Roquefort mould is added as a powder to the milk, and the curd is ladled into moulds before being naturally drained. Cheeses are brine-dipped twice, then turned and ripened for around three months before being scraped and wrapped. The result is a superb greeny-blue veined, mould-ripened product, an international prizewinner, described as 'Scotland's Roquefort'. *See also* DUNSYRE BLUE.

LANCASHIRE

Type: Cows milk, hard or semi-hard, full fat

When times were hard and butchers' meat scarce, Lancashire made do with its famous toasted cheese, the 'Leigh Toaster'. Lancashire can be softer than other English cheeses and spreads like butter when three months old. It has much in common with Caerphilly, except that it is allowed to mature to eight weeks or more. Lancashire was originally made from mixed curds, freshly separated curds being mixed with curd that had been kept for several days. In this way the acid that gives the cheese its markedly white colour was allowed to develop. Before the last war there were 200 farms making Lancashire in the old-fashioned way, from two-day-old curd, but when the Butlers of Lower Barker Farm decided to revive the craft in 1969 they were almost alone in their endeavours. It took time and trouble to make buttery and creamy Lancashire that could be matured for up to six months, whereas the mass-produced factory substitute was white, dry, acidic and more likely to be sold in six weeks. At the Nantwich Show, the judges now divide Lancashire into two classes, the new 'Acid' or 'Single Acid' Lancashire and the old-fashioned Farmhouse 'Fatty' Lancashire. The unpasteurised traditionals made by J.J. and R. KIRKHAM have been highly praised. *See also*: TOM BARRON FARMS (traditional), BUTLER'S FARMHOUSE (traditional and rindless), CARRON LODGE (traditional and rindless, DEW-LAY PRODUCTS (traditional), GRACEFIELD SELECT (traditional), GREENFIELDS DAIRY, SANDHAM'S (cloth-bound traditionals), SHORROCK'S LANCASHIRE CHEESE (unpasteurised traditionals), SINGLETON'S (traditional and rindless), WOLFEN MILL LANCASHIRE CHEESE (traditional and rindless).

LAUGHTON

Kevin and Alison Blunt, Greenacres Farm, Whitesmith, Lewes, East Sussex
Artisan maker using the farm's and other local milk. Visitors welcome
Type: Unpasteurised goats milk, soft, full fat, vegetarian

Made to the same recipe as GOLDEN CROSS, this is the 2½ lb (1.1 kg) log-shaped version for counter cutting. Mould-ripened cheese, similar to a Sainte-Maure, lightly dusted with charcoal before maturing for 4–5 weeks. *See also* CHABIS, FLOWER MAIRE.

LAURELS FARM CHESHIRE

Joseph Heler, Laurels Farm, Hatherton, Nantwich, Crewe, Cheshire
Creamery using the farm's own and other local milk. Visitors by appointment
Type: Cows milk, hard-pressed, full fat

Makers of fine Cheshire cheese since 1957, carrying on a tradition started by Joseph Heler's grandmother at the turn of the century. The farm milks around 500 cows but production was greatly expanded when a new dairy was opened in 1991. The dairy now produces 5,000 tonnes each year of Cheshire and other English territorial cheeses. The farm's Cheshire and Caerphilly cheese have both secured a first prize at the Nantwich Show, and the Cheshire with spring onion has been highly praised. Cheese can be bought direct from the farm but telephone (01270) 841500 to check opening times before calling.

LAVERBREAD CHEESE

Sue and Huw Jones, Llanboidy Cheese-makers, Cilowen-Uchaf, Login, Whitland, Dyfed
Artisan maker using the farm's own milk. Visitors welcome
Type: Unpasteurised cows milk, hard-pressed, full fat

Laverbread (Bara Lawr) is a misleading name, for this cheese does not resemble bread at all. Laver is a fine seaweed sometimes called sea-spinach. It clings to the rocks, resembling strands of silk, and has long been gathered for food. It used to be cured on the seashore in thatched drying houses, but now more controlled methods are used to remove sand and grit before the seaweed is boiled for 5–6 hours. Laverbread is sold in Swansea market (amongst other places) and looks for all the world like a dark-brown jelly. It has a taste all its own. Llanboidy Cheesemakers make 10 lb (4.5 kg) rounds of cheese containing genuine laverbread, matured for up to four months. *See also* LLANBOIDY.

LAVISTOWN

Olivia Goodwillie, Lavistown, Co. Kilkenny, Republic of Ireland
Artisan maker using the farm's own milk. Visitors by appointment
Type: Unpasteurised cows milk, semi-hard, full fat

Swaledale-type cheese, moist and creamy when young. The 3 lb (1.4 kg) rounds develop an old-fashioned Wensleydale crumbliness and a sharper flavour after six weeks.

LEAFIELD

Rodney Whitworth, Abbey Farm, Goosey, Faringdon, Oxfordshire
Artisan maker
Type: Ewes milk, hard-pressed, full fat, vegetarian

A 'character' cheese in all respects: the exterior rind is rugged, the body of the cheese firm and golden, the aroma delightfully flowery and the flavour dominant and lasting. Made in 8 in (20 cm) wheels which will mature to a great age. *See also* OXFORD BUTTONS.

LEGEND

J.J. Saunders, Emborough Farm Foods, Old Down Farm, Emborough, Somerset
Farmhouse maker

Type: Cows milk, hard-pressed, full fat

Emborough Farm has its own fanciful legend to explain the arrival of cheese-making in Somerset many centuries ago. Monks on a pilgrimage to Glastonbury Abbey took shelter in the caves of Cheddar Gorge during a storm. When the milk they were carrying in leather pouches was presented to the Bishop, it had magically turned to cheese. Emborough Farm produces an attractively black-waxed miniature Cheddar, which is presented in an intriguing hessian purse. An ideal gift and certainly a novel way to carry home your Cheddar cheese.

LEICESTER *see* RED LEICESTER

LINCOLNSHIRE POACHER

Simon Jones, F.W. Read & Sons, Ulceby Grange, Alford, Lincolnshire
Artisan maker using the farm's own milk
Type: Unpasteurised cows milk, hard-pressed, full fat

It was in 1917 that the Jones family began farming at Ulceby Grange, home of one of the very few cheeses made near the east coast of England. The farm's pedigree herd provides milk for this new Cheddar-type cheese, which is matured for 7–8 months and is close textured and firm flavoured, with a bitter-sweet finish that has been highly praised. Sold in 56 lb (25 kg) and 20 lb (9 kg) rounds, and 5 lb (2.3 kg) truckles. A favourite with Lincolnshire poachers everywhere!

LITTLE DERBY

Mr and Mrs D. Fowler, Forest Farm, Small Lane, Earlswood, West Midlands
Artisan maker using the farm's own milk. Visitors by appointment

Type: Cows milk, hard-pressed, full fat, vegetarian

Fowlers of Earlswood can claim to be the oldest cheesemaking family in Great Britain; they were making Derby cheese in the Peak District in 1840, and in 1918 they moved to Earlswood. In the nineteenth century, Derby cheese not made in the county of its birth was called Little Derby; after a gap of 50 years, the Fowlers brought this cheese back into manufacture. The milk comes from a Friesian herd grazing the rich Arden pastures, and the cheese is made without annatto colouring in the manner of the original Derby. The 28 lb (13 kg) truckles are dressed and turned regularly, and matured in the farm's cellars for at least seven months. The cheesecloth is removed and the cheeses are washed in red wine before being despatched. Good enough to take first prize at the Bakewell Show. Cheese can be bought at the farm but telephone (01564) 702329 to check opening times before calling.

LITTLE RYDINGS

Mary Holbrook, Sleight Farm House, Timsbury, Bath, Avon
Artisan maker using the farm's own milk
Type: Unpasteurised ewes milk, soft, medium fat

Camembert-style 7 oz (200 g) rounds, bloomy and soft-textured. The cheese is naturally ripened to a fuller flavour and the rind develops small brown freckles. *See also* MENDIP.

LLANBOIDY

Sue and Huw Jones, Llanboidy Cheese-makers, Cilowen-Uchaf, Login, Whitland, Dyfed
Artisan maker using the farm's own milk. Visitors by appointment

Type: Unpasteurised cows milk, hard-pressed, full fat, vegetarian

Llanboidy Farmhouse cheese is unique, probably the only cheese in the world made with milk from the rare Red Poll cattle. These are gentle, docile beasts, cross-bred from the old Norfolk and Suffolk cows. The 10 lb (4.5 kg) wheels of creamy cheese, which form a natural rind, are matured from 2–10 months. *See also* LAVERBREAD.

LLANGLOFFAN

Leon and Joan Downey, Llangloffan Farm, Castle Morris, Haverfordwest, Dyfed
Artisan maker using the farm's own milk. Visitors welcome
Type: Unpasteurised cows milk, hard-pressed, full fat, non-animal rennet

Leon and Joan Downey should go down in history as having brought Farmhouse cheesemaking back to Wales. They have featured on many television and radio programmes, extolling the virtues of cheese made on the farm. Back in the 1970s Leon was principal viola player with the Hallé Orchestra but now he makes traditional Farmhouse cheese instead of music. Many have followed the path the Downeys trod (not always with success) but it was they who gave the Principality back its cheesemaking heritage. Llangloffan Farmhouse cheese is hand-made, using milk from the Downeys' own herd of Jersey cows. Flaky and with a delightful flavour, it is finished with a natural crust. Red Llangloffan is the same cheese with additional chives and garlic. The farm has gained both HRH the Prince of Wales's Award and a business environment award. The milk and herbs are produced without artificial fertilisers or pesticides. Amongst those who have praised the cheese are Patrick Rance, Chris Kelly and Michael Barry (of the BBC programme *Food and Drink*),

Derek Cooper of Radio 4's *Food Programme*, Sandy Carr and Lucia van der Post.

The pride that Leon and Joan take in their craft is a delight to watch, and the Llangloffan Farmhouse Cheese Centre attracts thousands of visitors each year. So many, in fact, that it is one of the premier tourist attractions on the Pembrokeshire coast. There are facilities for all the family. Visitors can watch cheesemaking at the farm between April and September; but telephone (01348) 891241 before calling to check opening times. The farm shop is open all year, every day except Sunday.

LOCHABER SMOKED

Macdonald's Smoked Products, Glenuig, Lochailort, Inverness, Highland
Artisan maker and specialist smoker
Type: Cows milk, soft, full fat

Soft, cream cheese, rolled in oatmeal in the true Scottish manner and then smoked. Sold in 8 oz (225 g), 4 oz (110 g) and 2 oz (50 g) sizes, it has a shelf life of around four weeks. Mr Macdonald also produces smoked rounds of a Cheddar-type 'Islander' cheese.

LOCH ARTHUR FARMHOUSE CHEESE

Barry Graham, Loch Arthur Creamery, Camphill Village Trust, Beeswing, Dumfries and Galloway
Artisan maker using the farm's own milk. Visitors welcome
Type: Unpasteurised cows milk, hard-pressed, full fat, vegetarian

Loch Arthur Creamery was opened in 1985 by the Camphill Village Trust, which has established communities living and working with mentally handicapped adults. Their traditional cloth-bound Cheddar has been widely praised, winning prizes at the Royal Highland and Bakewell Shows. (Sadly, demand currently far outstrips supply.) The cheese is firm and dry, made only from the farm's small herd of Ayrshire cows, which has full organic DEMETER status. (The initials DEMETER signify a standard of soil management widely accepted throughout Europe, broadly equivalent to the Soil Association's accreditation in the UK.) The Cheddar is produced in 20 lb (9 kg) rounds and is also available with mixed herbs or caraway seeds. The farm also produces a rennet-free true lactic curd cheese and Loch Arthur Crannog, a fresh, soft cheese described as 'mild yet flavourful', which is available plain or with mixed herbs. Finished in 8 oz (225 g) waxed rounds. Cheese can be bought direct from the dairy, but telephone (01387) 776296 before calling to check availability.

LOCKERBIE CHEDDAR

The Cheese Company, Lockerbie Creamery, Dumfries and Galloway
Creamery
Type: Cows milk, hard-pressed, full fat

Lockerbie is a leading brand of Cheddar in Scotland. The mild or mature Cheddar (sometimes coloured with annatto) is available in most major stores. *See also* THE CHEESE COMPANY.

LODDISWELL CHEESE

Jocelyn and Bill Martin, Blackdown Farm, Rings Lane, Loddiswell, Kingsbridge, Devon
Artisan maker using the farm's own and other local milk. Visitors welcome
Type: Goats milk, soft, medium fat, vegetarian

Blackdown Farm is situated in South Hams, a beautiful part of South Devon, lying 650 ft (200 m) above sea level in the Devon hills. Jocelyn and Bill treat their animals more as pets than as farm stock, and the result is a superb range of goats cheeses. Pasteurised and raw milk types are available. Loddiswell Banon is an unpasteurised, full-fat goats cheese. The 2 oz (55 g) rounds are soft and unpressed, sometimes made with chives, garlic and herbs, or marinated in olive oil. Loddiswell Blackdown is made with pasteurised goats milk. A fresh and clean-tasting cheese, lightly pressed in 3 lb (1.5 kg) and 6 oz (170 g) rounds. Loddiswell Fresh Jersey is made with pasteurised cows milk from tried and trusted local herds. The Jersey milk makes for a rich and luscious cheese, available plain, with chives, garlic, or herbs and walnuts. Lightly pressed in 3 lb (1.5 kg) and 4 oz (100 g) rounds. Loddiswell Hazelwood is a Farmhouse cheese, also made with pasteurised cows milk. Mild but with a distinctive flavour, it is lightly pressed in 3 lb (1.5 kg) rounds. Visitors are welcomed and cheese can be bought at the farm, but telephone (01548) 821387 before calling to check opening times.

LOHOLONE, SPICED

David Reed, Home Farm, Beamish Museum, Beamish, Co. Durham
Artisan maker. Visitors welcome
Type: Unpasteurised cows milk, semi-soft, medium fat, vegetarian

Washed curd cheese containing a warming mixture of cumin and cloves. The fat content is reduced to approximately 38%. *See also* BEAMISH.

LONG CLAWSON CHEESES

Long Clawson Dairy, Melton Mowbray, Leicestershire
Creamery. Visitors by appointment
Type: Cows milk, semi-hard and hard-pressed, full fat

Long Clawson Dairy was founded as a farmers' co-operative in 1911 and is still going strong, with 50 members sending their milk to the dairies at Melton Mowbray and Harby. This is Britain's biggest producer of blue Stilton, the 'King of Cheeses'. Around 3,000 tonnes is made each year, with smaller quantities of vegetarian Stilton, white Stilton, white Stilton with citrus peel and BLUE VINNEY. Long Clawson also make an extensive range of specialist cheeses at their manufacturing unit at Bottesford. Many can be bought direct from the dairy (telephone (01664) 822332 for details) and there is also the superb Long Clawson Cheese Shop at 8 Windsor Street, Melton Mowbray. Telephone (01664) 62257 for opening times. *See also* BEAUCHAMP, BELLSHIRE, BELVOIR BLUE, CHEDDAR (MATURE WITH RICH FRUIT CAKE), CHESHIRE (BLUE), CHARNWOOD, COACHMAN, COTSWOLD, COTTAGE CHEESE, ENGLAND'S CHOICE, HIGHLAND CHOICE, HUNTSMAN, NUTCRACKER, NUTWOOD, PANEER, RED WINDSOR, RUTLAND, SHROPSHIRE BLUE, WHIRL, WENSLEYDALE (NEW RECIPE).

LONGLEY FARM COTTAGE CHEESE

J. and E. Dickenson, Longley Farm, Holmfirth, Huddersfield, West Yorkshire
Small creamery
Type: Cows milk, soft, low fat, vegetarian

The Dickenson family have been Yorkshire farmers for several generations and now employ their skills to make a renowned cottage cheese and other dairy products. They are the world's largest producers of Yorkshire Curd, the filling for the delightful curd tarts.

LONGMAN'S CHEDDAR (J. K. LONGMAN)

J.K. Longman, Ditcheat Hill Farm, Ditcheat, Shepton Mallet, Somerset
Farmhouse maker using the farm's own milk. Visitors by appointment

Type: Cows milk, hard-pressed, full fat, vegetarian

Makers of an excellent rind-on traditional Cheddar in 60 lb (27 kg) rounds. Production is around 400 tonnes each year. Cheese can be bought direct from the farm but only in the morning and not normally on Mondays. Best to telephone (01749) 860213 before calling.

LONGMAN'S CHEDDAR (W.H. LONGMAN & SONS)

W.H. Longman & Sons, North Leaze Farm, North Cadbury, Yeovil, Somerset
Farmhouse maker using the farm's own milk
Type: Cows milk, hard-pressed, full fat

Experienced makers of Cheddar cheese in rindless 40 lb (20 kg) blocks. Production is around 500 tonnes each year, normally made with animal rennet. It is not possible to buy cheese in small quantities at the farm.

LONGRIDGE FELL

J.M. Nuttall, Hartington Creamery, Buxton, Derbyshire
Creamery
Type: Cows milk, hard-pressed, full fat

Wensleydale-type cheese, made using a traditional Lancashire recipe, gently smoked over English oak for 18 hours. Soft, creamy, with mellow flavour. *See also* DAIRY CREST.

LOVINGTON FARMHOUSE CHEDDAR

Simon Barber, Lovington Farmhouse Cheesemakers, Lovington, Castle Cary, Somerset
Farmhouse maker using the farm's own milk

Type: Cows milk, hard-pressed, full fat, vegetarian

An experienced and respected maker, producing 1,000 tonnes of rindless Cheddar in 40 lb (20 kg) blocks per year. It is not possible to buy cheese in small quantities at the farm.

LOW-FAT CHEESES

Low-fat cheeses, other than those which have been traditionally made from skimmed milk or whey (e.g. COTTAGE CHEESE, DORSET BLUE VINNEY, RICOTTA), fall outside the scope of this book. Anyone concerned about their fat intake should buy the best cheese they can find and consume half as much as they would deem 'normal'. In this way they will continue to enjoy the pleasures of good taste and might even save money.

LUBBORN CHEESE *see* SOMERSET BRIE

LUNE VALLEY SMOKED COBBLES

Peter Gott, Sillfield Farm, Kendal, Cumbria
Artisan maker
Type: Unpasteurised cows milk, hard-pressed, full fat, vegetarian

Lune Valley Lancashire cheese is formed by hand into miniature rounds then lightly smoked over chips of beech and old oak whisky barrels. Available in four varieties: plain garlic, chilli and garlic, chives and onion, and hot black pepper.

LYE CROSS CHEDDAR

Alvis Brothers, Lye Cross Farm, Redhill, Bristol, Avon
Farmhouse maker using the farm's own milk. Visitors welcome

Type: Cows milk, hard-pressed, full fat, vegetarian

Alvis Brothers have been making excellent Cheddar cheese for over 30 years. Local farms supply 4,000 gallons (20,000 litres) of milk each day, enough to make around 1,500 tonnes of Cheddar a year in rindless 40 lb (20 kg) blocks. The curd is still turned and stacked by hand in a traditional cheddaring process, although only non-animal rennet is used. Alvis Brothers have gained a well-deserved reputation for using only milk that is extremely hygienic and antibiotic free. They rely on healthy cows, fed on natural foods (mostly grass), rather than risk taints from other feeds which could result in off-flavours or a soft and weak-bodied cheese that would not keep well. Their business is based on the provision of fresh, sweet, pure milk. Methods have been updated over the years but their cheesemaking continues to depend on a natural process. As Alvis Brothers say, 'Nature has no time for computerisation and monotonous conformity; only those who have experience and practical skills are able to succeed in making something that bit better.' The Cheddar is graded at various ages, to be sold as Mild, Mature (9–12 months), Extra Mature (12–14 months) or Vintage (over 14 months). It is generally supplied in rindless 10 lb (5 kg) blocks, or black-waxed 2.2 lb (1 kg) and 1.1 lb (500 g) miniatures. Oak-smoked Cheddar is available, in cut wedges. Lyegrano, produced on the same farm, is a very hard and granular, Italian-style cows milk cheese with a Parmesan-like flavour and aroma. Sold in rindless 40 lb (20 kg) blocks or ready-grated. Organic Mature Cheddar is also made in the farm's dairy, from milk certified organic to the standards of the Soil Association. It is sold in 10 lb (5 kg) or 5 lb (2.5 kg) rindless blocks and 11½ oz (325 g) portions. Alvis Brothers have an excellent farm shop, just off the A38 south of Bristol, which is well worth a visit. Telephone (01934) 862320 to check opening times.

LYMESWOLD, A LOST CHEESE

The story of Lymeswold is a sad one. It began life in Dairy Crest's research department at Crudgington near Telford and went on to take the country by storm. Launched as England's first new cheese for 200 years, it was universally acclaimed as a rival to imported blue cheeses and even gained a mention on the *Nine O'Clock News*. The cheese was moulded in short lengths of plastic drain-pipe (hardly traditional) but it made no matter, the orders just poured in. Exactly ten years later, by which time Lymeswold was largely forgotten, Dairy Crest announced that they were to cease manufacture. One might be allowed a wry smile at the rush of commentators who insisted that they had never liked the product and that it deserved to die. It was a different story during the heady days of 1982.

MAGDALEN FARM

John Woodward, Magdalen Farm, Winsham, Chard, Somerset
Artisan maker using the farm's own milk
Type: Cows milk, soft and hard-pressed, full fat, vegetarian

Magdalen Farm is an educational charity running on-farm training courses for young people. The farm is registered organic to the standards of the Soil Association and keeps a herd of 35 MRI (Dutch cross) cattle. The youngsters help to make a range of hard and soft cheeses which are sold in local shops.

MALTHOUSE COTTAGE FARM CHEESES

Jenny Ferris, Malthouse Cottage Farm, Ashington, Pulborough, West Sussex
Artisan maker using the farm's own milk. Visitors by appointment
Type: Goats milk, soft, full fat, vegetarian

Jenny Ferris saw a goat advertised in her local paper, bought it on impulse and now has a flock of 30 white Saanens and a thriving cheese business. Malthouse Soft is a Coulommier-type, with a mould-ripened crust. It is firm and mild when fresh, maturing to soft and tangy when ripe. Supplied in 4 oz (110 g) rounds, which when cut in half and grilled make a good first course. It also makes an excellent soufflé. The cheese is available rolled in herbs to form 5 oz (150 g) herb logs. Balls of Malthouse cheese are marinated in finest olive oil and aromatic herbs organically grown on the farm. These can be served from the jar or lightly grilled. They are supplied in 0.5 litre and 2 litre jars, which look great in the kitchen. The farm is certified organic to the standards of the Soil Association. *See also* BURNDELL.

MALVERN

Nick Hodgetts, Malvern Cheesewrights, Manor House, Lower Wick, Worcester
Artisan maker using the farm's own milk
Type: Unpasteurised ewes milk, semi-hard, full fat, vegetarian

Malvern cheese has been internationally acclaimed. Only milk from high health-status flocks is used in its manufacture. The recipe has been adapted from Wensleydale, and the cheese is smooth and lightly salted with a subtle Dales-type flavour. It matures to sweet nuttiness after 3–5 months. Available in 5 lb (2.5 kg) wheels, 3½ lb (1.5 kg) truckles and 14 oz (400 g) miniatures.

See also ELGAR, HEREFORD RED, SEVERN SISTERS, SINGLE WORCESTER, SYMONDS YAT, WORCESTERSHIRE GOLD.

MANCHEGO

Heritage Cheese, The Creamery, Glan-Yr-Afon Estate, Aberystwyth, Dyfed
Creamery
Type: Cows milk, hard-pressed, full fat

Manchego is Spain's oldest and most popular cheese, made in the central region of La Mancha from which it derives its name. Manchego is made in large rounds and develops a hard, yellow rind which often carries an elaborate pattern derived from the basket moulds. The cheese sometimes displays holes, in the Swiss manner. *See also* HERITAGE.

MARLOW

Stephen Fletcher, Ramhall Dairy Sheep, Ram Hall, Berkswell, West Midlands
Artisan maker using the farm's own milk
Type: Unpasteurised ewes milk, soft, full fat, vegetarian

Soft and mellow cheese, lightly tinted on the surface with annatto.

MARYLAND FARM CHEDDAR

Val Boothman, A.J. and R.G. Barber, Maryland Farm, Ditcheat, Somerset
Farmhouse maker using the farm's own and other local milk. Visitors welcome
Type: Cows milk, hard-pressed, full fat

One of the largest manufacturers of Farmhouse cheese in Somerset, producing around 5,000 tonnes each year of excellent Cheddar in rindless 40 lb (20 kg) blocks, with smaller volumes of the other English territorial cheeses. Paul Barber, 'Champion Farmer' in 1991, farms 2,000 acres and is a leading exponent of what could be termed 'the Somerset Triangle'. This form of husbandry is common enough in Somerset but requires highly efficient management. It works like this: (1) use milk from your own herd to make cheese, (2) feed the surplus whey to pigs, who thrive on it, (3) use the resulting pig slurry as a low-cost natural fertiliser which will improve grass yield, enabling the cows to provide more milk ... and back to step one. The cheese is sold under the Maryland Farm or Haystack labels, in 10 lb (5 kg) blocks or 4½ lb (2 kg) rounds, and frequently appears under supermarkets' own names. The farm also makes black-waxed truckles of mature Farmhouse Cheddar in 2 lb (1 kg) and 11½ lb (2 kg) sizes. A wide range of cheeses are on sale in the excellent farm shop, open Tuesday–Friday, and some items can be ordered by post. Telephone (01749) 860666 for details.

MATURE MEADOWS

Valerie Morris, Ashdale Cheese, Town Head Farm, Askwith, Otley, West Yorkshire
Artisan maker using the farm's own milk
Type: Unpasteurised goats milk, hard-pressed, full fat, vegetarian

Robust-flavoured cheese, designed for long keeping and matured for 6–12 months. Supplied in waxed 4 lb (1.8 kg) rounds and 10 oz (280 g) miniatures. *See also* ASHDALE.

McLELLAND SCOTTISH CHEESES

A. McLelland & Son Ltd, New Cheese Market, 80 Albion Street, Glasgow
Creamery proprietors and cheese traders
Type: All types of cheese

The leading Scottish cheese merchants since 1850, McLelland sell products from all over Scotland, including Arran, Dunlop, Galloway, Islay and Orkney. The company has worked hard to improve quality and expand the distribution of island cheeses, and the McLelland Cup (awarded annually) is one of Scotland's premier cheese awards. McLelland and MacCheddar rindless Cheddar is available white or coloured in 10 lb (5 kg) blocks.

MELDON

Rachel Stephens, Curworthy Cheese, Stockbeare Farm, Jacobstowe, Okehampton, Devon
Artisan maker using the farm's own milk
Type: Cows milk, semi-hard, full fat

CURWORTHY cheese (see entry) with whole-grain English mustard and lightly moistened with ale, producing an excellent blend of flavours. The cheese secured a first prize at the Royal Bath and West Show. Available in 1 lb (450 g) and 3 lb (1.4 kg) rounds.

MENALLACK FARMHOUSE

John and Caryl Minson, Menallack Farm, Treverva, Cornwall
Artisan maker using the farm's own milk. Visitors welcome
Type: Unpasteurised cows milk, soft, full fat, vegetarian

Soft and creamy, golden-rinded cheese, usually sold around eight weeks old. Sometimes made with added chives and garlic. It can be held back for over four months, by which time it has developed a deep and lasting bite. Also available smoked, the 5 lb (2.3 kg) truckles and 1 lb (450 g) miniatures are sold in the excellent farm shop (open all year) or can be despatched by post. Telephone (01326) 40333 for details. *See also* NANTERROW.

MENDIP

Mary Holbrook, Sleight Farm House, Timsbury, Bath, Avon
Artisan maker using the farm's own milk
Type: Unpasteurised goats milk, hard-pressed, full fat

Made in plastic colanders, which leave a distinctive 'basket' pattern on the oiled rind. The 5lb (2.3 kg) cheeses are pale yellow in colour and the creamy paste is dotted with small holes. Mendip is matured for 2–8 months but remains moist and mild. The farm also produces a number of naturally drained soft, fresh cheeses in 4 oz (110 g) rounds. These are sold plain, or with the addition of garlic and herbs, pepper, or rosemary. All products are made with natural sea-salt, adding a distinctive flavour and character. Only a few shops have the privilege of stocking Mary Holbrook's cheeses, for production is limited. No matter, excellence is worth seeking out. Olivia Mills, herself a cheesemaker and a leading international authority on sheep dairying, has described Mary Holbrook's cheeses as 'the best available anywhere'. Sleight Farm won a 'Best in Show' award in a specialist cheesemakers' competition, when a remarkable 300 varieties competed, and also secured a first prize at the International Food Exhibition. Mary's sheep and goats graze a hillside which has breathtaking views over the countryside south of Bath, not far from the farm where Joseph Harding and his family did so much to improve the quality of Cheddar. Cheese can sometimes be bought at the farm door but do telephone (01761) 470620 before calling to avoid a wasted journey. *See also* ASH PYRAMID, EMLETT, FETA, LITTLE RYDINGS, TYMSBORO', TYNING.

MENDIP FOODS *see* CATHEDRAL CITY

MERLIN

Gill Pateman, Merlin Cheeses, Tyn-y-Llwyn, Pontrhydygroes, Ystrad Meurig, Dyfed
Artisan maker using the farm's own milk. Visitors welcome
Type: Unpasteurised goats milk, hard-pressed, full fat, vegetarian

A superb range of 2 lb (1 kg) and 7 oz (200 g) round cheeses, waxed in different colours. Merlin in a black wax is a natural, white, Cheddar-type cheese, available fresh and mild, or rich and mature. Merlin in a yellow wax is a sweeter cheese with golden walnuts. Merlin in a red wax contains green olives. Merlin is also available smoked over a mixture of oak and ash, then rolled in paprika. Other varieties are enlivened with pineapple, ginger, pear and cinnamon, apricots, celery, garlic and chives, or herbs. Cheese can be bought at the farm; telephone (01974) 282636 to check opening times.

MERLIN'S SANDWICH

Don and Karen Ross, Little Acorn Products, Mesen Fach Farm, Bethania, Llanon, Dyfed
Artisan maker. Visitors by appointment
Type: Cows milk, hard-pressed, full fat, vegetarian

Claimed to be the ultimate sandwich, this is Cheddar cheese with horse-radish (an interesting combination) coloured by a ribbon of Cheddar with chives running through the centre. The 6 lb (2.7 kg) loaves will mature for up to six months. *See also* ACORN.

MILLEENS

Veronica and Norman Steele, Milleens Cheese, Eyeries, Beara, Co. Cork, Republic of Ireland
Artisan maker using the farm's own

and other local milk. Visitors by appointment
Type: Unpasteurised cows milk, soft, full fat

Created in 1978, Milleens is credited with being the first Irish Farmhouse cheese. It has been highly praised, Kathy Dineen in the *Irish Times* describing it as 'the most perfect cheese imaginable'. Milk from cows grazing the Beara Peninsula is used to make a cheese which is very buttery with a rich and flowery aroma and taste. The 3 lb (1.4 kg) rounds have a washed-rind finish in a distinctive orange colour. Milleens Dotes is the curious name given to small, washed-rind 8 oz (225 g) rounds of Milleens. A 'dote' was a little gift distributed at a wedding – how suitable!

MILLWAY STILTON

Millway Foods Ltd, Colston Lane, Harby, Melton Mowbray, Leicestershire
Creamery
Type: Cows milk, various types, full fat

Millway Foods are best known for Stilton; their dairy at Harby is one of the most technically advanced in the industry, producing over 20% of the Stilton sold in the UK. Stilton is available in a wide variety of cutting sizes and presentation packs, and the jars and casserole pots are particular favourites in the Christmas hamper. Stilton is also available made with vegetarian rennet. The company has successfully diversified into a range of speciality cheeses, collecting numerous awards for innovative products based on English territorial cheeses. Examples include: Stilton with Double Gloucester; Cheddar with elderberry wine or with pizza herbs; Double Gloucester with chives and onion, with mustard seed, or combined with soft cheese flavoured with garlic and herbs. There is also Red Leicester or Cheddar with walnuts and a smoked Cheddar

with paprika. *See also* SHROPSHIRE BLUE, STILTON (WHITE).

MIZEN

Sean Ferry and Bill Hogan, West Cork Natural Cheese, Schull, Co. Cork, Republic of Ireland
Artisan maker using local milk
Type: Unpasteurised cows milk, hard-pressed, medium fat

Sean and Bill studied the making of Sbrinz together in Switzerland, and now combine their skills to make this rock-hard, Swiss-style cheese. Matured for at least 18 months until slightly granulated but very smooth, with a sweet and sour interplay. Ideal grating or dessert cheese, sold in naturally rinded 40–110 lb (20–50 kg) cartwheels. *See also* DESMOND, GABRIEL.

MOILLON

Nachi Elkin, Gedi Enterprises, Plumridge Farm, Stagg Hill, Barnet, Hertfordshire
Artisan maker using the farm's own milk. Visitors welcome
Type: Goats milk, semi-soft, full fat, vegetarian

Mature and sharp, with the earthy quality of a French peasant cheese, Moillon has been compared with a Saint-Maure. Sold in 5 oz (150 g) logs. *See also* CHAVANNES.

MONKS OF STRATA FLORIDA

Don and Karen Ross, Little Acorn Products, Mesen Fach Farm, Bethania, Llanon, Dyfed
Artisan maker. Visitors by appointment
Type: Cows milk, hard-pressed, full fat, vegetarian

A range of cheeses taking their name

from the monks of Abbaty Ystrad Fflur, the Abbey of Cors Goch Glan Teifi. Choose from Welsh Cheddar with malt whisky and toasted oatmeal, or with Grand Marnier, apricots and crushed walnuts, or with wine, herbs and garlic, or with laverbread and white wine. All are available in black-waxed 6 lb (2.7 kg) rounds and 14 oz (400 g) miniatures. For a special occasion, the Welsh Cheddar is made by hand into 'truffles' with vine fruits or apricots, laced with Tia Maria or rum, and presented in beribboned jars. *See also* ACORN.

MONT BELAIR

Traditional Cheese Company, Robinhood Industrial Estate, Clondalkin, Dublin, Republic of Ireland
Artisan maker using the farm's own milk
Type: Cows milk, semi-hard, full fat, vegetarian

The Traditional Cheese Company are distributors of a wide range of Irish Farmhouse cheeses. Mont Belair is a high-quality Gouda-type, made for them in Co. Westmeath.

MONTEREY JACK

Type: Cows milk, hard-pressed, full fat

Monterey Jack is one result of the Californian Gold Rush. A distant relative of Cheddar, it was developed from *queso del pais* (literally, 'cheese of the country') made by Spanish priests in the eighteenth century. A Scot named Davy Jacks, who was a prominent dairy farmer in Monterey around the time of the Gold Rush, stamped his name on his cheese and, as they say, the rest is history. The mild and white cheese is made by the boiled-curd method. It tends not to shrink when grilled and is used in the USA for cheeseburgers, providing a better flavour than the processed cheese we substitute. *Makers*

include AERON VALLEY FARM, HERITAGE and SOUTH CAERNARFON CREAMERY.

MONTGOMERY'S
UNPASTEURISED CHEDDAR

J.A. and E. Montgomery, Manor Farm, North Cadbury, Somerset
Farmhouse maker using the farm's own milk. Visitors by appointment
Type: Unpasteurised cows milk, hard-pressed, full fat

Montgomery's are renowned for the excellence of their traditional cheese. They have collected many awards, amongst them first prize in a tasting organised by *Good Food* magazine. The 11-month-old cheese was judged to have an 'attractive, golden colour with a nice rind and marbled, flaky surface. Clean, strong flavour. Rich and rounded with buttery, nutty notes and a dry but creamy texture.' Cheese can be bought from the farm but telephone (01963) 440243 to check opening times. You can also buy from the post office across the road.

MOORE CHEESE

Susan Moore, Cranes Watering Farm, Starston, Harleston, Norfolk
Artisan maker using the farm's own milk. Visitors by appointment
Type: Unpasteurised cows milk, soft, full fat, vegetarian

A range of cheeses made from Channel Islands milk and cream. The cream cheese, made from thick Jersey cream, is scandalously rich and tempting, whether plain or with herbs and garlic. *See also* DEPWADE, GROVEHILL, PULHAM PEPPER, STARSTON, WAVENEY.

MOZZARELLA

Type: Cows milk, semi-hard, low fat, vegetarian

Mozzarella belongs to the drawn curd (pasta filata) family of cheeses. The curd is heated in hot whey until it becomes dough-like, after which it is kneaded like bread until it can be pulled into long threads and has a mouldable texture. Traditional Italian Mozzarella was moulded into balls, although it has appeared in animal shapes or even as statuettes of the saints. It was traditionally made from buffalo milk but cows milk is now used. Glynn Christian suggests eating the cheese with orange slices and chillies, but Mozzarella is mainly used as a pizza topping. The cheese should be pure white, with a soft plastic texture and a mild delicate flavour that is vaguely sweet. Mozzarella is not made to keep; it is sold when two or three days old, and the colour indicates how fresh it is. Look for white cheese, never yellow. Creameries making Mozzarella include: CARNEVALE, DANSCO TOLONA, Golden Foods (see AVONMORE), HERITAGE, KINGDOM CHEESE, OLYMPIA, SOUTH CAERNARFON CREAMERY, WATERFORD FOODS, WEST ULSTER FARMERS. Mozzarella nearly became the first cheese to be manufactured 'behind bars' when plans were laid for 1,000 tonnes per year to be made at East Sutton Park women's prison, near Maidstone in Kent. There was an adequate supply of raw material (it is little realised that HM prisons are major milk producers with 19 herds supplying over 2½ million gallons (12 million litres) of milk each year) but the project was short lived.

NANNY'S GOAT CHEDDAR

Graham Fry, Cricket Malherbie Farms, Nether Stowey, Bridgwater, Somerset
Farmhouse maker using local milk. Visitors welcome
Type: Goats milk, hard-pressed, full fat, vegetarian

There is a touch of humour in the name of this goats milk Cheddar. Winner of the United Kingdom Cheese Guild's trophy for the best goat cheese at the Good Food Show, Nanny's cheese is matured for 3–6 months and sold in 40 lb (20 kg) rindless blocks and 2 lb (1 kg) black-waxed rounds. *See also* CRICKET MALHERBIE CHEDDAR.

NANTERROW

John and Caryl Minson, Menallack Farm, Treverva, Cornwall
Artisan maker using the farm's own milk. Visitors welcome
Type: Unpasteurised ewes milk, fresh, soft, full fat, vegetarian

Unique Cornish Feta, not excessively salty, available plain or with parsley, chives and garlic. Sold in 1 lb (450 g) vacuum packs. *See also* MENALLACK FARMHOUSE.

NANTYBWLA FARMHOUSE CHEESE

Edward and Eiddwen Morgan, Nantybwla, College Road, Carmarthen, Dyfed
Artisan maker using the farm's own milk
Type: Unpasteurised cows milk, hard-pressed, full fat, vegetarian

The Morgans have taken many prizes for Caerphilly cheese at the Royal Welsh Show. Only milk from their show-winning herd of 40 Erie pedigree Holsteins is used in a recipe that has been handed down through many generations of the family. The cheese is sold in 10 lb (4.5 kg) wheels, 5 lb (2.3 kg) truckles and 14 oz (400 g) miniatures. Also available smoked, with added chives, or with added garlic. Cheese can be ordered by post; telephone (01267) 237905 for details.

NEPICAR

Harold Woolley, British Sheep Dairy Products, Nepicar Farm, Wrotham Heath, Kent
Artisan maker using the farm's own milk. Visitors by appointment
Type: Ewes milk, hard-pressed, full fat, vegetarian

Pale cream in colour and very firm-bodied, Nepicar is pressed in 4½ lb (2 kg) and 1.1 lb (500 g) rounds and matured for a minimum of 90 days before sale. *See also* CAROLINA, CECELIA.

NORTH BRADON CHEDDAR

North Bradon Farm, Isle Abbotts, Taunton, Somerset
Farmhouse makers and cheese traders. Visitors welcome
Type: Cows milk, hard-pressed, full fat, vegetarian

North Bradon Farm produces 2,500 tonnes per year of mild and mature Cheddar in rindless 40 lb (20 kg) blocks and 60 lb (27 kg) traditionals as well as a range of English territorial cheeses. Cheese can be bought from the farm shop Monday–Saturday but telephone (01460) 281688 to check opening times before calling.

NORTHUMBERLAND

Mark Robertson, Northumberland Cheese Company, Soppitt Farm, Otterburn, Northumberland
Artisan maker using the farm's own milk. Visitors welcome
Type: Cows milk, hard-pressed, medium fat, vegetarian

A washed-curd cheese, creamy and smooth, mild at first bite but with a well-rounded aftertaste. Available plain (sometimes wrapped in nettles), smoked, with chives, with peppers or with garlic. The 1.1 lb (0.5 kg), 2.2 lb (1 kg), 4½ lb (2 kg), and 22 lb (10 kg) rounds (elliptical in shape) are matured for at least one month in the farm's eighteenth-century cheese store. The dairy is a popular tourist attraction, with over 10,000 visitors each year, but telephone (01830) 520276 to check opening times before calling. *See also* COQUETDALE, ELSDON, REDESDALE.

NOSON LAWEN

Don and Karen Ross, Little Acorn Products, Mesen Fach Farm, Bethania, Llanon, Dyfed
Artisan maker. Visitors by appointment
Type: Cows milk, hard-pressed, full fat, vegetarian

Welsh Cheddar and cashew nuts, marbled with Worcester sauce. Presented in black-waxed 6 lb (2.7 kg) rounds and 14 oz (400 g) miniatures. *See also* ACORN.

NUNS OF CAEN

Charles Martell and Son, Laurel Farm, Dymock, Gloucestershire
Artisan maker using local milk
Type: Unpasteurised ewes milk, hard-pressed, full fat, vegetarian

With a washed-rind exterior and sweet and silky interior, this ewes milk cheese is made to a recipe first employed by the nuns of Caen in Normandy, who in the thirteenth century derived their income from taxes levied on Minchinhampton in Gloucestershire. (Minchin is Old English for nun.) In 1307 it was recorded that the nuns owned 1,886 sheep, and their surplus milk surely found its way into cheese. Nuns of Caen is supplied in 5 lb (2.3 kg) rounds. *See also* SINGLE GLOUCESTER.

NUTCRACKER

Long Clawson Dairy, Melton Mow-bray, Leicestershire
Creamery
Type: Cows milk, hard-pressed, full fat

Cheddar with walnuts. *See also* LONG CLAWSON.

NUTTALL'S FINE CHEESES

J.M. Nuttall, Hartington Creamery, Buxton, Derbyshire
Creamery
Type: Cows milk, various

John M. Nuttall of Dove Dairy, Hartington, was a Victorian master cheesemaker. He began making cheese in 1886 and went on to gain a royal warrant from George V and many show prizes in the 1920s and 30s. The company that bears his name is now the speciality division of DAIRY CREST. Nuttall's Stilton is famous internationally. Over 2,000 tonnes of white and blue Stilton is made each year at Hartington, and frequently wins prizes at agricultural shows. A lightly smoked Stilton, in 4½ lb (2 kg) wheels, is also available. The company also distributes Cheddar from the Sturminster Newton Creamery, together with STURMINSTER OAK SMOKED CHEDDAR, LONGRIDGE FELL smoked cheese and a smoked Brie. Nutttall's English territorial range includes Red Leicester, Double Gloucester, sage Derby, Caerphilly, Wensleydale, Cheshire, a single-day curd Lancashire and a traditional Lancashire made from a mixture of two days' curd. Cheese cannot be bought from the factory but 'Ye Olde Cheese Shoppe' is only a short distance away, right in the middle of Hartington village opposite the duck pond. Telephone (01298) 84935 for details of opening times.

NUTWOOD

Long Clawson Dairy, Melton Mow-bray, Leicestershire
Creamery
Type: Cows milk, hard-pressed, full fat

Cheddar, flavoured with cider, raisins and hazelnuts. *See also* LONG CLAWSON.

OLD CHARLEVILLE

Golden Vale, Charleville, Co. Cork, Republic of Ireland
Creamery
Type: Cows milk, hard-pressed, full fat

Mature Cheddar, minimum 12 months old, packed in 10 lb (5 kg) rindless wheels.

OLDE SUSSEX

Michael Turner, Turners Dairies, Myrtle Grove Farm, Patching, Worthing, West Sussex
Artisan maker using the farm's own milk
Type: Unpasteurised cows milk, hard-pressed, full fat, vegetarian

Hand-made and traditionally pressed cheese. Matured for five months to develop a firm body, natural rind and a strong, distinctive flavour. Produced in 8 lb (3.6 kg) rounds. The cheese is also available as Sussex Smokey in 5 lb (2.3 kg) rounds which have been naturally smoked over hardwoods. *See also* SCRUMPY SUSSEX, SOUTHDOWN.

OLDE YORK

Judy Bell, Shepherds Purse, Leachfield Grange, Bellfields, Newsham, Thirsk, North Yorkshire
Artisan maker
Type: Unpasteurised ewes milk, soft, full fat, vegetarian

A range of wonderfully soft and delicate cheeses made by the Coulommier method. Olde York is available made to the original recipe, or with garlic and pepper, chives, green peppercorns, and as a hint-of-mint cheese that serves as a palate-refresher between courses. The 1 lb (450 g) round cheeses are finished in various coloured waxes. *See also* SHEPHERDS PURSE.

OLD SCOTLAND

David Doble, Old Scotland Farm, Shere, Guildford, Surrey
Artisan maker
Type: Cows milk, hard-pressed, full fat, vegetarian

Friesian milk is used to make this intensely flavoured cheese. Highly recommended by one of the best cheese retailers, Kirsty Smith of The Little Deli Company (see p. 210).

OLD SHIRE

Gareth Evans, South Caernarfon Creameries, Rhydygwstl, Chwilog, Pwllheli, Gwynedd
Creamery
Type: Cows milk, hard-pressed, full fat

To meet the demand for extra-mature Cheddar, the superlative Old Shire is matured for at least 15 months before being sold in rindless blocks or 7 lb (3 kg) rounds which are finished with a distinctive green wax. *See also* SOUTH CAERNARFON CREAMERY.

OLD WORCESTER WHITE

Alyson Anstey, Anstey's of Worcester, Broomhall Farm, Worcester
Artisan maker using the farm's own milk. Visitors welcome
Type: Unpasteurised cows milk, hard-pressed, full fat, vegetarian

Made two miles south of the city of Worcester, from the milk of the farm's own Friesian herd. Worcester White is very creamy and has a mellow flavour; it is highly recommended for cooking. Made in 7 lb (3 kg) truckles, which are calico bandaged, and in smaller sizes. Cheese can be bought from the shop on the farm but telephone (01905) 820232 to check opening times. *See also* DOUBLE WORCESTER, WORCESTER SAUCE CHEESE.

OL' SMOKY CHEDDAR

Graham Fry, Cricket Malherbie Farms, Nether Stowey, Bridgwater, Somerset
Farmhouse maker using the farm's own and other local milk. Visitors welcome
Type: Cows milk, hard-pressed, full fat, vegetarian

The famous CRICKET MALHERBIE CHEDDAR, naturally smoked over oak chippings. Sold in 10 oz (270 g) waxed miniatures.

OLYMPIA ITALIAN-STYLE CHEESES

Olympia Food Products, Olympia House, Manton Lane, Bedford, Bedfordshire
Creamery
Type: Cows milk, various, vegetarian

Makers of traditional Italian cheeses, producing around 2,000 tonnes of Mozzarella and smaller quantities of Ricotta and other varieties each year.

ORKNEY CHEDDAR

Kirkwall Creamery, Orkney
Creamery using local milk
Type: Cows milk, hard-pressed, full fat

Most of the milk produced on Orkney goes to the creamery at Kirkwall, the most northerly production point in the

UK. The creamery produces a rindless Cheddar cheese which has often taken the highest honours at dairy shows.

OXFORD BUTTONS

Rodney Whitworth, Abbey Farm, Goosey, Faringdon, Oxfordshire
Artisan maker
Type: Ewes milk, soft, medium fat, vegetarian

Silky-smooth cheese with a 'sweet' finish, an ideal companion to fresh fruit. The 7 oz (200 g) rounds are made to be eaten young and fresh. *See also* LEAFIELD.

PANEER

Type: Cows milk, semi-hard, full fat, vegetarian

Surati Paneer is India's best-known cheese, traditionally made from buffalo milk but now produced from cows milk, which is separated by the action of acetic acid. The curds are ripened in the whey before being strained and pressed. Makers include HERITAGE, HUNDALEE and LONG CLAWSON.

PANT-YS-GAWN FARM

Bryson Craske, Abergavenny Fine Foods, Castle Meadows Park, Abergavenny, Gwent
Artisan maker using the farm's own milk. Visitors welcome
Type: Goats milk, soft, full fat, vegetarian

Pant-ys-gawn means 'hollow in the sunshine' and the farm where this cheese is made lies in the heart of the Brecon Beacons National Park. The cheese is creamy, with a clean, mild taste that is guaranteed to be free from any 'off' flavours. Available in 1.1 lb (500 g) logs. Varieties include plain, herb, black pepper, garlic and chives, and citrus pepper. The farm also produces gourmet bite-sized portions marinated in aromatic oil with red chillies and decorative sprigs of rosemary. The bites are not 'oily' to the taste but carry a delicate and unusual flavour. The farm also makes miniature Welsh Cheddars, in 14 oz (400 g) and 7 oz (200 g) sizes from cows milk. *See also* CASTLE MEADOWS CAERPHILLY.

PARKHAM FARM CHEDDAR

David Willes, Raddy Farm, Instow, Bideford, Devon
Farmhouse maker using the farm's own milk. Visitors by appointment
Type: Cows milk, hard-pressed, full fat, vegetarian

Long-established makers of Cheddar in 40 lb (20 kg) rindless blocks, producing around 12,000 tonnes a year. Cheese can be bought at the farm but telephone (01271) 860433 before calling.

PECORINO *see* CWMTAWE PECORINO

PENBRYN

Anne Degan, Ty-hen Penbryn, Sarnau, Dyfed
Artisan maker using farm's own milk
Type: Unpasteurised cows milk, hard, full fat, vegetarian

Organically produced Gouda-type, delicately flavoured and without the waxy (some might say rubbery) texture of the mass-produced product.

PENCARREG

Dougal Campbell, Welsh Organic Foods, Llambed Industrial Estate, Lampeter, Dyfed
Artisan maker using organic milk

Type: Cows milk, soft, full fat, vegetarian

This 'Welsh Brie' is mould-ripened, has a rich flavour and is claimed to be the only organic Brie-type cheese produced in Europe. Made from the milk of five farms in Wales and Shropshire, each of them accredited organic to the standards of the Soil Association. The makers recommend that Pencarreg be allowed to develop its full flavour out of the refrigerator before cutting and serving. Pencarreg Blue is a unique, organic, blue Brie. Both cheeses are sold in 4 lb (1.8 kg) ovals for counter cutting, 7 oz (200 g) miniatures or 6 oz (170 g) cut wedges, but the blue variety is also available in an attractive 10 oz (300 g) presentation box in a distinctive dark-blue and gold livery. Cheese can be ordered by post; telephone (01570) 422772 for details.

PENTLAND BRIE, PENTLAND CAMEMBERT

Rosemary and Mike Marwick, Howgate Cheeses, Camperdown Creamery, Faraday Street, Dundee
Artisan maker
Type: Unpasteurised cows milk, semi-soft, full fat, vegetarian

For those who prefer the richer and fuller flavour of unpasteurised cheeses, Howgate produce raw milk versions of their bloomy-rinded cheeses. Runny and sticky when fully ripe, the Brie is made in 3 lb (1.4 kg) rounds and the Camembert in 2 lb (900 g) rounds.

PEN Y BONT

John and Jenny White, Mount Pleasant, Pen y Bont, Carmarthen, Dyfed
Artisan maker using the farm's own milk
Type: Unpasteurised goats milk, semi-hard, full fat, vegetarian

Goats tended by organic methods, grazing naturally managed pastures, provide the milk for this white, Dales-type cheese. Normally sold mild at around two weeks but will mature on to develop a firmer flavour. Produced in 4 lb (1.8 kg) flat discs.

PERROCHE

Charles Westhead, Neals Yard Creamery, Everlands Estate, Idle Hill, Sevenoaks, Kent
Artisan maker
Type: Unpasteurised goats and cows milk, soft, medium fat, vegetarian

Soft and moist cheese. The curds are drained and sold within a few days, providing a fresh taste with a hint of almonds. The cheese is made in 4 oz (110 g) rounds or 1 lb (450 g) logs. Varieties available include plain or rolled in fresh herbs, with a choice of tarragon (highly praised), oregano, dill and rosemary. All are to be eaten fresh.

PICK AND MIX CHEESES

Small portions of wrapped cheese are commonly sold as inexpensive 'pick and mix' cheeses. This is a good idea, in principle, as it provides an opportunity to try a new cheese. In reality, however, such products are nowhere near as satisfactory as tasting samples from a well-stocked cheese counter. Many of the pick and mix cheeses are of indifferent quality, unlikely to lead to serious cheese purchases. Nevertheless, they generate sales of some £30 million per year, mainly through larger stores.

PILGRIMS CHOICE CHEDDAR

North Downs Dairy, Grove Dairy Farm, Bobbing Hill, Sittingbourne, Kent
Cheese trader and packer
Type: Cows milk, hard-pressed, full fat (various)

North Downs Dairy operates a modern cheese-packing facility at Wincanton in Somerset. Their Pilgrims Choice label is already a familiar sight on the delicatessen counters of many super-markets and smaller stores, and continues to grow in popularity. North Downs Dairy specialises in rindless cheese, made by creamery or farm-house makers. There are mild and mature Cheddars, a vintage Cheddar and other English cheeses, all of which can be supplied in 10 lb (5 kg) and 5 lb (2.5 kg) blocks or in a range of prepacked wedges.

PLAS DAIRY FARM CHEESES *see* LACTIC CURD

PLUMLEY

R. Threadgold, Boydells Dairy Farm, Wethersfield, Braintree, Essex
Artisan maker using the farm's own milk. Visitors by appointment
Type: Ewes milk, soft, full fat, vege-tarian

Prizewinning Coulommier-type cheese, available plain, with chives or with garlic and herbs. The cheese is mainly sold direct from the farm; telephone (01371) 850481 before calling to check opening times.

POETH MEL

Peter Sayer, Welsh Farmhouse Cheese, Maesllyn, Llandysul, Dyfed
Artisan maker using local milk. Visitors welcome
Type: Unpasteurised cows milk, hard-

pressed, full fat, vegetarian

Caerphilly cheese with added Welsh honey and mustard seeds. Sold in red-waxed 5 lb (2.3 kg) rounds or 1 lb (450 g) miniatures. *See also* ST EMELYN.

PROVOLONE

Heritage Cheeses, The Creamery, Glan-Yr-Afon Estate, Aberystwyth, Dyfed
Creamery
Type: Cows milk, semi-soft, medium fat, vegetarian

Italian-style pasta filata (drawn curd) cheese with a shiny, yellow rind and a creamy-white interior. The young cheese is mild and smooth cutting but well-aged Provolone becomes granular in texture and has a robust flavour. *See also* HERITAGE.

PULHAM PEPPER

Susan Moore, Cranes Watering Farm, Starston, Harleston, Norfolk
Artisan maker using the farm's own milk. Visitors by appointment
Type: Unpasteurised cows milk, semi-soft, full fat, vegetarian

A Norfolk milk cheese, made from the milk of Jersey and Guernsey cows. Lightly salted, the 8 oz (225 g) rounds are dusted with cracked peppercorns. *See also* MOORE CHEESE.

QUANTOCK BLUE

Alan and Kay Duffield, Exmoor Blue Cheese, Willett Farm, Lydeard St Lawrence, Somerset
Artisan maker. Visitors by appoint-ment
Type: Unpasteurised ewes milk, soft, full fat, vegetarian

In between the Quantock and the Brendon Hills nestles the Vale of

Taunton Deane, perfect dairying country. The Duffields have been making cheese here since 1985 and have built an enviable reputation for their products. Quantock Blue is unpressed cheese made with the blue mould *Penicillium roqueforti*. Sold in 4½ lb (2 kg) discs. Alan Duffield won a second prize at the Bath and West Show with this cheese, which has been described as powerful and spicy. *See also* BABY BRENDON, BRENDON BLUE, COLEFORD BLUE, EXMOOR GOATS CHEESE IN OIL, GOLD TOP BLUE, JERSEY BLUE, SOMERSET BLUE.

QUICKE'S TRADITIONAL CHEDDAR

J.G. Quicke & Partners, Home Farm, Newton St Cyres, Exeter, Devon
Farmhouse maker using the farm's own milk. Visitors welcome
Type: Cows milk, hard-pressed, full fat, vegetarian

The Quicke family have been farming 1,500 acres at Home Farm, Newton St Cyres, for over 400 years. They are the only commercial producers of Farmhouse Cheddar left in Devon, with milk from their own herd of 300 Holstein/Friesian cows being used to make cheese every morning of the year, apart from two weeks in August, when milk supplies are at their lowest. They mix the morning milk with the evening milk from the previous day and use small open vats, to give their cheesemaker maximum control. Total production is around 600 tonnes each year, about 10% of which is made with unpasteurised milk. The Cheddar is sold as mellow at 6–8 months, and mature at 9–12 months. They also make mild Cheddar, a herb Cheddar (with chives, thyme, oregano and parsley) and, just to prove how versatile they are, Double Gloucester and Red Leicester. The Cheddar is also available smoked over oak chippings, when it is called Woodley, which would

seem to be a most appropriate name. The Quicke family can be justly proud of their Cheddar, with over 30 prizes having been won since 1973, including the crowning achievement in the industry, Supreme Champion at the Royal Bath and West Show, two years running. Selection packs of the cheeses can be ordered by post and there is an excellent farm shop where cheese may be purchased. Telephone (01392) 851655 for details of opening times. *See also* SINGLE DEVON.

QUIVVY

Silke Cropp, Corleggy, Belturbet, Co. Cavan, Republic of Ireland
Artisan maker using the farm's own milk. Visitors by appointment
Type: Goats milk, soft, full fat, vegetarian

Soft balls of goats cheese, packed in a glass jar with oil, fresh herbs, red peppercorns and edible flowers. *See also* CORLEGGY, DRUMLIN.

RACHEL'S DAIRY COTTAGE CHEESE

Rachel and Gareth Rowlands, Rachel's Dairy, Brynllys Farm, Borth, Dyfed
Artisan maker. Visitors welcome
Type: Cows milk, soft, low fat, vegetarian

Brynllys Farm has been run by the same family for four generations. Their 250 acres and milking herd of 75 Guernsey cows are managed to the standards of the Soil Association. Brynllys is possibly the oldest organic farm in Britain and, after more than 50 years, the Rowlands know that organic farming is no passing fashion. Their cottage cheese, made at the dairy in nearby Aberystwyth, has been highly praised, coming first in a survey organised by the BBC's *Good Food* magazine. There is an excellent farm shop and the farm is open to visitors but telephone (01970) 871489 to check opening times.

RAINES DAIRY SOFT CHEESES

Raines Dairy Products, Raine House, Crown Road, Enfield, Middlesex
Creamery
Type: Cows milk, soft or semi-soft

Manufacturers of cottage cheese and soft cheese, mainly sold under supermarket own brands.

RED CHEDDAR *see* COLOURED CHEESES

REDESDALE

Mark Robertson, Northumberland Cheese Company, Soppitt Farm, Otterburn, Northumberland
Artisan maker using the farm's own milk. Visitors welcome
Type: Unpasteurised ewes milk, hard-pressed, full fat, vegetarian

Mark Robertson started producing cheese in 1985 and now his products are exported all over the world. Redesdale is an elliptical, brine-washed cheese, delicate and subtle when young but strong and fully flavoured at only four months, without the aroma of wet carpet that accompanies some ewes milk products. Sometimes mixed herbs are added to the curd. Available in three sizes: 6 lb (2.75 kg), 2.2 lb (1 kg) and 1.1 lb (500 g). *See also* NORTHUMBERLAND.

RED LEICESTER

Type: Cows milk, hard-pressed, full fat

Leicester cheese, with its mild flavour and vivid red colour, used to be nearly as popular as Cheddar. Early in the eighteenth century a special cheese fair was held at Leicester each Michaelmas and the volume of business became so great that in 1759 a full-time cheese market was built. To ensure that standards of quality and weight were maintained, the town crier used to read the punishments that would befall anyone caught trying to pass off cheese that was not up to the mark. Leicester is the only cheese that ever caused a riot. In 1776 food was scarce and a crowd of 4,000 protesters attempted to seize a large quantity of cheese from the Old Bell Inn near the city centre. The magistrates read the Riot Act and troops were called in to quell the mob. The following day four women were imprisoned for their part in the only 'cheese riot' in British history. Sad to relate, there is very little Leicester cheese actually made in the county, although TUXFORD AND TEBBUTT's product was highly praised by Patrick Rance in *The Great British Cheese Book*. J.M. NUTTALL produce a particularly good example, in the traditional flat 33 lb (15 kg) disc, which has won prizes at the Royal Bath and West Show and been chosen as Supreme Champion at the Nantwich Show. Other makers include BELTON CHEESE, BUTLERS FARMHOUSE LANCASHIRE, FOUNTAINS DAIRY, Golden Foods (see AVONMORE), LAURELS FARM, QUICKE'S TRADITIONAL CHEDDAR.

RED WINDSOR

Long Clawson Dairy, Melton Mowbray, Leicestershire
Creamery
Type: Cows milk, hard-pressed, full fat

It was in 1968 that Mr Baddiley, the owner of Tythby Dairy (now merged with Long Clawson), was approached to develop a new product by Mr Adamson of Charles Liles and Company. He decided on a Cheddar cheese with elderberry wine, giving a ruddy, veined appearance and a sweet taste. Red Windsor grew in popularity and is now part of a 'family' of blended cheeses. *See also* LONG CLAWSON.

REECE'S SPECIALITY CHEESES

Reece's Creamery, Hampton, Malpas, Cheshire
Creamery
Type: Cows milk, hard-pressed, various

Producers of a wide range of English territorials, many with additives, including waxed and presentation cheeses. *See also* THE CHEESE COMPANY.

RHIWFELEN

Peter Sayer, Welsh Farmhouse Cheese, Maesllyn, Llandysul, Dyfed
Artisan maker. Visitors welcome
Type: Unpasteurised cows milk, hard-pressed, full fat, vegetarian

Matured Welsh Cheddar, made using local milk, with added apricots and brandy. Sold in yellow-waxed 5 lb (2.3 kg) rounds or 1 lb (450 g) miniatures. *See also* ST EMELYN.

RHODES CHEESE *see* CARRON LODGE

RIBBLESDALE

Chris and Iain Hill, Ribblesdale Cheesemakers, Ashes Farm, Horton in Ribblesdale, North Yorkshire
Artisan maker. Visitors welcome
Type: Cows, ewes and goats milk versions, hard-pressed, full fat, vegetarian

Ashes Farm lies in a bleak spot, high in the Pennines, amidst a country of glacial drumlins, limestone crags and curlews. The hard, dry Craven cheese (once called Old Whangby, meaning 'old leather') was made here for count-less generations. Ribblesdale Cows Milk Cheese is made by hand; it is an old Dales-type cheese with a crumbly yet creamy texture that melts in the mouth. The 4 lb (1.8 kg) wheels are sometimes black-waxed, and sometimes made with added garlic. Ribblesdale Goats Milk Cheese, although hard-pressed, is unusually delicate and mild for a goat cheese. Iain Hill uses an exclusive recipe and the end result has the character of a fresh Caerphilly. The 3½ lb (1.6 kg) wheels are produced plain, with garlic, or smoked. Ribblesdale Ewes Milk Cheese is hard and has a firm nutty flavour. The 3 lb (1.4 kg) rounds are normally red-waxed. Part of the production is sent to Iain's son Adrian, who smokes the cheeses over oak and ash to produce Ribblesdale Smoked. Cheese can be ordered by post, telephone (01729) 860231 for full details. *See also* ASHES WENSLEYDALE.

RICHARD III WENSLEYDALE

Mrs Suzanne Stirke, Fortmayne Cottage, Newton le Willows, North Yorkshire
Artisan maker using the farm's own milk
Type: Cows milk, hard-pressed, full fat, vegetarian

A true Wensleydale from the Dales, made totally by hand, with natural seasalt. Finished in 5 lb (2.3 kg) rounds. *See also* YORVIK.

RICHMOND SMOKED

David and Mandy Reed, Swaledale Cheese Company, Mercury Road, Richmond, North Yorkshire
Artisan maker
Type: Cows milk, semi-soft, full fat, vegetarian

Swaledale cheeses are made entirely by hand (a two-day process), then turned daily for a month before reaching maturity and becoming ready to be smoked over beech chips. A prize-winner at Nantwich, this cheese has a creamy texture and a warm russet colour. It is sold in vacuum packs and red-waxed rounds, 1 lb (450 g) or 3½ lb (1.6 kg) in weight. *See also* BEAMISH, SWALEDALE.

RICOTTA

Type: Ewes or cows milk, semi-soft, low fat

Best described as Italian cottage cheese, Ricotta was traditionally made from the whey drained from the curd when making Provolone. It is now produced in Britain, still from the surplus whey of another cheese. Whey contains protein, called lactalbumin, which coagulates like the white of an egg when the milk is heated. Acids such as vinegar and whole milk may be added to improve the balance and fat content. Ricotta is normally made from cows milk; it is not ripened and is pure white in colour. The finished product is only 4–10% fat, has a fine, slightly moist texture and a bland sweet flavour. It has a short life and needs using quickly. Just occasionally, you might see the cured and salted version, called dry Ricotta, sold as a grating cheese. Makers using cows milk include CRICKET MALHERBIE, Giovanni Irranca (see CWMTAWE), Island Cheese Company (see KILBRIDE) and OLYMPIA. Sussex High Weald Dairy (see SUSSEX SLIPCOTE) make a ewes milk ricotta.

RING

Eileen and Tom Harty, Gortnadiha House, Ring, Co. Waterford, Republic of Ireland
Artisan maker using the farm's own milk. Visitors by appointment
Type: Unpasteurised cows milk, semi-hard, full fat

Hand-made in the Gaeltacht area of Waterford, using methods derived from the last century, this is a cheese with a rich, distinctive, tongue-tingling spicy and nutty flavour which has been likened to mature Gouda. Sold in 9 lb (4 kg) cylinders.

ROMANY

D. John Davidge, Ilchester Cheese Company, Ilchester, Somerset
Specialist dairy making character cheeses
Type: Cows milk, hard-pressed, full fat

Layers of Double Gloucester and Caerphilly, laced with chopped onions and chives. *See also* ILCHESTER.

ROSARY

Clare Moody, The Rosary, Landford, Salisbury, Wiltshire
Artisan maker using local milk
Type: Goats milk, soft, full fat, vegetarian

Creamy and mild-flavoured, Rosary is decorated with a sprig of fresh herbs. Made in 10 oz (275 g) small rounds and a 2.2 lb (1 kg) cutting size. Also available in a mature version or with a sprinkling of garlic and herbs. Rosary with an ash coating has taken a first prize at the Royal Bath and West Show.

ROUBILIAC

Nachi Elkin, Gedi Enterprises, Plumridge Farm, Stagg Hill, Barnet, Hertfordshire
Artisan maker using the farm's own milk. Visitors welcome
Type: Goats milk, semi-soft, full fat, vegetarian

Fresh cheese with a bright, white appearance and a tangy flavour. The 5 oz (150 g) logs are available lightly coated with black pepper, red and green peppers, garlic or fine herbs, and formed into small balls which are marinated in olive oil. *See also* CHAVANNES.

ROUND TOWER

Nan O'Donovan, Bride View House, Farranmareen, Enniskean, Co. Cork, Republic of Ireland
Artisan maker using the farm's own milk
Type: Unpasteurised cows milk, hard-pressed, full fat, vegetarian

Rich and sweet-tasting Gouda-type cheese. Available in waxed 4 lb (1.8 kg) rounds, matured for up to a year.

RUSTIC

J.J. Saunders, Emborough Farm Foods, Old Down Farm, Emborough, Somerset
Farmhouse maker
Type: Cows milk, semi-hard, full fat

Cheese with spring onion, chives and sun-dried tomatoes. Normally sold ready-grated. *See also* SAUNDERS' CHEDDAR.

RUTLAND

Long Clawson Dairy, Melton Mowbray, Leicestershire
Creamery
Type: Cows milk, hard-pressed, full fat

A blend of Cheddar with beer, garlic and parsley. *See also* LONG CLAWSON

RYEFIELD

Anne and John Brodie, Ryefield House, Virginia, Co. Cavan, Republic of Ireland
Artisan maker using the farm's own milk
Type: Unpasteurised cows milk, hard-pressed, full fat, vegetarian

Cheddar-type Farmhouse cheese, pitched and turned by hand. Matured for at least four months, Ryefield is deep orange in colour and slightly crumbly in texture, with a good finish on the palate. Available in black-waxed 5 lb (2.5 kg) rounds and 10 oz (280 g) miniatures. *See also* BOILIE.

ST ANDREWS

Rosemary and Mike Marwick, Howgate Cheeses, Camperdown Creamery, Faraday Street, Dundee
Artisan maker
Type: Cows milk, soft, full fat, vegetarian

Washed-rind cheese with an attractive pink surface bloom and just a trace of white mould. Smooth, creamy, mellow flavour. Available in 5 lb (2.3 kg) rounds and 12 oz (340 g) miniatures. St Andrews Blanc is a *Tomme bianche*, slightly stronger and with a bloomy rind. Pasteurised and raw milk versions of both cheeses are made. *See also* HOWGATE.

ST BRENDAN BRIE

Patrick Berridge, Carrigbyrne Farmhouse, Adamstown, Enniscorthy, Co. Wexford, Republic of Ireland
Farmhouse maker using the farm's own milk. Visitors by appointment
Type: Cows milk, soft, full fat

Monastic associations have led to numerous cheeses being given saints' names, in Ireland as elsewhere. Cheese has been made in this area for many centuries, and parts of Carrigbyrne Farmhouse date back to 1750, although the making of mould-ripened cheeses is a recent introduction. This Brie-type cheese is available in 3 lb (1.4 kg) rounds. *See also* ST KILLIAN.

ST DAVID

Bryson Craske, Abergavenny Fine Foods, Castle Meadows Park, Abergavenny, Gwent
Artisan maker. Visitors welcome
Type: Cows milk, soft, full fat, vegetarian

Buttery textured, washed-rind cheese with a tangy but delicate flavour, in 5 lb (2.5 kg) rounds and 5 oz (150 g) portions. The makers recommend that the cheese be allowed to develop at room temperature for a couple of days before cutting and serving. *See also* CASTLE MEADOWS CAERPHILLY.

ST EMELYN

Peter Sayer, Welsh Farmhouse Cheese, Maesllyn, Llandysul, Dyfed
Artisan maker. Visitors welcome
Type: Unpasteurised cows milk, hard-pressed, full fat, vegetarian

Peter Sayer makes his Caerphilly in a traditional way, largely by hand and using local milk, but he is not afraid to enliven the cheese with new flavours. St Emelyn is made with the addition of garlic and leek, attractively waxed in two-tone green and white. St Ishmael is made with the local edible seaweed called laverbread and is clear-waxed. St Tyssul is the smoked version of the plain Caerphilly. All the cheeses are made in 5 lb (2.3 kg) rounds and 1 lb (450 g) miniatures. Visitors are welcome to call at the farm to buy cheese but telephone (01239) 858841 first to check opening times. *See also* ANADL-Y-DDRAIG, CAETHWAS, CAWS TARRON, GLASGWM, POETH MEL, RHIWFELEN, YNSMON.

ST FINAN'S

Leyhead Sheep Dairy, Lumphanan, Grampian
Artisan maker using the farm's own milk
Type: Ewes milk, various types, full fat, vegetarian

The Leyhead flock of British Friesland ewes graze south-facing, clover-rich pastures high above Deeside. The soft cheeses, in a range of flavours, are all in 6 oz (170 g) wheels. They include St Finan's Armenica (with apricots), St Finan's Broomhill (plain, soft cheese, ideal for spreading and for sauces), St Finan's Garlic (with freshly crushed garlic) and St Finan's Peperita (with coarsely ground black pepper). There are also hard cheeses, pressed under original granite presses, matured on the farm and finished with a wax coating. These are sold in 3½ lb (1.6 kg) half-cheeses or cut wedges, and include St Finan's Original (close-textured Farmhouse cheese, well matured and clear-waxed), St Finan's Blanchory Black (with black peppercorns, black-waxed), St Finan's Caraway (with caraway seeds, based on a traditional Aberdeenshire 'carvi' cheese, clear-waxed), and St Finan's Herb (marbled with layers of green herbs, clear-waxed). The farm also produces two cows milk cheeses, St Finan's Jersey Coo, made from the milk of a single Jersey cow (supplies are limited!), flavoured with fresh garlic and rolled in parsley, and St Finan's Oatmeal (without the garlic but rolled in pinhead oatmeal).

ST GEDI

Nachi Elkin, Gedi Enterprises, Plumridge Farm, Stagg Hill, Barnet, Hertfordshire
Artisan maker using the farm's own milk. Visitors welcome
Type: Goats milk, semi-soft, full fat, vegetarian

Few cheesemakers can match the success of Nachi Elkin at a recent Bakewell Show: three first prizes and three third prizes on one day. The downy-coated 9 oz (250 g) rounds of St Gedi are mild, smooth and silky when young but will mature to a deep richness. *See also* CHAVANNES.

ST GEORGE

Lyn and Jenny Jenner, Nut Knowle Farm, World's End, Gun Hill, Horam, East Sussex
Artisan maker using the farm's own milk
Type: Goats milk, soft, full fat, vegetarian

Mould-ripened cheese, made and packed in 9 oz (250 g) woodchip boxes in the style of Camembert. Also made in 2.2 lb (1 kg) logs. *See also* CAPRINI.

ST ILLTYD

Bryson Craske, Abergavenny Fine Foods, Castle Meadows Park, Abergavenny, Gwent
Artisan maker. Visitors welcome
Type: Cows milk, hard-pressed, full fat, vegetarian

Mature Cheddar milled with garlic, herbs and Welsh wine. (One of my family's favourites.) Supplied in blackwaxed 10 lb (4.5 kg) and 5 lb (2.3 kg) drums. St Illtyd lived around 490 AD and figured in the early Christian Church in Wales. *See also* CASTLE MEADOWS CAERPHILLY.

ST IVEL

Unigate/St Ivel, Interface Business Park, Wootton Bassett, Swindon, Wiltshire
Major creamery proprietor manufacturing at several locations

The patron saint of cheese is St Candida (her shrine stands within the parish church of Whitchurch Canonicorum in Dorset) but modern commentators might be forgiven for thinking it is St Ivel! Alas, there is no such saint in the calendar. St Ivel was a jolly monk found in the humorous writings of a Mr Barrett, a director of Aplin and Barrett Dairies, and his name was derived from the Saxon name for the river Yeo in Somerset, variously spelt Yeo, Yivell or Ivel. No book on cheese could ignore St Ivel, which now forms part of Unigate PLC, for every part of the dairy industry has been touched by this producer. Cow and Gate, Moonraker, Wiltshire United Dairies and Aplin and Barrett are just some of the names that it has embraced. The company used to manufacture cheese in 16 creameries located across the country but these were sold to the Milk Marketing Board in 1979. St Ivel recently returned to hard-cheese manufacture at Haverfordwest in west Wales, Lisnaskea in Northern Ireland and Wexford in the Irish Republic. The Wexford plant alone produces 10,000 tonnes of cheese each year. St Ivel manufactures soft cheese and cottage cheese in south Wales and at Evercreech in Somerset. Indeed, the St Ivel label can be seen on virtually every type of dairy product. The prepacked wedges of cheese are stocked in a wide variety of food stores, and 10 lb (4.5 kg) blocks of St Ivel rindless Cheddar appear on many counters. One item in the range, St Ivel 'Ninety Plus' Mature Cheddar, owes its name to the grading scheme which awards Cheddar cheese points out of a hundred for quality.

ST KILLIAN

Patrick Berridge, Carrigbyrne Farmhouse, Adamstown, Enniscorthy, Co. Wexford, Republic of Ireland
Farmhouse maker using the farm's own milk. Visitors by appointment
Type: Cows milk, soft, full fat

The biggest-selling Farmhouse cheese in Ireland. Made from the milk of the Carrigbyrne dairy herd, St Killian is a sweet and creamy Camembert-type, sold in a hexagonal roll. Said by Michael Bateman to have a pleasing 'mushroomy' taste. *See also* ST BRENDAN.

ST MARTIN

Eileen O'Brien, Carnames, Kilrush, Co. Clare, Republic of Ireland
Artisan maker using the farm's own milk
Type: Cows milk, hard-pressed, full fat

Gouda-type cheese praised for its sweet, buttery flavour. Available in 3 lb (1.5 kg), 2.2 lb (1 kg) and 1.1 lb (500 g) rounds.

ST MAURE

Lyn and Jenny Jenner, Nut Knowle Farm, World's End, Gun Hill, Horam, East Sussex
Artisan maker using the farm's own milk
Type: Goats milk, soft, full fat, vegetarian

Creamy cheese in 9 oz (250 g) logs. Ideal for the cheeseboard or for cooking. *See also* CAPRINI.

ST PETROC

Elize Jungheim, Trehill Farm, Sampford Courtnay, Okehampton, Devon
Artisan maker. Visitors welcome
Type: Cows milk, semi-hard, full fat, vegetarian

This cheese, with its saintly name, combines two of the best things from Devon: rich milk from a pedigree Friesian herd and Buckfast tonic wine. The wine is added at the curd stage, giving the cheese a slight sweetness, almost Swiss in character, as well as providing a rich infusion of herbs and a distinctive red marbling. The 5 lb

(2.3 kg), 3 lb (1.4 kg) and 1 lb (450 g) truckles are red waxed with a black top. Cheese can be bought at the farm shop, which is open all year, or at Natural Life Cheeses (close to Tavistock Pannier Market), or ordered by post. Telephone (01837) 840684 for details. *See also* TREHILL.

ST TOLA

Meg and Derek Gordon, Inagh, Co, Clare, Republic of Ireland
Artisan maker using the farm's own milk
Type: Goats milk, semi-soft, full fat

Fresh-tasting cheese, made from the milk of a prizewinning goat flock.

SAGE DERBY

Type: Cows milk, hard-pressed, full fat

Sage Derby used to be flavoured with finely chopped sage leaves, or streaked with ground sage and spinach juice. Now it is likely to be marbled with sage oil. It has a perfumed flavour all its own, and is well worth trying grated over a tomato salad. Makers include KNOLTON FARMHOUSE and TIMES PAST.

SAGE LANCASHIRE

Type: Cows milk, hard-pressed, full fat

Lancashire cheese with fresh sage leaves or sage oil. Makers include TOM BARRON FARMS, BUTLER'S FARMHOUSE, Rhodes Cheese (see CARRON LODGE) and J.J. Sandham (see SANDHAM'S TRADITIONAL).

SALMON LEAP

Golden Cow Dairies, Artabrackagh Road, Portadown, Co. Armagh, Northern Ireland

Creamery
Type: Cows milk, soft, full fat

A blend of smoked Irish salmon, fresh cream and cheese, in 5 oz (150 g) logs. *See also* COLERAINE.

SANDHAM'S TRADITIONAL LANCASHIRE

J.J. Sandham, Rostock Dairy, Garstang Road, Barton, Preston, Lancashire
Small creamery
Type: Cows milk, semi-hard, full fat, vegetarian

The small family firm of J.J. Sandham started making their Lancashire cheese over 60 years ago. Like so many others, they were robbed of their birthright during the years of the Second World War, but they regained their milk supply and their heritage in the mid-1950s. No less than five family members still have a hand in the business, and a family recipe is used to make their distinctive, buttery cheese, which is mild and creamy. There is also a sharper 'tasty' variety for sterner palates. Garlic or sage are sometimes added. Quality is guaranteed by the family's knowledge of their product. Total production is around 200 tonnes each year.

SAUNDERS' CHEDDAR

J.J. Saunders, Emborough Farm Foods, Old Down Farm, Emborough, Somerset
Farmhouse maker using the farm's own milk
Type: Cows milk, hard-pressed, full fat

J.J. Saunders are one of the larger cheesemakers in Somerset, making around 3,000 tonnes each year. Their Cheddar meets the demand for stronger cheese in the South-west. They have been runners-up at the Bath and West and Nantwich Shows on many occasions, and in 1991 Saunders'

Cheddar was selected as 'Champion Cheese' at the Scottish Cheesemakers Show. This was the first time the Scottish judges had picked a Somerset Farmhouse cheese in the show's 26-year history. As well as securing the McLelland Championship Cup outright, they won the W.R. Grace prize for the best rindless block and the Hansen Centenary prize for white rindless mature. *See also* CROSSELLE, JACANTI.

SCOTTISH OAK SMOKED CHEDDAR

Derek and Ann Brow, The Ingle Smokehouses, Arran Place, Perth, Tayside
Artisan maker
Type: Cows milk, semi-hard, full fat

A delight to both the palate and the eye, this is a superbly presented Cheddar from the Scottish islands, naturally smoked over oak chippings. The oak might even come from old whisky barrels! Also available made with vegetarian rennet. *See also* GOWRIE.

SCOTTISH PRIDE CHEESES

Scottish Pride Ltd, 190 Helen Street, Glasgow
Major creamery proprietor manufacturing at several locations

Scottish Pride operates creameries at CAMPBELTOWN, Rothesay and Arran. A wide range of dairy products are manufactured, with rindless Cheddar and Dunlop being the most important cheeses.

SCRUMPY SUSSEX

Michael Turner, Turner's Dairies, Myrtle Grove Farm, Patching, Worthing, West Sussex

Artisan maker using the farm's own milk
Type: Unpasteurised cows milk, hard-pressed, full fat, vegetarian

Hand-made and traditionally pressed cheese with Sussex cider, mixed herbs and just a touch of garlic added at the curd stage, giving a far more distinctive flavour than cheese blended with extra ingredients after pressing. Finished in 5 lb (2.3 kg) rounds. *See also* OLDE SUSSEX, SOUTHDOWN.

SEVERN SISTERS

Nick Hodgetts, Malvern Cheesewrights, Manor House, Lower Wick, Worcester
Artisan maker using the farm's own milk
Type: Unpasteurised cows milk, hard-pressed, full fat, vegetarian

This extremely smooth and moist cheese is made by Richard Rogers. The rounds are matured for five months and finished with a distinctive green wax. *See also* MALVERN.

SHANNON VALE

Kerrygold, Grattan House, Lower Mount Street, Dublin, Republic of Ireland
Major creamery proprietor manufacturing at several locations
Type: Cows milk, semi-hard, full fat

Smooth, oak-smoked, Cheddar-type cheese in 6½ lb (3 kg) wheels. *See also* KERRYGOLD.

SHARPHAM

Debbie Mumford, Sharpham Creamery, Ashprington, Totnes, Devon
Artisan maker using the farm's own milk
Type: Unpasteurised cows milk, semi-soft, full fat, vegetarian

The Sharpham Estate includes 500 acres of pasture, vineyards, orchards, woodland and garden, lying in the valley of the river Dart. The dairy farm has 70 acres of permanent pasture, providing grazing for 50 Jersey cows whose milk is used to make this Coulommier-type cheese. Sharpham has been a prizewinner at many shows and was praised by Patrick Rance, who said it was 'as good as the best Brie de Montereau'. Ripened for 2–3 weeks before sale, it is available in 2.2 lb (1 kg) or 1.1 lb (500 g) rounds and 9 oz (250 g) squares. Normally only available March–January.

SHEPHERDS PURSE FARM-HOUSE WENSLEYDALE

Judy Bell, Shepherds Purse, Leachfield Grange, Newsham, Thirsk, North Yorkshire
Artisan maker
Type: Ewes milk, hard-pressed, full fat, vegetarian

Shepherds Purse is a family firm that has achieved a string of honours for its cheeses. This original Wensleydale, made from ewes milk as it was in the twelfth century, is firm and sometimes flaky, with a clean, sharp flavour. Matured for at least four weeks before sale, it is available in 3½ lb (1.6 kg) rounds and 10 oz (280 g) baby cheeses. *See also* HERRIOT FARMHOUSE, OLDE YORK, YORKSHIRE BLUE.

SHORROCK'S LANCASHIRE CHEESE

W.R. Shorrock, New House Farm, Ford Lane, Goosnargh, Preston, Lancashire
Farmhouse maker using the farm's own milk
Type: Unpasteurised cows milk, hard-pressed, full fat, vegetarian

Small but highly regarded manufacturer of traditional Lancashire cheese in 40 lb (20 kg) and 20 lb (9 kg) cylindricals. Production is around 100 tonnes each year. Cheese cannot be bought direct from the farm but is available from Goosnargh Post Office Stores nearby.

SHROPSHIRE BLUE

Type: Cows milk, semi-hard, full fat

Shropshire Blue is a misnomer as the cheese was first produced in Scotland. *Penicillium roqueforti* produces the blue veins, and annatto gives a golden-orange colour. Ripened for 10–12 weeks, when it is said that the cheese has 'a bit more bite than Stilton'. Makers include COLSTON BASSETT, CROPWELL BISHOP, LONG CLAWSON, MILLWAY and TUXFORD AND TEBBUTT.

SINGLE DEVON

J.G. Quicke and Partners, Home Farm, Newton St Cyres, Exeter, Devon
Farmhouse maker using the farm's own milk. Visitors welcome
Type: Cows milk, hard-pressed, medium fat, vegetarian

Local cows, fed on locally grown maize, lucerne, wheat and grass give an individual flavour to this new Devon cheese, which has proved popular with visitors to the farm. About a quarter of the cream is removed by drawing milk from the bottom of the vat, producing a lower-fat cheese. The curd is scalded to a lesser degree than Cheddar, allowing the acidity to rise and giving a stronger flavour. The cheese is made largely by hand, pressed for a full three days and finished with a natural rind. The end product is best eaten young, when it is close-textured and waxy, retaining a light hint of acid. *See also* QUICKE'S TRADITIONAL CHEDDAR.

SINGLE GLOUCESTER

Charles Martell and Son, Laurel Farm, Dymock, Gloucestershire
Artisan maker using the farm's own milk
Type: Cows milk, hard-pressed, full fat, vegetarian

Single Gloucester is now firmly back on the menu, thanks to the efforts of Charles Martell, and likely to receive a Protection of Designated Origin before long. What was once a poor man's alternative to the superior Double Gloucester is now a sought-after cheese in its own right. The cheese is sometimes produced with the traditional coating of nettles on the 8 lb (3.6 kg) wheels. Laurel Farm successfully re-creates a number of 'lost' cheeses; *see also* CLOISTERS, DOUBLE BERKELEY, HEREFORD HOP, NUNS OF CAEN, STINKING BISHOP.

SINGLETON'S 'FARM MAID' CHEESES

Alan Riding, Singleton's Dairy, Mill Farm, Preston Road, Longridge, Preston, Lancashire
Creamery
Type: Cows milk, hard-pressed, full fat, vegetarian

The Riding family began making cheese in the 1920s. The dairy now produces around 2,500 tonnes of cheese a year, including traditional and 'new' Lancashire, Cheshire, Cheddar, a Lancashire with sweet pickle, Red Leicester with herbs and garlic and a Double Gloucester with chives and onion. *See also* BLEASDALE and TRUCKLEDOWN.

SINGLE WORCESTER

Nick Hodgetts, Malvern Cheesewrights,

Manor House, Lower Wick, Worcester
Artisan maker using the farm's own milk
Type: Unpasteurised cows milk, hard-pressed, full fat, vegetarian

The recent discovery of a recipe used by Cistercian monks in south Worcestershire has led to the revival of this neighbour to Double Gloucester. Very creamy and only lightly salted, it has a distinctive and unusual tangy flavour. Finished with a thin, natural rind. *See also* MALVERN.

SKIRRID

Don and Karen Ross, Little Acorn Products, Mesen Fach Farm, Bethania, Llanon, Dyfed
Artisan maker. Visitors by appointment
Type: Unpasteurised ewes milk, semi-hard, full fat, vegetarian

Mild and clean-flavoured cheese marinated in Old English mead. Made in 5 lb (2.3 kg) truckles, which are close-textured and easy to slice. Delicious served with oatmeal crackers or Bath Oliver biscuits. Matures for up to four months. Originally produced at Grosmont in the Gwent hills, the cheese takes its name from the nearby Skirrid Mountain. *See also* ACORN.

SLEIGHT FARM *see* MENDIP

SMART'S GLOUCESTER CHEESE

Diana Smart, Old Ley Court, Birdwood, Churcham, Gloucestershire
Artisan maker using the farm's own milk. Visitors by appointment
Type: Unpasteurised cows milk, hard-pressed, full fat, vegetarian

Gloucester cheese, single or double, was once almost as important to the county as the woollen industry, but today only a couple of makers remain in the Severn Vale. Diana Smart uses a recipe that has been handed down over several generations for her hand-made Gloucester cheese. Double Gloucester is made from full-cream milk but the Single Gloucester uses skimmed milk from the previous evening mixed with the morning's whole milk to produce a low-fat cheese with a creamy flavour. The whole process, which starts immediately after morning milking, takes about nine hours to complete. After pressing in a Victorian press for two days, during which time the cheeses are turned twice, the Single Gloucester is matured for up to six weeks and the Double Gloucester for up to six months more. Total production is around one tonne each month. Cheese can be bought at the farm and it is sometimes possible to watch cheese-making but visitors are asked to telephone (01452) 750225 before calling.

SOMERFIELD VINTAGE EXTRA MATURE CHEDDAR

Somerfield Stores, PO Box 708, Bristol, Avon
Type: Cows milk, hard-pressed, full fat, vegetarian

Supermarket own-label products fall outside the scope of this book (not least because the actual manufacturers may change without prior notice), but the excellence of this vintage Cheddar merits its inclusion. Specially made on a farm in south Somerset, it is aged for 15 months and skilfully graded to ensure a rich, deep flavour. Packed in 6½ lb (3 kg) blocks with a maroon wrapper and stocked by most of the larger Somerfield/Gateway stores in the UK.

SOMERSET BLUE

Alan and Kay Duffield, Exmoor Blue

Cheese, Willett Farm, Lydeard St Lawrence, Somerset
Artisan maker using the farm's own milk. Visitors by appointment
Type: Unpasteurised cows milk, hard-pressed, full fat, vegetarian

Blue cheese made from the milk of a single Jersey herd using *Penicillium roqueforti* in the manner of Stilton. The 9 lb (4 kg) rounds have a creamy texture and stunning blue tang due to the exclusive use of Jersey cows milk. *See also* QUANTOCK BLUE.

SOMERSET BRIE

Lubborn Cheese, North Street, Crewkerne, Somerset
Small creamery
Type: Cows milk, soft, full-fat, vegetarian

Brie is a soft-paste cheese, the curd filled into moulds and the whey allowed to drain away naturally. As the cheese matures, over several weeks, the characteristic white fur of *Penicillium candidum* forms on the surface. The mould growth might once have been natural but the spores are now distributed by a spray in commercial manufacture. At Lubborn Cheese they use traditional French methods to produce Somerset Brie. Made in the familiar wheels, it becomes soft and develops a rich flavour, just like its cousin from across the Channel. A blue Brie is also available. *See also* CAPRICORN.

SOMERSET CREAMERIES *see*
CROPWELL BISHOP

SOMERTON

D. John Davidge, Ilchester Cheese Company, Ilchester, Somerset
Specialist dairy making character cheeses

Type: Cows milk, hard-pressed, full fat

The Saxon capital of Wessex lends its name to this mellow Cheddar blended with garlic and herbs for extra piquancy. *See also* ILCHESTER.

SOUTH CAERNARFON CREAMERY CHEESES

Gareth Evans, South Caernarfon Creameries, Rhydygwstl, Chwilog, Pwllheli, Gwynedd
Creamery using local milk
Type: Cows milk, hard-pressed, full fat

South Caernarfon Creameries is a farmers' co-operative on the Llyn Peninsula, established in 1938. Over 200 local farms supply milk, producing around 4,000 tonnes of Cheddar, Monterey Jack and other cheeses each year. *See also* OLD SHIRE.

SOUTHDOWN

Michael Turner, Turner's Dairies, Myrtle Grove Farm, Patching, Worthing, West Sussex
Artisan maker using local milk
Type: Ewes milk, hard-pressed, full fat, vegetarian

Made by hand and traditionally pressed, this cheese is rich and smooth, and lightly smoked to impart a delicate flavour. Sold in 3 lb (1.4 kg) rounds. *See also* OLDE SUSSEX, SCRUMPY SUSSEX.

SPELGA COTTAGE CHEESE

Dramona Quality Foods, Antrim Road, Belfast, Northern Ireland
Major creamery proprietor
Type: Cows milk, soft, low fat

Dramona Quality Foods produces flavoured and plain cottage cheeses under the SPELGA label. *See also* BARON'S TABLE, DRAMONA.

SPENWOOD

Mrs Anne Wigmore, Village Maid, The Cottage, Basingstoke Road, Riseley, Berkshire
Artisan maker using milk from a single herd
Type: Unpasteurised ewes milk, hard-pressed, full fat, vegetarian

Traditionally made cheese; the 5 lb (2.3 kg) rounds are matured for six months to produce a natural rind and a unique flavour which has been likened to a young Parmesan. The cheese, which derives its name from Spencers Wood, has received many accolades: first in its class at Nantwich, winner of the 1991 Big Cheese Award (sponsored by *The Guardian*) and given a three-star rating in a survey conducted by *The Independent on Sunday. See also* WELLINGTON.

STAFFORDSHIRE ORGANIC

Michael and Betty Deaville, New House Farm, Acton, Newcastle-under-Lyme, Staffordshire
Artisan maker. Visitors by appointment
Type: Unpasteurised cows milk, hard-pressed, medium fat, vegetarian

Traditional county name for an organic cheese made from Soil-Association-standard milk and sea-salt. Traditionally cloth-bound and supplied in round truckles of 40 lb (20 kg), 20 lb (9 kg), or 3 lb (1.4 kg). As well as being sold plain, the cheese is available flavoured with chives, wild garlic or mixed herbs. It can be bought on the farm and tours of the dairy can sometimes be arranged but telephone (01782) 680366 first for details.

STARSTON

Susan Moore, Cranes Watering Farm, Starston, Harleston, Norfolk
Artisan maker using the farm's own milk. Visitors by appointment
Type: Unpasteurised cows milk, soft, full fat, vegetarian

Starston is made from the milk of Jersey and Guernsey cows with a little added salt, employing a recipe for a Norfolk milk cheese. The cheese is named after its home village, which has a sign showing cattle crossing The Beck, a local tributary of the river Waveney. Visitors assume that the sign depicts the cows of Cranes Watering Farm but it really depicts the steers that give Starston its name, and you don't get milk from steers! *See also* MOORE CHEESE.

STICHILL

Brenda Leddy, Garden Cottage Farm, Stichill, Kelso, Borders
Artisan maker using the farm's own milk
Type: Unpasteurised cows milk, hard-pressed, full fat, vegetarian

Hand-made cheese, produced by Mrs Leddy and her daughter. They use only milk from the famous Stichill Jersey herd in their Cheshire-style product. It has a delightful aftertaste of cider apples. Said to be at its best when matured for 10 months.

STILTON

Made in the Vale of Belvoir
Type: Cows milk, semi-hard, full fat

The 'king' of English cheeses. The best Stilton is made from summer milk, ready to be enjoyed at Christmas. Look for cheese that is pure white with an even covering of blue veins radiating out from the centre. Stilton cheese needs to be kept quite dry and cool, for it has a tendency to absorb moisture, leading to discoloration inside the rind. Cheese that is dark brown around the perimeter is past its best. It is most important to allow Stilton to warm to room temperature before serving if you want to fully appreciate the flavour. Cut it with a knife, like any other cheese, and do not scoop from the centre. Enjoy it with a glass of port if you will, but avoid the affectation of wasting fine port and fine cheese by pouring one over the other. Only dairies around the Vale of Belvoir are allowed to describe their cheese as Stilton, and they include some of the most illustrious names in cheese-making. *See* COLSTON BASSETT, CROPWELL BISHOP, LONG CLAWSON, MILLWAY, NUTTALL'S FINE CHEESES, ST IVEL, TUXFORD AND TEBBUTT. Patrick Rance, author of *The Great British Cheese Book*, makes special mention of the Stilton produced by Margaret Callow at WEBSTERS of Saxelby, the smallest Stilton maker.

STILTON (WHITE)

Millway Foods Ltd, Colston Lane, Harby, Melton Mowbray, Leicestershire
Creamery
Type: Cows milk, semi-hard, full fat

All the Stilton makers produce white Stilton. Lacking the strength and tang of blue Stilton, it is a light, crumbly, versatile cheese that combines well with many flavours. Millway Foods pack their white Stilton in 9 lb (4 kg) rounds and a range of cut sizes. In addition to the plain variety, it is available with apricots, garlic and herbs, garlic and mushroom, peach and pear, stem ginger or tikka spices. *See also* MILLWAY STILTON.

STINKING BISHOP

Charles Martell and Son, Laurel Farm, Dymock, Gloucestershire
Artisan maker using the farm's own milk
Type: Cows milk, soft, full fat

Named after one of the hundred or so varieties of pear that used to be grown around the Gloucestershire–Herefordshire border for the making of perry, Stinking Bishop is derived from a cheese once made by Cistercian monks in the village of Dymock. The 9 lb (4 kg) wheels are matured in humid cave-like conditions whilst the rind is washed in perry to encourage the pungent and spirited aroma. *See also* SINGLE GLOUCESTER.

STRATHKINNESS

Rosemary and Mike Marwick, Howgate Cheeses, Camperdown Creamery, Faraday Street, Dundee
Artisan maker
Type: Cows milk, semi-soft, full fat, vegetarian

Matured for six months or more, Strathkinness has a mellow but full flavour. The flat 40 lb (20 kg) rounds sometimes display small natural holes, in the Emmental manner. Pasteurised and raw milk versions are made but only in limited quantities. *See also* HOWGATE.

STURMINSTER OAK SMOKED CHEDDAR

Sturminster Newton Creamery, Sturminster Newton, Dorset
Creamery
Type: Cows milk, hard-pressed, full fat

Sturminster Newton draws milk from 50 farms around the Blackmore Vale and is Dairy Crest's centre for traditional Cheddar production. Some is cut into rounds and slowly smoked over oak, without artificial flavourings or colourings. The gleaming 15 lb (7 kg) flat discs look for all the world as if they have received a coat of ship's varnish! *See also* DAIRY CREST.

SUSSEX SLIPCOTE

Mark Hardy, Sussex High Weald Dairy, Putlands Farm, Duddleswell, Uckfield, East Sussex
Artisan maker using the farm's own milk. Visitors by appointment
Type: Unpasteurised ewes milk, soft, full fat, vegetarian

Slipcote is an intriguing name, and the recipe for this cheese dates back to the sixteenth century. Young cheese that came on too fast literally burst out of the cheesecloth, and became known as Slip-coat or Slip-cote ever after. An unripened cheese, similar to Colwick or York, it would always have been eaten fresh, the curds left for 24 hours to develop a junket-like texture and then spread on bread. Today's Slipcote is still light and fresh but has a three-week shelf life; the 2 lb (900 g) rolls and 4 oz (110 g) rounds are sold plain, or coated in cracked peppercorns or herbs and garlic. This cheese was a first prizewinner at the London International Cheese Show three years running. *See also* DUDDLESWELL.

SUSSEX YEOMAN

Lyn and Jenny Jenner, Nut Knowle Farm, World's End, Gun Hill, Horam, East Sussex
Artisan maker using the farm's own milk
Type: Goats milk, hard-pressed, full fat, vegetarian

Long-keeping cheese, made to a Swiss recipe and matured for several months to a strong, rich flavour. Available in 3½ lb (1.6 kg) rounds or 1 lb (450 g) miniatures. *See also* CAPRINI.

SWALEDALE

David and Mandy Reed, Swaledale Cheese Company, Mercury Road, Richmond, North Yorkshire
Artisan maker
Type: Cows milk, semi-soft, full fat

It was in early 1985 that David and Mandy Reed began making their traditional Dales cheeses. When Marjorie Longstaff of Harkerside in Upper Swaledale announced that she was to retire, it was feared that traditional Swaledale might disappear for ever, but the Reeds revived production, using her methods. They now make two cheeses, one from cows milk and the other from ewes milk. The cows graze the upland slopes of the Yorkshire Dales National Park, in an area designated 'environmentally sensitive' and where farmers are discouraged from using artificial fertilisers. Swaledale Cows Milk Cheese is mild, moist, semi-soft (one writer described it as 'springy') and slightly sharp. The 1 lb (450 g) and 4 lb (1.8 kg) rounds retain the slightly crumbly texture that larger commercial producers seem unable to copy. Variants are available with garlic and chives or with applemint herb. All cheeses are available in traditional cloth binding or white wax. Swaledale Old Peculier is soaked in Theakstons Old Peculier ale (a pint of ale to every 5 lb of curd!) and presented in a black-waxed round. Swaledale Ewes Milk Cheese is soft, creamy and even-textured. It is smoother and softer than any cows milk Wensleydale. Sometimes smoked and available in traditional cloth binding or white wax. *See also* BEAMISH, RICHMOND SMOKED.

SWINZIE

Ann Dorward, Dunlop Dairy, West Clerkland, Stewarton, Strathclyde
Artisan maker using the farm's own milk
Type: Ewes milk, hard-pressed, full fat

Rich and creamy product, sold in 4½ lb (2 kg) rounds. Developed by Ann Dorward in 1989, and named after a nearby burn, it has won first prize at

the Nantwich Show. *See also*
DUNLOPPE.

SYMONDS YAT

Nick Hodgetts, Malvern Cheesewrights,
Manor House, Lower Wick, Worcester
Artisan maker
Type: Unpasteurised goats milk, semi-
soft, full fat

Fresh and clean-tasting, lemony
cheese. Made on the farm seasonally.
See also MALVERN.

TALA

Heather White, Tala Cheese, North Beer
Farm, Boyton, Launceston, Cornwall
Artisan maker using the farm's own
milk
Type: Ewes milk, hard, full fat, vege-
tarian

First produced in 1989, Tala cheese
takes its name from Tala Water, a tiny
stream which runs through a hidden
valley near Launceston, in the upper
reaches of the river Tamar. This is a
washed-curd cheese, smooth and
mellow, made from the milk of British
Friesland ewes, which tends to be mild
but can be matured. The 5 lb (2.3 kg)
rounds and 14 oz (400 g) miniatures
(ideal presents) have a natural, clean
rind. Also available smoked.

TEIFI FARMHOUSE CHEESE

John and Patrice Savage-Onstwedder,
Glynhynod Organic Farmers, Ffostrasol,
Llandysul, Dyfed
Artisan maker using the farm's own
milk. Visitors by appointment
Type: Unpasteurised cows milk, semi-
hard, full fat, vegetarian

Teifi is, without doubt, a connoisseur's
cheese, selected by *The Independent* as
one of the top ten Farmhouse cheeses.

Patrice trained in Holland and her
cheese is a Gouda-type, organically
made with milk from the Friesian herd
of Rhydgoch Farm, a near neighbour.
The recipe employs traditional starter
(to avoid bitterness later on), vegetarian rennet and sea-salt. The curd is
cut by hand as the action of a curd mill
can lead to a drier cheese. Teifi is
creamy in texture; the aroma suggests
flowers and meadow grasses and the
finish is rich and satisfying. Sizes available include 40 lb (20 kg), 8 lb (3.6 kg),
2 lb (900 g) and 1 lb (450 g) wheels,
some produced in 12 varieties,
including plain, garlic, garlic and onion,
celery and garlic, chives, sweet pepper,
mustard seed, cumin seed, nettles and
laverbread (seaweed). Teifi with cumin
seed was Prince Charles's favourite at
the Royal Welsh Show so the product
has the benefit of royal approval. It was
entered in the Gouda class at the
Nantwich International Cheese Show
and might have won, except that out of
1,000 cheeses present, this was the only
one to be stolen. Obviously the thief
knew a good bit of cheese when he saw
it! Teifi Mature is the only cheese (in
my researches) that claims to possess
aphrodisiac qualities. As some cheeses
have a slight ammonia content, this
may have some basis in fact. A chemical
called phenylethylamine is produced in
the human brain when lovers are in a
state of excitement, and mature cheese
could stimulate its manufacture.
Hundreds of customers have remarked
that whereas normal cheese gives them
headaches or migraine, Teifi has no
such ill effects.

TETBURY SMOKED CHEESES

Philip Grant, House of Cheese, Church
Street, Tetbury, Gloucestershire
Specialist retailer
Type: Smoked cheeses, various

The smoking of cheese requires
considerable delicacy of touch if the
result is to be a success. The prizewin-

ning House of Cheese offers a selection of naturally smoked cheeses which are particularly good, and the smoked Single Gloucester is outstanding.

TEVIOTDALE

John and Christian Curtis, Easter Weens Farm, Bonchester Bridge, Hawick, Borders
Artisan maker using the farm's own milk. Visitors by appointment
Type: Unpasteurised cows milk, semi-hard, full fat

Jersey milk cheese, finished with a natural white crust. This area has been farmed for 2,000 years, the pastures of Bonchester Bridge being protected by Bonchester Hill which stands guard over this wild border country. *See also* BONCHESTER.

THISTLEDOWN

Valerie Morris, Ashdale Cheese, Town Head Farm, Askwith, Otley, West Yorkshire
Artisan maker using local milk
Type: Unpasteurised goats milk, soft, full fat, vegetarian

Orange-waxed 10 oz (300 g) rounds of soft, fresh cheese. *See also* ASHDALE.

THORN BUSH FARM

Chris Williams, Thorn Bush Farm, Slebech, Haverfordwest, Dyfed
Artisan maker using the farm's own milk
Type: Ewes milk, semi-soft, full fat, vegetarian

New maker (1995) commencing production of semi-soft cheese.

TICKLEMORE GOAT CHEESE

Robin Congdon, Ticklemore Cheese, Ticklemore Street, Totnes, Devon
Artisan maker. Visitors welcome
Type: Unpasteurised goats milk, hard-pressed, full fat

Made by hand, pressed in unusual 5 lb (2.3 kg) spheres in basket moulds and allowed to develop a natural rind, this cheese is matured for 2½ months minimum, resulting in a very smooth texture and a medium mature flavour. Normally only available June to January. Ticorino, from the same maker, is a hard-pressed, full-fat, unpasteurised ewes milk cheese. It has a full, mature flavour and is normally only available in limited quantities from June to January. A range of hand-made cheeses is also produced in this small dairy, using milk from three local farms. Some of the cheeses are only available seasonally but the cheese shop is open all year and has rightly become a Mecca for lovers of good food. Telephone (01803) 865926 to check opening times. *See also* BEENLEIGH BLUE, DEVON BLUE, DEVON RUSTIC, HARBOURNE BLUE.

TIMES PAST CHEDDAR

Peppy D'Ovidio, Times Past Cheese Dairy, Westfield Lane, Draycott, Cheddar, Somerset
Artisan maker using milk from six farms in the Cheddar Valley. Visitors welcome
Type: Unpasteurised cows milk, hard-pressed, full fat

The old complaint that too little Cheddar cheese is made in the village of Cheddar is well nigh answered by Times Past Dairy, just a few minutes' walk from Cheddar village. Peppy D'Ovidio, with his 25 years of experience, is regarded as one of the finest cheesemakers in Britain. His traditional cloth-bound Cheddar is available in 52 lb (24 kg), 9 lb (4 kg) and the famous 4½ lb (2 kg) truckles which are especially popular with visitors. Traditional versions of the UK territorial cheeses are also made: Red Leicester, Double Gloucester and Cheshire can be made from pasteurised milk when required. Cheese can be bought at the dairy, 9 am to 3 pm weekdays, or ordered by post. Telephone (01934) 743465 for details.

TOBERMORY TRUCKLES

Jeffrey Reade, Sgriob-Ruadh Farm, Tobermory, Isle of Mull
Artisan maker using the farm's own milk. Visitors welcome
Type: Unpasteurised cows milk, hard-pressed, full fat

Hand-made Farmhouse cheese, strong and full of flavour. The dark-green waxed truckles are dressed with Mackenzie tartan ribbon; the black-waxed truckles carry a Royal Stuart tartan ribbon. Both are made in 1 lb (450 g) or 7 oz (200 g) sizes. *See also* ISLE OF MULL.

TOM BARRON'S FARMHOUSE LANCASHIRE CHEESE

K.W. Leeming, Ambrose Hall Farm, Woodplumpton, Preston, Lancashire
Farmhouse maker using the farm's own milk
Type: Cows milk, hard-pressed, full fat, vegetarian

Prizewinning makers of traditional Lancashire cheese, in 40 lb (20 kg) and 20 lb (9 kg) rounds, just recovering from a disastrous fire. Garlic or sage varieties are sometimes available. Normal production is around 200 tonnes each year.

TORVILLE

R.A. Duckett and Co., Walnut Tree Farm, Heath House, Wedmore, Somerset
Artisan maker using the farm's own milk. Visitors by appointment
Type: Cows milk, hard-pressed, full fat, vegetarian

Rind-washed version of the famous Caerphilly made by Chris Duckett, finished with a 'kneecracker' cider wash, which imparts a distinct scrumpy flavour. *See also* DUCKETT'S.

TOWER FARMS CHEDDAR

Arthur Peters, Deans Cross, Lydeard St Lawrence, Taunton, Somerset
Creamery
Type: Cows milk, hard-pressed, full fat

Nestling in the hollow between the Quantocks and the Brendon Hills lies some of the most peaceful countryside in Somerset. The land is rich and well watered, growing lush grass and ensuring rich milk. Right at the heart of all this plenty, Tower Farms make their Somerset Cheddar. Production is in rindless 40 lb (20 kg) blocks.

TREHILL

Elize Jungheim, Trehill Farm, Sampford Courtnay, Okehampton, Devon
Artisan maker using local milk. Visitors welcome
Type: Cows milk, semi-hard, full fat, vegetarian

Garry and Elize Jungheim are champions of country food, responsible for exhibitions in nearby Tavistock town hall to promote the sale of Devon fare. Trehill is made from pedigree Friesian milk, giving it a buttery taste and texture, and lightly flavoured with garlic and chives. Available in green-waxed 5 lb (2.3 kg), 3 lb (1.4 kg) and 1 lb (450 g) truckles. Trehill St Rumon is made to the same recipe but flavoured with parsley, celery and chives; it is available in the same sizes but red-waxed. Cheese can be bought at the farm shop, which is open all year, or at Natural Life Cheeses near Tavistock Pannier Market, or ordered by post. Telephone (01837) 840684 for details. *See also* DEVON COUNTRY, ST PETROC.

TRUCKLEDOWN

1920 Cheesemakers, Mill Farm, Preston Road, Longridge, Lancashire
Creamery
Type: Cows milk, semi-hard, full fat, vegetarian

Introduced at the 1993 International Food Exhibition and based on a compilation of old family recipes, Truckledown is a delicately flavoured and creamy cheese with a delightful touch of crumbliness in the texture. Sold in traditional round bandaged and waxed truckles. *See also* SINGLETON'S.

TUDOR SMOKED

Karen and Don Ross, Little Acorn Products, Mesen Fach Farm, Bethania, Llanon, Dyfed
Artisan maker. Visitors by appointment
Type: Ewes milk, hard-pressed, full fat, vegetarian

Prizewinning cheese, pressed in 2½ lb (1.1 kg) truckles and cold-smoked over oak chippings to impart a deep flavour. Matures for up to three months. *See also* ACORN.

TUXFORD AND TEBBUTT STILTON

Tuxford and Tebbutt, Thorpe End, Melton Mowbray, Leicestershire
Creamery
Type: Cows milk, semi-hard, full fat

The frontage of Tuxford and Tebbutt's dairy at Melton Mowbray has remained largely unaltered since it was built in 1780. Originally the company manufactured pork pies, Melton Mowbray's other famous product, but they now produce around 13% of all Stilton manufactured in Britain, much of it going for export. The cheese is made largely as it has been for 150 years, but with the assistance of modern controls and storage facilities. Cheese can be bought from the factory shop on most days but visitors are advised to telephone (01664) 500555 to check opening times. *See also* THE CHEESE COMPANY.

TWO CHURCHES

Donal Hayes, Liathmore Cheese, Two-mile-borris, Thurles, Co. Tipperary, Republic of Ireland
Artsian maker using the farm's own milk. Visitors by appointment
Type: Cows milk, soft, low fat, vegetarian

Six generations have farmed the land where the eleventh-century Liathmore Abbey once stood. The history of the site goes back yet further; the ruins of a fifth-century oratory are still to be seen. In recognition of these two buildings, the cheese is appropriately called Two Churches. The farm's own pedigree herd provides the milk for this soft and creamy cheese, made without rennet, in 10 lb (5 kg) or 4½ lb (2 kg) tubs. *See also* COOLBAWN.

TYMSBORO'

Mary Holbrook, Sleight Farm House, Timsbury, Bath, Avon
Artisan maker using the farm's own milk
Type: Unpasteurised goats milk, soft, full fat

Small pyramids of soft cheese, ripened

in the farm's cellars until they develop a natural crust. A spontaneous blue mould sometimes appears. *See also* MENDIP.

TYNEDALE SPA

Jayne Burrough and Diane Gerrard, Irthingspa Dairy Goats, Holme View, Gilsland, Cumbria
Artisan maker. Visitors welcome
Type: Cows milk, hard-pressed, full fat, vegetarian

Creamy and crumbly cheese, available plain or smoked in 5 lb (2.3 kg), 2 lb (900 g) and 1 lb (450 g) rounds. *See also* IRTHINGSPA.

TY'N GRUG FARMHOUSE CHEDDAR

Dougal and Alex Campbell, Welsh Organic Foods, Tregaron Road, Lampeter, Dyfed
Artisan maker using the farm's own milk. Visitors by appointment
Type: Unpasteurised cows milk, hard-pressed, full fat, vegetarian

The Campbells gained their experience of cheesemaking over ten years ago in Switzerland. Amongst the peaks and chalets, they learnt to handle brown cows with large bells and make cheese without starters whilst the curd was separated in copper vats heated over wood fires. Dougal's first job was learning to build the log fire so that it was hot enough to scald the curd without burning the whey in the bottom of the vat. The second essential skill was learning to make cheese without soot or ash floating around on the top! With the luxuries of mains gas and water, Dougal is now able to produce cheese in a more leisurely manner. This is rich, organic Cheddar with a superb aroma and delicious acidity. Highly praised for its rich, full taste and slightly grainy texture, it is available in mature or medium-mature, 30 lb (14 kg) rounds, 6 lb (2.7 kg) truckles and smaller vacuum portions.

TYNING

Mary Holbrook, Sleight Farm House, Timsbury, Bath, Avon
Artisan maker using the farm's own milk
Type: Unpasteurised ewes milk, hard, full fat

An unpressed cheese, made in 6 lb (2.7 kg) basket moulds and matured for 6–12 months, by which time it has acquired a hard texture and an intense flavour, reminiscent of an Italian Pecorino. A prizewinner at the Nantwich Show. *See also* MENDIP.

TYNWALDE SMOKED CHEDDAR

Ellan Vannin Farms, Isle of Man Milk Marketing Association, Tremode, Isle of Man
Creamery using local milk
Type: Cows milk, hard-pressed, full fat, vegetarian

Milk from the island's farms is collected to produce over 2,000 tonnes of cheese per year, mainly Cheddar and other English territorials in 40 lb (20 kg) blocks and 7 lb (3 kg) wheels. Tynwalde (named after the Isle of Man parliament) is available in attractive black-waxed 6 oz (170 g) rounds. It is slowly smoked over oak. *See also* DRUIDALE.

UNIGATE *see* ST IVEL

VEGETARIAN CHEESE *see p. 24*

VELDE

Nachi Elkin, Gedi Enterprises,

Plumridge Farm, Stagg Hill, Barnet, Hertfordshire
Artisan maker using the farm's own milk. Visitors welcome
Type: Goats milk, semi-soft, full fat, vegetarian

Mild and smooth goat cheese. The 4½ oz (120 g) rounds are dusted with a charcoal coating (entirely edible) which adds a nutty character. *See also* CHAVANNES.

VERGIN

Rachel Stephens, Curworthy Cheese, Stockbeare Farm, Jacobstowe, Okehampton, Devon
Artisan maker using the farm's own milk
Type: Cows milk, semi-hard, full fat

CURWORTHY cheese enlivened by a bright-gold label, shiny red wax, and the addition of stem ginger. Hot stuff! Available in 7 oz (200 g) waxed miniatures.

VINTAGE

D. John Davidge, Ilchester Cheese Company, Ilchester, Somerset
Specialist dairy making character cheeses
Type: Cows milk, hard-pressed, full fat

Mature Cheddar cheese richly veined with ruby port wine. *See also* ILCHESTER.

VULSCOMBE

Josephine and Graham Townsend, Higher Vulscombe Farm, Cruwys Morchard, Devon
Artisan maker using the farm's own milk
Type: Unpasteurised goats milk, hard-pressed, full fat, vegetarian

Rennet-free, lactic curd cheese, formed in 6 oz (170 g) cylinders, highly praised by *Good Cheese* magazine. Sold plain or with the addition of garlic, fresh organic herbs or crushed black peppercorns. The farm is run according to organic methods and cheese may be bought direct, but telephone (01884) 252505 to check opening times.

WALDA

Olivia Mills, Brebilait Products, Wield Wood Estate, Alresford, Hampshire
Artisan maker using the farm's own milk. Visitors by appointment
Type: Heat-treated ewes milk, semi-hard, full fat, vegetarian

Olivia Mills is a leading international authority on sheep dairying, secretary of the British Sheep Dairying Association and, need I say, a formidable champion of ewes milk cheeses. Her own flocks graze natural pasture and are managed in sympathy with organic principles. The milk is not pasteurised but 'thermalised', i.e. heat treated at a lower temperature which is sufficient to kill coliform bacteria but retains the milk's local character. Cheese is made by hand and not pressed other than under its own weight in the 'Dutch' method. The 7 lb (3 kg), 4½ lb (2 kg) and 2.2 lb (1 kg) rounds are pressed in Gouda moulds and dressed with a clear wax. They are clean cutting, slightly crumbly and have the rich aroma and slight sweetness typical of ewes milk products. They have achieved awards at every major cheese show. Green peppers or caraway seeds are occasionally added, and part of the production is matured for as long as three years, by which time it has become a superb grating cheese. Cheese has been made on this farm since medieval times, when the village was known as Wald or Walda, hence the name of the modern product. Cheese can be bought at the farm but telephone (01420) 563151 before calling to check opening times.

WALDORF

D. John Davidge, Ilchester Cheese Company, Ilchester, Somerset
Specialist dairy making character cheeses
Type: Cows milk, hard-pressed, full fat, vegetarian

Inspired by the world-famous salad, Waldorf is a mellow, crumbly blend of mature Cheddar cheese with apple, pineapple, roasted hazelnuts and celery. *See also* ILCHESTER.

WARREN FARM CHEDDAR

Phillip Cook, A.H. Warren Ltd, Coombe Farm, Crewkerne, Somerset
Farmhouse maker using the farm's own milk
Type: Cows milk, hard-pressed, full fat, vegetarian

A rindless Cheddar cheese made largely by traditional methods. The dairy was established by the late Mr A.H. Warren, one of the founding fathers of the Farmhouse Cheese-makers scheme. The 1,800 cows in the milking herd benefit from the right basics: 3,000 acres of unspoilt grassland and the highest standards of animal husbandry. Their feed (mostly natural silage) is formulated and mixed on site; they have their own vet on call and the dairy is equipped with a modern laboratory. The result is superb-quality milk, which goes into the making of Cheddar cheese 365 days a year. Warren's is the largest operation in Somerset still making cheese by manual methods; the cheddaring is done on open tables. Other manufacturers have adopted more economic Tower systems, but the taste and texture of Warren Farm Cheddar show the advantages of doing it the old way. Even though modern retailing demands cheese in rindless 40 lb (20 kg) blocks, Warren's can rightly claim still to be making 'real' Farm-house Cheddar cheese, sensibly concentrating on the longer-keeping variety. The cheese is matured on the farm, in temperature- and humidity-controlled stores, then despatched at 10–15 months. Sizes available include 40 lb (20 kg), 10 lb (5 kg) and prepacked consumer wedges and there is a limited production of miniature black-waxed truckles in various sizes. It is not possible to buy cheese direct from the farm in small quantities.

WATERFORD FOODS

Waterford Foods, 35 Steps, Magherin Road, Lurgan, Craigavon, Co. Armagh, Northern Ireland
Major creamery proprietor manufacturing at several locations
Type: Cows milk, semi-soft, full fat, vegetarian

Manufacturer of Mozzarella, producing around 7,000 tonnes each year.

WATERLOO

Mrs Anne Wigmore, Village Maid, The Cottage, Basingstoke Road, Riseley, Berkshire
Artisan maker using milk from a single herd
Type: Unpasteurised cows milk, soft, full fat, vegetarian

Guernsey milk from the Duke of Wellington's estate is used to make this washed-curd cheese. Rich and golden in colour, creamy in texture and mild in taste. Available in 2½ lb (1.1 kg) and 1 lb (450 g) rounds. *See also* WELLINGTON.

WAVENEY

Susan Moore, Cranes Watering Farm, Starston, Harleston, Norfolk
Artisan maker using the farm's own milk. Visitors by appointment
Type: Unpasteurised cows milk, semi-soft, full fat, vegetarian

A Norfolk milk cheese, made from the milk of Jersey and Guernsey cows that graze the banks of the river Waveney, which divides Norfolk from Suffolk. Slightly salted and made in alternate annatto-coloured and plain layers. *See also* MOORE CHEESE.

WEBSTERS DAIRY STILTON

Margaret Callow, Websters Dairy, Saxelby, Melton Mowbray, Leicestershire
Small creamery using local milk
Type: Cows milk, semi-hard, full fat

The smallest of the blue Stilton makers and, by many accounts, the best of them all. Cheese has been made at the dairy for over 125 years (some parts of the building date back to the seventeenth century). Made using local milk, Websters Stilton is buttery-textured and exceptionally creamy. Around seventy 15 lb (7 kg) truckles are produced each day, available white or well-blued. Stilton made with non-animal rennet and 4½ lb (2 kg) miniatures are available to order.

WEDMORE

R.A. Duckett and Co., Walnut Tree Farm, Heath House, Wedmore, Somerset
Farmhouse maker using the farm's own milk. Visitors by appointment
Type: Unpasteurised cows milk, hard-pressed, full fat, vegetarian

This is a Caerphilly with a layer of chopped chives, which impart a delicate flavour that improves with age. Pressed in 7 in (18 cm) discs. *See also* DUCKETT'S.

WELLINGTON

Mrs Anne Wigmore, Village Maid, The Cottage, Basingstoke Road, Riseley, Berkshire
Artisan maker using milk from a single herd

Type: Unpasteurised cows milk, hard pressed, full fat, vegetarian

Anne Wigmore has been making cheese since 1985, following 10 years in dairy research at Reading University. What began as home cheesemaking has expanded to the point where there are 1,000 cheeses maturing in her store. Wellington is traditionally made and matured for six months. It has a full flavour, likened to a cross between Cheddar and Double Gloucester, and a natural rind. Its aroma is described as fruity. The cheese goes well with a ripe Comice pear. Anne uses milk from the Duke of Wellington's herd of Guernsey cows, and the cheese is matured in the cellars of the Duke's ancestral home, Stratfield Saye. *See also* SPENWOOD, WATERLOO, WIGMORE.

WELSH RAREBIT

Bryson Craske, Abergavenny Fine Foods, Castle Meadows Park, Abergavenny, Gwent
Artisan maker. Visitors welcome
Type: Cows milk, hard-pressed with other ingredients, vegetarian

Made to a traditional Welsh recipe, ready to spread on hot toast. Turns golden brown when grilled. Also superb as a sauce for cauliflower cheese. *See also* CASTLE MEADOWS CAERPHILLY.

WENSLEYDALE (BLUE)

J.M. Nutall, Hartington Creamery, Buxton, Derbyshire
Creamery
Type: Cows milk, semi-hard, low fat

Nuttalls have revived the manufacture of a blue-veined Dales cheese. Traditionally presented in cloth-bound 13 lb (6 kg) rounds, the cheese has a low fat content and a mild, honey flavour when young, which ripens to a rich flavour as it matures. *See also* DAIRY CREST.

WENSLEYDALE (COWS MILK)

Richard Clark, Wensleydale Dairy Products, Gayle Lane, Hawes, North Yorkshire
Small creamery using local milk. Visitors welcome
Type: Cows milk, semi-hard, full fat

Amongst the staff of Wensleydale Creamery are descendants of Kit Calvert, and much is made of the heritage left by the 'King of Wensleydale'. A new creamery was completed in 1993, although the cheese is still made largely by hand. It is matured for two weeks, retaining a slightly flaky texture and honeyed aroma. A fuller flavoured 'original' Wensleydale, matured for 16 weeks, and a smoked variety are also made. A visitor centre with a restaurant, a museum of cheese-making and a viewing gallery over the dairy have been provided to cater for the many tourists who flock to the Dales. Telephone (01969) 667664 to check opening times. Fortunately the interest in reviving Dales cheeses is not confined to one maker alone and other excellent products are made. *See entries for* FOUNTAINS DAIRY, GREENFIELDS DAIRY, KNOLTON FARMHOUSE, LAURELS FARM and RICHARD III.

WENSLEYDALE (COWS AND EWES MILK)

Mark Robertson, Northumberland Cheeses Company, Soppitt Farm, Otterburn, Northumberland
Artisan maker using the farm's own milk
Type: Cows milk, hard-pressed, full fat, vegetarian

The mixing of cows and ewes milk results in a cheese with the classic Wensleydale acidity but a deeper and more mature flavour. The 7 lb (3 kg) and 2 lb (850 g) truckles are hand-salted and cloth-wrapped. *See also* NORTHUMBERLAND.

WENSLEYDALE (EWES MILK)

Type: Ewes milk, semi-hard, full fat

Wensleydale should be mild, creamy and white, made from a finely cut curd that is only lightly pressed, retaining the high moisture content that gives a crumbly and flaky texture. It is best eaten fresh, to fully savour the honey aftertaste, and is particularly good with apple pie or a crisp fresh apple. Artisan makers include ASHES and SHEPHERDS PURSE.

WENSLEYDALE (NEW RECIPE)

Long Clawson Dairy, Melton Mowbray, Leicestershire
Creamery
Type: Cows milk, semi-hard, full fat

Long Clawson's 'New Recipe' collection forms part of an ongoing research and development programme. Wensleydale with apricots was launched in 1992, and has now been joined by Wensleydale with stem ginger. Supplied in 10 in (25 cm) half-moons.

WEST HIGHLAND SOFT CHEESES

Kathy Biss, West Highland Dairy, Achmore, Stromeferry, By Kyle of Lochalsh, Highland
Artisan maker using the farm's own milk. Visitors welcome
Type: Pasteurised, various milks, vegetarian

A range of soft cheeses, cows milk Crowdie prominent amongst them as befits a farm this far north. Fresh curd and Coulommier-type cheeses are made from cows, goats, or the farm's own ewes milk in various styles. Call at the farm shop to see the range. Telephone (01599) 577203 to check opening times. *See also* ASCAIG, CREAGMHOL.

WESTMORLAND WONDERS

Peter Gott, Sillfield Farm, Endmoor, Crooklands, Cumbria
Artisan maker
Type: Unpasteurised cows milk, semi-soft, full fat, vegetarian

Soft cheeses in a dazzling variety of flavours, formed into rounds and lightly waxed. Varieties include apricot, cajun spice, chilli and garlic, chives and onions, garlic, hot black pepper, peach and pear, and sweet pickle.

WEST ULSTER FARMERS MOZZARELLA

Dromore Road, Irvinestown, Co. Fermanagh, Northern Ireland
Creamery
Type: Cows milk, soft and semi-soft, full fat

A farmers' co-operative, manufacturing around 6,000 tonnes of Mozzarella each year. Cottage cheese is also made, albeit on a much smaller scale.

WESTWAY DAIRY MATURE CHEDDAR

David Gillard, Westway Dairy Company Ltd, Westway Farm, Bishop Sutton, Avon
Farmhouse cheese specialist
Type: Cows milk, hard-pressed, full fat, vegetarian

Specialist suppliers of Farmhouse Cheddar, using their grading skills and close connections with local farms to bring Cheddar aged from 8–18 months to market. Range includes traditional Cheddar and rindless Cheddar in 40 lb (20 kg) or 6½ lb (3 kg) counter-cutting blocks and prepacked wedges. They also produce ready-grated cheese. Westway Cheddar is sold by several supermarket groups and a number of specialist retailers. Cheese cannot be bought direct from the farm but Westway operates a number of excellent cheese stalls within the markets of Cardiff, Gloucester, Newport and Worcester. David Gillard is credited with making the most expensive purchase of English cheese on record. On 3 June 1988, at the Royal Bath and West Show, the champion cheeses were auctioned and cheese factors competed for them. Mr Gillard was a successful bidder, paying £210 for a 15 lb (6.8 kg) Double Gloucester cheese, equal to £14 per pound. *See also* ISLE OF ATHELNEY and CHEDDAR (TASTY).

WHITE STILTON *see* STILTON (WHITE)

WHIRL

Long Clawson Dairy, Melton Mowbray, Leicestershire
Creamery
Type: Cows milk, soft, full fat

Red Leicester or Double Gloucester cheese, formed into rolls with a swirl of flavoured, full-fat, soft cheese as a filling. Varieties include Leicester with soft cheese, herbs and garlic; Leicester with soft cheese, onions and chives; Leicester with soft cheese and celery; Double Gloucester with smoked salmon. *See also* LONG CLAWSON

WIGMORE

Mrs Anne Wigmore, Village Maid, The Cottage, Basingstoke Road, Riseley, Berkshire
Artisan maker using milk from a single herd

Type: Unpasteurised ewes milk, semi-soft, full fat, vegetarian

A creamy, soft, Reblochon-type cheese with a flowery aroma. It has a naturally soft rind and is matured for 4–6 weeks. Available in 3½ lb (1.6 kg) and 1 lb (450 g) rounds. *See also* WATERLOO.

WILLOWDOWN

Margaret Willcock, Humphreys Farm, Nutley, Uckfield, East Sussex
Artisan maker using the farm's own milk. Visitors welcome
Type: Unpasteurised goats milk, medium fat, vegetarian

Willowdown Soft is a fresh-tasting cheese, ideal for spreading, and comes in 4 oz (100 g) cylinders; it is also available with garlic and herbs. Willowdown Hard Pressed is sold in 2 lb (900 g) cylinders. Margaret Willcock regularly shows her British Saanen goats, all descended from two she 'rescued' 20 years ago, and has exported stock to Zambia, Spain and Portugal. Foreign travel is no problem; her husband used to pilot DC10s! The animals are organically fed, grazing herbal-mix paddocks in rotation. When Margaret and her husband started cheesemaking they couldn't find suitable goat cheese recipes (many seemed bent on imitating cows milk products), so they took the bull by the horns (ouch!) and asked the French Goat Association for advice. They struggled through a French instruction book with the help of a dictionary, eventually discovering the recipes they use for Willowdown. Margaret used to mix her own concentrates in a cement mixer, but now a local miller makes up feeds to her direction. Cheese can be bought at the farm and tours of the dairy can be arranged but telephone (01825) 712432 first for details of opening times.

WINDSOR'S CHESHIRE CHEESE

W.J. and T.E. Windsor, The Lodge Farm, Black Park, Whitchurch, Shropshire
Farmhouse maker using the farm's own milk. Visitors by appointment
Type: Cows milk, hard-pressed, full fat

Specialist makers of traditional Cheshire cheese, in 52 lb (24 kg) rounds and smaller sizes. Production is around 300 tonnes per year. Cheese cannot be bought direct from the farm but parties are sometimes taken round the dairy. Telephone (01948) 662958 for details.

WOLFEN MILL LANCASHIRE CHEESE

Procter and Son, Wolfen Mill Dairy, Chipping, Lancashire
Small creamery using local milk
Type: Cows milk, hard or semi-hard, full fat

In the Forest of Bowland, the wind blows fresh, the rain falls softly and the grass grows green. Near the village of Chipping, in the heart of Bowland, lies Wolfen Mill Dairy. Local farms supply 4,000 gallons (20,000 litres) of milk each day, much of it going into the Lancashire cheese that the family have been making here for generations. Theirs is a fine-textured, creamy Lancashire, made by the two-day curd method and pressed in 28 lb (13 kg) rounds. The dairy also manufactures a Lancashire with onion, Double Gloucester and Red Leicester cheeses.

WORCESTER SAUCE CHEESE

Alyson Anstey, Anstey's of Worcester, Broomhall Farm, Worcester
Artisan maker using the farm's own milk. Visitors welcome
Type: Unpasteurised cows milk, hard-pressed, full fat, vegetarian

Old Worcester White cheese marbled with the 'Original and genuine Lea and Perrins Worcestershire sauce'. A prizewinner at the Nantwich Show, supplied in cloth-bound 6½ lb (3 kg) rounds and mini-truckles. *See also* OLD WORCESTER WHITE.

WORCESTERSHIRE GOLD

Nick Hodgetts, Malvern Cheesewrights, Manor Farm, Lower Wick, Worcester
Artisan maker using the farm's own milk
Type: Unpasteurised cows milk, semi-hard, full fat, vegetarian

Superb creamy, golden cheese made with milk from Sandwell Priory, where cheese was made by Cistercian monks in the Middle Ages. The Jersey herd grazes unspoilt pasture, rich with natural herbs. After the cheese has matured for 3–4 months it develops a delightful herby scent accompanied by a rich, clean aftertaste. Available in 5 lb (2.3 kg) wheels, 3 lb (1.5 kg) truckles and 14 oz (400 g) miniatures. *See also* MALVERN.

WYKE FARMHOUSE CHEDDAR

John Clothier, White House Farm, Wyke Champflower, Bruton, Somerset

On-farm creamery
Type: Cows milk, hard-pressed, full fat

During the Middle Ages the quaintly named village of Wyke Champflower was held by a knight from Champfleury in Normandy. Wyke (or wick) means a group of outlying farm buildings and probably indicates a place where cheese was made. Cheese has certainly been made here since the 1930s, when Ivy Clothier began winning prizes at agricultural shows for the exceptional quality of her Cheddar. The tradition continues, but very differently now as the third gener-ation of the Clothier family make 7,000 tonnes of cheese each year in 40 lb (20 kg) rindless blocks. They farm 2,000 acres of Somerset and Dorset, milking around 1,300 cows, but this only provides a fraction of their require-ments and over 70 local farms supply the balance. The dairy is equipped with five Cheddarmaster towers. Wyke Farmhouse rindless Cheddar is to be found in many supermarkets and has been selected as Supreme Champion at the Royal Bath and West Show. Cider Cheddar is one of the farm's speciali-ties, combining both the things for which Somerset is famous.

YARG

Michael and Margaret Horrell, Lynher Valley Dairy, Upton Cross, Liskeard, Cornwall
Artisan maker using the farm's own milk. Visitors welcome
Type: Cows milk, hard, full fat, vege-tarian

Light, creamy, mould-ripened cheese, the only product still coated with nettle leaves in the traditional way. The nettles were said to have the practical advantages of keeping the cheese moist and warding off flies in days gone by. It was Alan and Jennie Gray who invented Yarg in 1982, christening the new cheese with a reversal of their own surname. When the Gray family ceased manufacture it was taken up by the Horrells. *See also* CORNISH SOFT CHEESE.

YEOMAN

D. John Davidge, Ilchester Cheese Company, Ilchester, Somerset
Specialist dairy making character cheeses
Type: Cows milk, hard-pressed, full fat

Cheddar blended with sweet pickle in 5 lb (2.5 kg) wheels. *See also* ILCHESTER.

Y-FENNI

Bryson Craske, Abergavenny Fine Foods, Castle Meadows Park, Abergavenny, Gwent
Artisan maker. Visitors welcome
Type: Cows milk, hard-pressed, full fat, vegetarian

Mature Cheddar blended with wholegrain mustard and Welsh ale. *See also* CASTLE MEADOWS CAERPHILLY.

YNSMON

Peter Sayer, Welsh Farmhouse Cheese, Maesllyn, Llandysul, Dyfed
Artisan maker. Visitors welcome
Type: Unpasteurised cows milk, hard-pressed, full fat, vegetarian

Matured Welsh Cheddar, made using local milk, with added coarse-grain mustard seed and Welsh ale. Sold in burgundy-waxed 5 lb (2.3 kg) rounds or 1 lb (450 g) miniatures. *See also* ST EMELYN.

YORKSHIRE BLUE

Judy Bell, Shepherds Purse, Leachfield Grange, Bellfields, Newsham, Thirsk, North Yorkshire
Artisan maker
Type: Ewes milk, hard-pressed, full fat, vegetarian

Developed in 1990 but produced by traditional methods, Yorkshire Blue re-creates the true Wensleydale which was originally a ewes milk cheese. *Penicillium roqueforti* is added to the curd and the cheeses are spiked with stainless-steel wires in the manner of Stilton. At 12 weeks Yorkshire Blue is slightly crumbly with a mild tang and sweet taste, but then goes on to develop a distinctive 'sheepy' mellowness without sharpness or acidity. Sold in 8 lb (3.6 kg) rounds. From the same dairy comes Yorkshire Feta, a semi-soft, low-fat cheese, made with vegetarian rennet and brined less heavily than is normal. Creamy-textured, piquant and slightly acid, it usually comes in a two-toned green and white wax so that it has a longer life. Sold in 2½ lb (1.1 kg) or 1 lb (450 g) drums. Yorkshire Lowlands Farmhouse Cheese is made from unpasteurised ewes milk. It is hard-pressed and full fat, with vegetarian rennet. Traditionally hand-made and matured for 3–6 months, the cheese has a 'nutty and woody' flavour and firm texture. Finished in bright poppy-red wax, in 3½ lb (1.6 kg) rounds and 10 oz (280 g) baby cheeses. *See also* SHEPHERDS PURSE.

YORVIK

Mrs Suzanne Stirke, Fortmayne Cottage, Newton le Willows, North Yorkshire
Artisan maker using the farm's own milk
Type: Cows milk, soft, full fat, vegetarian

The old name for York provides the new name for a very traditional way of presenting cheese. York cheese used to be made by the farmers' wives in the Dales, who used their bread tins as moulds. A layer of cream was placed between two layers of cheese, and this would turn yellow with time. The resulting striped cheese was turned out and sliced like cake. Suzanne Stirke has re-created the cheese, except that it is now a layer of annatto-coloured curd with a scattering of chives that makes the stripe through the 1 lb (450 g) round cheeses. *See also* RICHARD III.

Good Places to Buy Cheese

The directory on pp. 95–201 lists around 1,000 cheeses, but where to buy them? No retailer could stock them all; some outlets stock only a few but the better shops offer an interesting display, backed by staff who have a sound working knowledge of what they sell. It is the smaller retailers who score highly on both counts, although the large supermarkets, who supply most of our cheese, have some outstanding branches. The displays at Tesco's in Chorley, Lancashire, and West Amersham, Buckinghamshire, for example, have been awarded prizes. Asda deserve a mention for their innovative counters and incredible variety, including 40 types of cut Cheddar in larger branches. The larger Co-op stores have good displays, Portsmouth and Plymouth being particularly worthy of note. Somerfield/Gateway Stores stock a truly outstanding vintage mature Cheddar and praise must be given to Safeway for the sheer effort they have put into developing the market for cheese. I cannot pretend that my list is complete, for there are many good places to buy cheese, and I apologise if your favourite counter is omitted.

ENGLAND

Avon

Alvis Brothers Farm Shop, Lye Cross Farm, Redhill, Bristol
Cheese Cottage, 42 High Street, Midsomer Norton
Felix van den Berghe, 40 High Street, Westbury on Trym, Bristol (Alan Brown)
Fine Cheese Company, 29 Walcot Street, Bath (Tony Down)
Nibbles, Guildhall Market, Bath
Paxton & Whitfield, 1 John Street, Bath
Sanders Superstore, Lympsham, Weston-super-Mare

Berkshire

County Delicacies, 35 St Mary's Butts, Reading
Old Dairy Farm Shop, Pathhill Farm, Whitchurch-on-Thames, nr
  Reading (Mrs E. Rose)

Cambridgeshire

Essentially English, 106 West Street, Oundle, Peterborough

Channel Islands

D.W.R. Best Ltd, 39–40 Meat Market, St Peter Port, Guernsey

Cheshire

J.H. Bickley, High Street, Malpas (John Huxley)
Cheese Shop, 116 Northgate Street, Chester (Carole Faulkner)
Godfrey C. Williams & Son, 9–11 The Square, Sandbach
Good Food, 68 Chestergate, Macclesfield
Mottersheads, Stall 3, The Market, Warrington
Warhams of Nantwich (S.J. Biggins), Warrington Market

Cornwall

Carley and Co., 34–6 St Austell Street, Truro
Cheese Board, Pannier Market, Lemon Quay, Truro
Lynher Valley Dairy, Netherton Farm, Upton Cross, Liskeard (Michael
  Horrell)
Menallack Farm, Treverva (John and Caryl Minson)

Cumbria

Cheeseboard, 18 Covered Market, Scotch Street, Carlisle
Cheese Stall, The Market, Dalton Road, Barrow-in-Furness (Peter
  Gott)
Butterworth's, 50 Quarry Rigg, Bowness-on-Windermere
James and John Graham, 7–8 Carvyles Court, Carlisle

also at Finkle Street, Kendal
6–7 Market Square, Penrith
The Lakes Fine Fresh Food Store, Tithebarn Street, Keswick
Thornby Moor Dairy, Crofton Hall, Thursby, Carlisle (Mrs Carolyn
   Fairbairn)

Derbyshire

Chatsworth House Farm Shop, Stud Farm, Pilsley, Bakewell
Cheeseboard Delicatessen, 22 Market Place, Ashbourne
Food and Wine Shop, Cliff House, Terrace Road, Buxton (Peter
   Pugson)
Gallery Cheese Shop, The Wardwick, Derby (Terry Millner)
St James Delicatessen, 9–11 St James Street, Derby (Ken Davis)
Ye Olde Cheese Shoppe, Hartington, Buxton

Devon

Barnstaple Delicatessen, Butchers Row, Barnstaple (Les and Ann Lyn)
Blackdown Goat Centre, Rings Lane, Loddiswell, Kingsbridge (William
   Martin)
Blacks of Chagford, 28 The Square, Chagford
Brian Ford, Seven Brethren Bank, Barnstaple
Churston Delicatessen, Churston, Paignton
Hungry Palate, 31 Market Avenue, Plymouth (Roger Cashman)
Mange Tout Delicatessen, 84 Fore Street, Kingsbridge (Debbie Sharley)
Natural Life Cheeses, The Pannier Market, Tavistock (Elize Jungheim)
Normans, Station Road, Budleigh Salterton (and branches throughout
   the West Country)
Plymco Superstore, Plympton, Plymouth (and the larger branches of
   Plymouth and South Devon Co-op)
J.G. Quicke Farm Shop, Woodley, Newton St Cyres, Exeter
Ticklemore Cheese Shop, 1 Ticklemore Street, Totnes
Watty's Delicatessen, 16 Catherine Street, Exeter

Dorset

Down to Earth, Princes Street, Dorchester (David Nestling)
Farmer Bailey's Cheese Centre, 54 High Street, Shaftesbury
Sabins Fine Foods, 5 Hound Street, Sherborne (David Kiddie)

Durham

Cheeseboard, In-Shops, 154–6 Front Street, Chester-le-Street
Home Farm Shop, Beamish Outdoor Museum, Beamish
Partners (Talbot Gray Ltd), 26 Horsemarket, Barnard Castle
Philberts, 9 Grange Road, Darlington

Essex

Chisnells Delicatessen, 12 Market Row, Saffron Walden (Chris
    Chisnell)
Fiveways Superstore, Manningtree
Guntons, 81–3 Crouch Street, Colchester (Mr G.A. Gunton)
Harrison's, Commercial Road, Westcliff-on-Sea

Gloucestershire

Birdwood House Farm Shop, Birdwood, Huntley (Melissa Ravenhill)
Bomfords, 61 Cricklade Street, Cirencester
Carol's Delicatessen, Chickabiddy Lane, Southam
Hania Cheese, The Shambles Market, Stroud (Fridays only)
Hamptons Delicatessen, 1 Digbeth Street, Stow-on-the-Wold
House of Cheese, 13 Church Street, Tetbury (Philip Grant)
Westway Dairy, Eastgate Market, Gloucester
Windrush Wines, The Ox House, Market Square, Northleach

Hampshire

Harvest Delicatessen, 46 West Street, Alresford (Jeff Webb)
Havant Hypermarket and larger branches of Portsea Island Co-op
Kimbridge Farm Shop, Kimbridge, nr Romsey (Anne Humbert)
La Fromage, 172 Albert Road, Southsea (Mr Hewitt)

Hereford and Worcester

Anstey's of Worcester, Broomhall Farm, Worcester (Alyson Anstey)
Green Link Organic Food, 9 Graham Road, Great Malvern
J's Delicatessen, 16 High Street, Droitwich (Janet Slater)
La Fromagerie, Malvern Link
Doug Morgan, The Butter Market, Hereford
Mousetrap, 1 Bewell Square, Hereford

Mousetrap, 3 School Lane, Leominster (Mark and Karen Hindle)
Organic Options, 15 Broad Street, Leominster
Robbins, Port Street, Evesham
Westway Dairy, The Shambles Market, Worcester

Kent

James's of Beckenham, 188 High Street, Beckenham (John Sanders)
Little Deli, 86 High Street, Edenbridge (Suzy Roberts)
Perfect Partners, 7 Stone Street, Cranbrook (Richard Clark)

Lancashire

Greenfields Dairy, Skye House Lane, Goosnargh, Preston (Peter
    Procter)
Preston Market (numerous cheese stalls, well worth a visit)
John Rose, Spar Supermarket, Lancaster University

Leicestershire

Cheese Cottage, 6 Churchgate, Loughborough
Clawson Cheese Shop, 8 Windsor Street, Melton Mowbray
Emmerson & West, 7 Northampton Road, Market Harborough
Christopher James, 606 Queen's Road, Leicester
Leicester City Centre Market (a delight to browse round, has several
    cheese stalls)
Long Clawson Dairy (factory shop), Melton Mowbray
David North, Station Road, Rothley
Uppingham Delicatessen, 29 High Street East, Uppingham

Lincolnshire

Commestibles, 82 Bailgate, Lincoln (Kate O'Meara)

London area

Barstow & Barr, 24 Liverpool Road, N1
Bumble Bee, 30 Brecknock Road, N7 (Iain Olgivie)
Cheeseboard, Royal Hill, Greenwich
Gedi Enterprises, Plumridge Farm, Stagg Hill, Barnet
Harrods Fromagerie, Brompton Road, Knightsbridge SW1

Jereboams, 24 Bute Street, SW6
Jereboams, 51 Elizabeth Street, SW1
La Fromagerie, 62 Talbot Road, Highgate, N6 (Patricia Michelson)
Mortimer & Bennett, 33 Turnham Green Terrace, W4 (Dan Mortimer
   and Di Bennett)
Mr. Christian's, 11 Elgin Crescent, W1 (Greg Scott)
Neals Yard Dairy, 17 Shorts Gardens, WC2
Paxton & Whitfield, 93 Jermyn Street, W1
Real Cheese, Wimbledon
Selfridges Food Hall, Oxford Street, W1
Villandry, 89 Marylebone High Street, W1 (Jean Charles)

Manchester

Cheese Hamlet, 706 Wilmslow Road, Didsbury (Arthur Axon)

Norfolk

Cranes Watering Farm, Rushall Road, Starston, Harleston
Humble Pie Foods, Burnham Market, Norfolk
The Mousetrap, 2 St Gregory's Alley, Norwich (Mr Hatch)
Roys of Wroxham, Out of Town Centre, Wroxham
   also at Roys, Easton Centre, Church Lane, Easton

Northumberland

C'est Cheese, Market Street, Hexham
Corbridge Larder, Heron House, Hill Street, Corbridge
The Food Shop, Berwick-upon-Tweed
Real Cheese Shop, 6 Oldgate, Morpeth
Redesdale Pantry, Otterburn
Robb & Son, Fore Street, Hexham

Nottinghamshire

Cheese Cuisine, 10 Saracens Head Yard, Newark (Louise Hanson)
Cheese Shop, 14 Market Street, Bingham (Hans Hanson)
Traditional Foods, 99 Melton Road, West Bridgford
Whitewell's Delicatessen, Canning Circus, 7–9 Ilkeston Road,
   Nottingham
   also at 93 Melton Road, West Bridgford

Oxfordshire

Carter & Son, 3 Marlborough Street, Faringdon
Delikatesserie, 239 Banbury Road, Summertown, Oxford
Gluttons, 110 Walton Street, Oxford
The Granary, 30 High Street, Watlington (Robert Francis)
Oxford Cheese Company, The Covered Market, Oxford
What's for Dinner, 23 Market Place, Henley on Thames (Carolyn and
    Mark Sinclair)
Wells Stores, 29 Stert Street, Abingdon (Gill Draycott)
Wyatt's Farm Shop, Long Compton

Shropshire

Cook'n'Carve, Under the Clock Market, Shrewsbury
Good Cheese from Wales, Under the Clock Market, Shrewsbury
    (Karen Ross)
T.O. Williams, Williams of Wem, High Street, Wem

Somerset

Robin Boswell, Food and Wine Shop, High Street, Yeovil
The Cheddar Cheese Company Ltd, The Gorge, Cheddar (trading as
    The Original Cheddar Cheese and Cider Depot in William Small's
    old shop)
Cheese and Wine Shop, South Street, Wellington (Peter and Geraldine
    Orr)
Chewton Dairy Farm, Priory Farm, Chewton Mendip
County Stores, North Street, Taunton
Cricket Malherbie Farm Shop, Stowey Court Farm, Nether Stowey,
    Bridgwater
Delicatessen, 36 High Street, Shepton Mallet
Laurel Bank Dairy, Queen Street, Wells (Mike Pullin)
Manor Court Delicatessen, 9 Fore Street, Chard
Martin's Market Place, Castle Cary (R. and J. Lovegrove)
Maryland Farm, Ditcheat, Shepton Mallet (A.R. and J.G. Barber)
Red House Farm Shop, Stratton-on-the-Fosse (V.M. Creed)
Jon Thorners Farm Shop, Pylle, Shepton Mallet
Times Past Cheese Dairy, Westfield Lane, Draycott, Cheddar (Peppy
    D'Ovidio)
Tower Farms Cash & Carry, Dean's Cross, Lydeard St Lawrence,
    Taunton
Truckle of Cheese, Glastonbury

Suffolk

Cheese Shop, 74 Beccles Road, Oulton Broad, Lowestoft
Solar Superstore (Ipswich Cooperative Society), Ipswich

Surrey

Cheese World, Milkhouse Gate, 142 High Street, Guildford
Eastside Cheese, 59 Station Road, East Oxted
Fine Cheese, Reigate
La Charcuterie, High Street, Cranleigh (Ian McCall)
Parson's Pantry, 12 Upper Church Lane, Farnham
Pyramide, 98 High Street, Chobham (John Watt)
Secretts Garden Centre, Old Portsmouth Road, Milford, Godalming
Vivians, 2 Worple Way, Richmond

Sussex, East

Brighton Co-op, Peacehaven
The Cheese Shop, 17 Kensington Gardens, Brighton (Peter Bone)
Corbin's, Uckfield (Adrian Corbin)
Greenacres Farm, Whitesmith, Lewes (Kevin and Alison Blunt)
Heathfield Delicatessen, High Street, Heathfield
Humpheys Farm, Nutley, Uckfield (Margaret Willcock)
Infinity Foods, North Street, Brighton
Le Gourmet, 159 Dyke Road, Hove
Middle Farm, Firle, Lewes
Say Cheese, Gardner Street, Herstmonceux, Hailsham (David and
    Eleanor Robins)
Say Cheese, 4 Riverside, High Street, Lewes
Seasons, Hartfield Road, Forest Row
Wealden Wholefoods, High Street, Wadhurst

Sussex, West

Chichester Delicatessen, Sadlers Walk, Chichester
Horsham Cheese Shop, The Carfax, Horsham
Pallant Cheese & Wine, Arundel
Post Office Stores, Haywards Heath

Tyneside and Cleveland

Fenwicks, 39 Northumberland Street, Newcastle-upon-Tyne
Darras Larder, 13 The Broadway, Darras Hall, Ponteland, Newcastle-
    upon-Tyne
Not Just Cheese, 141 Elwick Road, Hartlepool

Warwickshire

C. Bunting, High Street, Alcester
Paxton & Whitfield, 13 Wood Street, Stratford-upon-Avon
Wass and Wass, 24–6 Sheep Street, Shipston on Stour (Gill Wass)

West Midlands

Harvest Country, 4 Lonsdale Road, Harbourne, Birmingham (Jim
    Harness)
Langmans Fine Cheese, 3 Manor Walk, Solihull
Little Deli Company, 3 Belwell Lane, Four Oaks, Sutton Coldfield
    (Kirsty Smith)
Ryton Organic Gardens, Ryton-on-Dunsmore, Coventry (Henry
    Atkinson)
Southfield Nurseries, Kenilworth, Balsall Common, Berkswell

Wiltshire

Cheeseboard, 30 Silver Street, Bradford-on-Avon
Fromagerie, High Street, Malmesbury
L'Herrison, 90–2 Crane Street, Salisbury (Alan Pitcairn)
Mackintosh of Marlborough, High Street, Marlborough (Nigel
    Mackintosh)

Yorkshire

Chapman and Quinn, 8–9 Harrogate Market Hall, Harrogate
Cheese Board, 21 Victoria Road, Scarborough
Czwicks, Commercial Street, Brighouse
Dairy Farm Shop, Market Place, Knaresborough (Mark and Lisa
    Wilson)
Deli and Wine Shop, 23 Wheelgate, Malton (Glenn Stott)
Farm Dairy, 3 Market Place, Knaresborough (Mark Wilson)

Farndale Dairy, Oak House Farm, Farndale (Kath Wright)
Fayre Do's, 13 Silver Street, Wakefield
Hopkins & Porter, The Old Stable, Ripley Castle, Ripley (Mervyn and
  Katherine Morse)
Herriot's, 4 John Street, Harrogate
Howards, 61 Clifton Road, York
Hunters, 13 Market Place, Helmsley
  also at 160 Main Street, Boston Spa
Lewis & Cooper, 92 High Street, Northallerton (Tony Howard)
Mary's of Richmond, Market Place, Richmond
Milburn & Sons, The Green, Hutton Rudby
Patton & Birch, The Cheeseboard, Victoria Road, Scarborough
Queen's Kitchen, 2 Queen's Court, Bingley
Silver Hill Dairy, Eccleshall Road South, Sheffield (Suzanne Hill)
Smith, R.V., 10 Butcher's Row, Kirkgate Market, Leeds (and branches)
Stephane's Sandwiches, 77 Low Petergate, York
York Beer Shop, 28 Sandringham Street, York

IRELAND

Buckley's, Chatham Street, Dublin
Caviston's, Sandycove, nr Dublin
Country Choice, Nenagh, Co. Tipperary
Eats of Eden, Spaights Buildings, Limerick City
Iago's, English Market, Cork
Mannings Emporium, Ballylickey, Bantry, Co. Cork
McCambridge's, Shop Street, Galway
Ryefield Foods, Mother Redcap's Market, Back Lane, Dublin
Vernons Stores, Clontarf, nr Dublin

SCOTLAND

Brody & Brody, The Square, Kelso, Borders
Cheesemongers, 30 Victoria Street, Edinburgh (Iain Mellis)
Island Cheese Company, Home Farm, Brodick, Isle of Arran (Ian and
  Allison McChlery)
Nastuiks International, 62 West Harbour Road, Morningside, Edinburgh
Roots and Fruits, 451 Great Western Road, Glasgow
Great Glen Fine Foods, Old Ferry Road, North Ballachulish,
  Invernesshire (Douglas Locke)
Sgriob-ruadh Farm, Tobermory, Isle of Mull (Jeff Reade)

Valvona & Crolla, 19 Elm Row, Edinburgh
West Highland Dairy, Achmore, Stromeferry, Ross-shire (David and
   Kathy Biss)

WALES

Abergavenny Fine Foods, 4 Castle Meadows Park, Abergavenny, Gwent
Farmhouse Cheese Stall, Carmarthen Market (John Savage
   Onstwedder)
Howell's Food Hall, Cardiff
Good Food, Middleton Street, Llandrindod Wells, Powys
Leslie Gwynne, The Square, Talgarth, Powys
Hay Whole Foods, Lion Street, Hay-on-Wye, Powys
Irma Fingal Rock, 64 Monnow Street, Monmouth, Gwent
Llangloffan Farm, Castle Morris, Haverfordwest, Dyfed (Leon and
   Joan Downey)
Merlin Cheeses, Tyn-y-Llwyn, Pontrhydygroes, Ystrad Meurig, Dyfed
   (Gill Pateman)
Siop Tandderwen, High Street, Betws-y-coed, Gwynedd
Welsh Wine Cellar, Pier Street, Aberystwyth, Dyfed
Castle Stores, King Street, Llandovery, Dyfed
Westway Dairy, 98 Central Market, Cardiff
   also at The Covered Market, Newport, Gwent

Bibliography

Books on Cheese

Biss, Kathy, *Practical Cheesemaking*, Crowood Press (1988)

Black, Maggie, *Paxton and Whitfield's Fine Cheese*, Webb & Bower (1989)

Calvert, Kit, *Wensleydale Cheese*, Dalesman (1977)

Cheke, Val, *The Story of Cheesemaking in Britain*, Routledge & Kegan Paul (1959)

Davis, J.G., *Cheese*, Churchill (1965)

Foulkes, F.W., *Hooked on Cheese*, Shropshire Libraries (1985)

Jones, Evan, *The Book of Cheese*, Macmillan (1980)

Layton, T.A., *Choose Your Cheese*, Gerald Duckworth (1957)

Maddever, Kate, *Farmhouse Cheesemaker's Manual*, MMB (1988)

Marquis, V. and Haskell, P., *The Cheese Book*, Leslie Frewin (1967)

Nillson, Anne, *Home Cheesemaking*, Woodbridge Press (1979)

Ogilvy, Susan, *Making Cheeses*, Batsford (1976)

Rance, Patrick, *The Great British Cheese Book*, Macmillan (1982)

Robinson, R. and Tamine, A., (eds), *Feta and Related Cheeses*, Ellis Horswood (1991)

Scott, R., *Cheesemaking Practice*, Elsevier (1981)

Squire, John, *Cheddar Gorge*, Collins (1937)

Sutherland-Thompson, G., *Grading Dairy Produce*, Crosby Lockwood (1925)

Thear, Katie (ed.), *The Home Dairying Book*, Broad Leys (1978)

Walker-Tisdale, C.W. and Robinson, T., *The Practice of Soft Cheesemaking*, North (1918)

Walker-Tisdale, C.W. and Woodnutt, W., *Practical Cheesemaking*, Allen & Unwin (1917)

BOOKS ON FARMING, FOOD AND NUTRITION

Brigden, Roy, *Victorian Farms*, Crowood Press (1986)

Drummond, J., and Wilbraham, A., *The Englishman's Food*, Jonathan Cape (1939)

Fussell, G.E., *The English Dairy Farm 1500–1900*, Cass (1966)

Hartley, Dorothy, *Food in England*, Macdonald (1956)

Howell, Chris, *Memories of Cheddar*, self-published (1984)

Morris, Chris, *Dairy Farming in Gloucestershire*, Gloucester Folk Museum (1983)

Salmon, Jill, *The Goatkeeper's Guide*, David & Charles (1981)

Schwartz, Oded, *In Search of Plenty*, Kyle Cathie (1992)

Sheldon, J.P., *British Dairying*, Crosby Lockwood (1896)

Street, L., and Singer, A., *The Backyard Dairy Book*, Prism (1975)

Tannahill, Reay, *Food in History*, Penguin (1988)

Thomason, A.G., *The Small Dairy Farm*, A. & C. Black (1955)

Whitlock, Ralph, *The English Farm*, J.M. Dent (1983)

OTHER SOURCES

Baker, Stanley, *Milk to Market*, Heinemann (1973)

Barty-King, Hugh, *Making Provision*, Quiller Press (1986)

Bines, Young and Law, *Comparison of Recombinant Chymosin and Calf Rennet*, AFRC Institute of Food Research (1988)

Keevil, Ambrose, *The Story of Fitch-Lovell*, Phillimore (1972)

Murray, A.H., *World Handbook of Dairying*, Clare's, Wells (1936)

Wilson, Barry, *Dairy Industry Newsletter* (fortnightly)

Wright, Rebecca (ed.), *Dairy Industries International* (monthly), Wilmington Publishing